POLITICS OF NATION BUILDING IN INDIA

POLITICS OF NATION BUILDING IN INDIA

Shibani Kinkar Chaube

GYAN

Politics of Nation Building in India

ISBN: 978-81-212-1143-7

Published in 2012 in India by
Gyan Publishing House,
23 Main, Ansari Road, Darya Ganj,
New Delhi-110002
Phones : 23282060, 23261060
Fax : 011-23285914
E-mail: books@gyanbooks.com
Website: www.gyanbooks.com

Laser Typesetting by: Quick Media, Delhi
Printed at : Chawla Offset Printers, Delhi

Dedicated

To

Amartya

and

Ishan

Preface

Nation-building is a composite word that appeared in the social sciences in the 1960s to describe an old programme of social, economic and political construction undertaken by the leaders of newly independent countries through building of democratic and development-oriented institutions and policies. In reply to the British denial of nationhood to the Indians, in the 1920s Surendra Nath Banerjee declared that India was a nation in the making. The Karachi Resolution of the Indian National Congress announced a programme for achievement of fundamental rights that included social, economic and political rights of Indians. In 1932 Mohandas Karamchand Gandhi undertook the programme of constructive work. In 1938 Subhas Chandra Bose, president, All-India Congress Committee, established a National Planning Committee under Jawaharlal Nehru. All these steps led to the massive work of the Constituent Assembly of India, the setting up of the planning commission, administrative reforms, local self-government institutions and general elections. A new coinage was 'national integration' in 1961 when a commission carrying that name was instituted in order to tame communal violence. 'Nation building', initially with a hyphen, entered the social science literature in the 1960s.

'Nation' belongs to the domain of politics, democratic politics for that. The reference point of the modern nations is the state defined by territory though there are tiny stateless peoples all over the world and there are secessionist tribes with claim to nationhood. But 'nation building' is a complex and an elaborate process with a heavy emphasis on the leadership. It involves most other social sciences as well as political science. There is a choice on the definition. Some nations have chosen to live in secular states, some have defined their states in terms of religious faiths and some nations have chosen to define themselves in terms of tribal affinity. Islamic states, for instance, use *Shari'ah law* or the *Quran* as a basis of *legislation* (e.g., *Saudi Arabia*). There are some states which have adopted Islam as state religion (like Pakistan), where application of Shari'ah laws/courts has been a contentious issue. Several African nations are but glorified federations of tribes. India has been constituted as a secular state but there are strong ethno-cultural strains, produced by the vastness and diversity of her territory and population, on her secular aspirations.

The papers included in the volume, with focus on the political aspect of nation building, were written over four decades. They are being published, after minor revisions, at the initiative of Gyan Publishing House. Some of the empirical details may have become slightly out of date. The broad arguments in them, I believe, have been sustained over the period.

Shibani Kinkar Chaube

Acknowledgement

The author is thankful to the editors and publishers of the undermentioned books and journals for originally publishing the articles included in this volume.

1. Politics among the Social Sciences: A Historical Overview, in Sudipta Kaviraj, Partha Chatterjee, Shibani Kinkar Chaube, Sobhanlal Datta Gupta, *The State of Political Theory: Some Marxist Essays*. Calcutta: Research India Publications, 1978.
2. The Raja and the Raj: Conflict and Collaboration, *Granthana, Vol. VI, Nos. 1 & 2, January 1999.*
3. Personalistic Ethics of Gandhi's Political Philosophy. *The Journal of the Indian Academy of Philosophy, Vol. XXXIV, Nos. 1 & 2, 1995.*
4. The Indian Constitution through Half a Century, *Man and Development, September 2000.*
5. Basic Structure, Judicial Review and Supreme Court: Limits of Privileges and Power of the Indian Parliament. *Keynote address delivered at the inauguration of the 9th Annual Conference of West Bengal Political Science Association on 17th March 2007.*
6. The Supreme Court, Federalism in India, *Trends in Social Science Research, Vol. 1, No. 1, June 1994.*
7. Nation Building and Ethno-Cultural Tensions in South Asia, in Girin Phukon (Ed.), *Ethnicity and Polity in South Asia. New Delhi: South Asia Publishers, 2002.*
8. The Ethnic Problem in India: A Historical Perspective, *Social Research, January-March 1982.*
9. Colonial Context of Regionalism; The Australian and the Indian Experience in Ian Copland and John Rickard (Eds.), *Federalism: Comparative Perspectives from India and Australia, New Delhi: Manohar, 1999.*
10. The Cultural Frame and the Dynamics of Federalism in India, *Social Science Probings, June 1984.*

11. The National and Ethnic Problems of India and Canada, *Social Science Probings, March 1994–December 1995.*
12. Caste, Politics and Indian Federation in Rsheeduddun Khan (Ed.), *Rethinking Indian Federalism. Shimla: Inter-University Centre of Humanities and Social Sciences, Indian Institute of Advanced Study, 1997.*
13. The Domain of Secularism: Religion, State and Society in India, *Social Science Probings, Vol. 7-8, 1990-1991.*
14. Communalism and Secularism in India, in *Fifty Years of India's Freedom* Edited by K. Raghavendra Rao, Ashok K. Maiti, Debabrata Pands, N.P. Chaube, Indian Academy of Social Sciences, Allahabad, 1997.
15. Minority Problem in India: An Overview, in Radharaman Chakravarti and Durga Prasad Bhattacharya (Eds.), *Society, Revolution and the Future. A bunch of essays in honour of the birth centenary of scholar, journalist, patriot Dr. Dhirendranath Sen. Kolkata; Dr. Dhirendranath Sen Centenary Committee, 2003.*
16. Tribal Movements: Social and Political in *Social Movements in Contemporary India.* Calcutta. K.P. Bagchi & Co, 1999.
17. Inter-ethnic Politics in Northeast India, *International Journal of Modern Sociology, Autumn 1975, Vol. II.*
18. India and Her Neighbours: Linkages and Fissures, *Social Science Probings, 18, 1, June 2006.*
19. Social Tensions in Calcutta, *Indian Journal of Social Work. Vol. XLIV, No. 2 (July 1983).* A briefer version of *Violence, Crime and Labour Unrest in Calcutta: A Comparative Analysis in Social Tensions in Jean Racine (Ed.), Calcutta, 1981, New Delhi: Concept Publishing Company, 1990.*
20. Social Unrest in India in *Social Unrest: Proceedings of the first Inter-Congress (Eds. Ajit K. Danda, Satyabrata Chakrabarti, Arabinda Basu. Kolkata; Indian National Confederation and Academy of Anthropologists 2006.*

Contents

1

Politics among the Social Sciences : A Historical Overview*

The Disintegration of Political Economy

It is customary for anyone writing on political theory to stress, at the first opportunity, the distinction between theory and thought. A thought is an intellectual exercise of a general order encompassing desire, speculation, comment, criticism and explanation. A theory is, more than anything else, a 'logical file of knowledge' with explanatory purpose. While such knowledge may lead to the other variants of thought, its immediate concern is restricted to verifiability.[1] It is with the realisation of this distinction that the birth of the modern social sciences—economics, sociology including anthropology, and political science—is historically associated.

Of course, until the late nineteenth century there was no detailed specialisation and what passed for 'the social science' was the broad discipline of political economy informed by a sense of history. David Ricardo's *Principles of Political Economy and Taxation* (London, 1817) exhibits a deep awareness of the interrelation between the polity and the economy of a society. According to one view, political economy was the product of European mercantilism—the 'managed economies' preceding the industrial revolution—and 'aimed to maximise the profitability of the nation for the use of the monarch'.[2] The name 'classical political economy', however, is given to the theory of the industrial revolution originating from the philosophy of John Locke and flowering in the writings of Adam Smith and David Ricardo. The

* The writer has benefited from discussions with his colleagues at the CSSSC. Among them Professor Amiya Bagchi, Professor Asok Sen, Dr Partha Chatterjee and Dr Sobhanlal Datta Gupta have read the first draft of the paper. The responsibility for any remaining defects belongs to the writer.

basic assumption of the 'classics' was that the state was 'the creature of economic power no less than its master'.[3]

One major problem of theory in social sciences, rarely admitted, is the role of philosophy. Philosophy enters social sciences at two stages : (1) building of hypotheses and (2) their verification. The first entry is more easily detectable than the second. Assuming that *complete* knowledge of things can hardly be gathered, social scientists of necessity satisfy themselves with the knowledge 'sufficient' for the construction of a theory. The hypotheses determine the logic of filing such knowledge which, in its turn, depends upon the social scientists' world-view. Verification of the hypotheses in terms of the reality in the social sciences is easily vulnurable to the social scientist's perception of his universe that is composed of human relationships rather than physical objects. When Adam Smith was reflecting the spirit of the industrial revolution by advocating *laissez faire,* he was clearly assuming a primacy of the economy which, to him, could take care of itself without state intervention.[4] His basic assumption, evidently, was the permanence of capitalism.

Scott Greer, a sociologist and critic of 'economic determinism', finds in classical political economy itself the germ of separation between politics and economics since it was with the classics that 'Economics developed around the notion of the self-regulating system of production, distribution, consumption and saving'.[5] Quite logically, he places Marx in the tradition of the 'classics'. 'Marx was, in his convictions .concerning the primacy and autonomy of the economic system, a direct descendant of Adam Smith'.[6] It is to Marx that the crisis of political economy is most frequently ascribed. It is, however, equally ignored that with all its merits classical political economy left severe gaps in its theoretical framework which only Marx could expose.

The principal concepts of economics over nearly the past two hundred years, according to Roll, have been 'private property and enterprise, private exchange, the market economy'.[7] Of these three, the first two are evidently articles of faith, the last an all-purpose theoretical framework. Yet there have been shifts of emphasis. Thus, although Adam Smith wanted an uninterrupted operation of the economic market, he explained its mechanism 'by more fundamental concepts, either relating to human conduct or derived from a view of society and its historical development'.[8] The quest for such a fundamental law based the supply and demand theory of the market on the theory of exchange value which led to the development of two different kinds of labour theories of value in the hands of Ricardo and Marx. Both Ricardo and Marx demonstrated that the surplus value of labour was appropriated by the capitalist owners of industry. Ricardo, like Smith, believed in the permanence of capitalism and the 'iron law of wages' appeared to him rational. Thus, political economy, in its later days, was identified with 'shallow dogmatism by which well-to-do people in 'the first half of Queen Victoria's reign tried to convince working men that any change in the distribution of the good things of life was "scientifically impossible."[9] Marx reacted by refuting these 'laws of political economy'as irrational. They did not appreciate the real value of labour.[9a]

The crisis of political economy developed slowly. James Mill's *Elements of Political Economy,* published in 1821, is the 'last expression of unquestioning faith in the Ricardian school'. Soon the vicious capitalist 'trade cycle' set in and the optimism of the classics started to dissolve. In England and France 'the influence of classical political economy makes itself felt in an unsuspected quarter : the infant working-class movement; and, as a reaction, a powerful apologetic strain makes itself felt in the growth of an economic orthodoxy'.[10] It was in the year of continental revolution (1848) that *The Communist Manifesto* was published. In the same year John Stuart Mill's *Principles of Political Economy* diluted some of the basic premises of classical political economy.

Not until the lapse of half a century after James Mill was capitalist economy restored to another generally accepted theory—the neoclassical economics. The chief innovation of the neoclassical school was the reduction of the entire set of problems of economics—production, distribution, exchange and consumption—to marginal analysis. 'Behind demand is marginal utility, reflected in the demand prices of buyers (the price at which given quantities will be demanded); behind supply is marginal effort and sacrifice, reflected in the supply prices (the prices at which given quantities will be forthcoming)'.[11] The net effect of the innovation was the elimination of the great problem of classical political economy—the problem of distribution—through its reformulation in terms of marginal returns. The 'classics' viewed it as a problem of the social structure. The 'neoclassics' reduced it to the problems of individual preferences and bargains. The orientation of the economists thus changed from the society toward the individual.[12] The structural problem was finally eliminated through the reduction of the problem of distribution into the theory of employment.

Crisis of Identity of Social Sciences

The unifying element between political economy and the earlier tradition of social thought was the acknowledgement of the interdependence between individual action and the social structure. The negative aspects of this interdependence, were the source of all social criticisms and reform/revolutionary programmes. Marxism was the strongest form of such criticism and programme. 'The most outstanding works of the late nineteenth and the early twentieth century emerged from the arguments against Marx'.[13] Neoclassical economics ignored the Marxist challenge by taking the social structure as 'given' and concentrating on the problem of individual choice. Thus emerged 'a subjective theory of value ... only compatible with an individualist view of society' : in some of its more extreme formulations it even became 'atomistic'.[14]

The impact of the emergence of neoclassical economics was a crisis of identity for political science which now became engaged in the study of governmental institutions without regard to social realities. The hiatus between the two offsprings of political economy was sought to be filled by the new science of sociology,[15] derived from the writings of Herbert Spencer. Even in sociology there appeared a split between the structuralist bias of Emile Durkheim and the emphasis put by Max Weber on human action. Spencer differed from Marx : but the difference rested in Spencer's prognosis of the individuation of society and Marx's emphasis on class contradiction. The social structure was of primary concern to both of them. Durkheim was concerned with the stability of the social structure. Weber, on the other hand, took the social structure as 'given' and concentrated primarily on 'action' with reference to individual psychology.[16]

At the turn of the century, psychology itself was getting a

new shape under the impact of the behaviourists who redefined their subject as 'the science of action'—action flowing from motor responses to situational stimuli rather than the unquantifiable faculties of the brain. Though 'behaviourism' in psychology sprang from Pavlov's emphasis on the association of biological acts with situational stimuli, it should be noted that the more sustained influence of psychology on the social sciences in general was that of the individualistic Watsonian variety of behaviourism as modified by the premises of psycho-analysis about 'instinct' as the motivator of action.[17]

There remained, however, one methodological problem : how precisely is individual behaviour quantifiable in psychological terms? In physics, the source of all scientific aspirations of the social sciences, it has been established that the behaviour of light particles is measurable not individually, but in quantum. Pareto, one of the fathers of neo-classical economics, confessed that utility is measurable not cardinally, but ordinally. He thought that a 'scale of preferences' is *sufficient* for economic analysis. The best result that can be achieved from this kind of psycho-mechanics is, therefore, probabilistic.

Seeking to redirect the attention of political science from institutions to the new developments in psychology, Graham Wallas, father of modern political science, recalled that 'The thinkers of the past, from Plato to Bentham, had each his view of human nature, and he made those views the basis of their speculations on government'.[18] A linkage was thus established by the 'new political science' with the general emphasis of the other social sciences on the psychological aspect of action. Yet the early political behaviourists could not altogether ignore the structural aspects of their themes. Wallas's contemporary in the United States, Arthur Bentley, wrote that political behaviour could be meaningful only when it was organised in 'groups' around definite interests.[19] To the extent that Bentley's behaviour was derived from interests structured around pragmatic groups rather than classes, his theory was 'a convenient dilution of Marxism', but 'hardly ... a substantial alternative'.[20] According to Giovanni Sartori, 'the interest terminology either leads to fuzzy theorizing or acquires its substance from the more or less covert assumption that interest generally is "economic interest."'[21]

The behavioural paradox was exposed when Charles Beard, a second-generation new political scientist, wrote *An Economic Interpretation of the Constitution of the USA* clearly depicting the functional correlation between the federal structure of the USA and the victory of the big moneyholders over smaller proprietors and farmers in the battle over the conversion of the USA from a confederation into a federation. The thesis went against the popular American myth that the federation was a victory of straight-thinking Americans over the narrow-minded ones and was roundly condemned by conservative Americans, at the same time being admired by the leftists. In the 1935 edition of his book, Beard tried to make amends but reminded his critics that the idea that economic difference could give birth to political division was as old as at least Hamilton's *Federalist Paper* No. 10.[22] Beard was rejected by the behaviourists who reduced 'interests'to the rather abstract category of 'attitudes'. L.L. Thurstone, who proposed the term, defined it as 'the sum total of a man's inclinations and feelings, prejudices or bias, preconceived notions, ideas, fears, threats, and convictions about a specific topic'. Richard Jensen comments that 'Since the scientific methodology of the day in psychology (and in most sciences) did not stress the analysis of mutual interaction of a number of variables and constraints within a unified system, Thurstone's formulation proved satisfactory to the political scientists'.[23]

There is indeed a very positive value of the behavioural approach which represented 'a break with the social absolutism and moralism of Christian theology'. As LaPiere correctly stresses : 'If the important aspect of any social structure is its functions, it follows that no structure can be judged in terms of structure alone'.[24] The behavioural approach destroyed the 'sanctity' of any established social-political institution and could encourage rational assessment of such institutions. This comment is even more applicable to Freud who did a great deal to destroy the 'holiness' of society.

Here precisely lies the rub. The 'functionalist' theory that developed after World War I, first in anthropology, then in sociology and finally in the other social sciences, rejected the scientific potential of this theory of action. Robert Merton, a functionalist sociologist, condemned the political implications of

Freud's doctrine as anarchistic.[25] Talcott Parsons came out heavily against the behavioural school. Unless behaviour is viewed in terms of interaction, it has little relevance to the social sciences.[26] David Easton, who developed the concept of 'the political system', accorded behaviour the status of 'data' while, at the same time, making a distinction between 'behavioralism' and the 'outmoded behaviorist views'.[27] Against mounting attack the political behaviourists beat a retreat. In 1956, a *Reader in Political Behavior* admitted the importance of the structural and situational variants in the political process which have been of interest to the political scientists.[28] In 1961, Dahl signed the epitaph of the 'behavioral protest' with the kind assurance that its point had been taken in the 'main body of political science'.[29] Two years later a leading behaviouralist called his method a 'persuasion'.[30]

A Theory of Action

In 1937 a 'voluntaristic theory of action' consistent with the concern for institutional integration was floated by the Harvard sociologist, Talcott Parsons.[31] Combining the positivistic tradition of Vilfredo Pareto and Emile Durkheim and the idealistic tradition of Max Weber, Parsons formulated the action theory in the following form :

1. Behaviour is oriented to the attainment of ends or goals or other anticipated states of affairs.
2. It takes place in situations.
3. It is normatively [teleologically] regulated.
4. It involves expenditure of energy or effort or motivation.[32]

The robust element in the theory of action was its liberal dynamism. 'As process, action is, in fact, the process of alteration of the conditional elements in the direction of conformity with norms [goals]. Elimination of the normative aspect altogether eliminates the concept of action itself and leads to the radical positivistic position. Elimination of the conditions of the tension from that side, equally eliminates action itself and results in idealistic emanationism.'[33] In just over a decade, however, Parsons became sceptical of its significance. 'A central problem...has been, and is, how to bring theory of this sort closer to the possibilities of guiding of and testing and refinement by technical research, especially with the use of technically refined instruments of observation and of the ordering and empirical analysis of observational data'.[34]

Although in 1938 Einstein spoke of the 'decline in the mechanical view' in physics[35], there was a definite movement towards the same view in the US social sciences. In 1948 Parsons sponsored an interdisciplinary manifesto of some US sociologists, anthropologists and psychologists on a mechanical *general theory of action* which the authors called 'structural-functional'.[36] The relevant data about human action in society being 'highly fragmentary, though by no means absent', the theory of action had of necessity to be ordered into an 'empirical-theoretical' rather than a perfectly theoretical scheme in the sense of classical mechanics. If the purpose of a theory of action was to identify the circumstances in which an action tends to be recurrent, it would not be enough to say that 'in the long run only behavior which is adequately rewarded will tend to persist'.[37] It would be necessary to know the reward structure and its relation to the value and role structure in the society under study. 'This is the most promising path to the extension of the empirical relevance of generalizations from the one structural case to families of structural cases'.[38] It was hoped that the progress of knowledge would ultimately facilitate the growth of a perfect theory. The test of the significance of this theory, meanwhile,

> takes the form of the "functional" relevance of the process. The test is to ask the question, what would be the differential consequences for the system of two or more alternative outcomes of a dynamic process. Such consequences will be found to fit into the terms of maintenance of stability or production of change, of integration or disruption of the system in some sense.[39]

Harald Mey thinks that Parsons moves in the wrong direction when he surrenders the dynamic principle (in *The Structure of Social Action)* of interrelationship between person and society in favour of a 'one-sided imprint-system of society on to person'.[40] In the new scheme of things action becomes 'role' and psychology, particularly Freud's psychoanalysis, acquires a prominent position.[41] Three major 'points of reference' emerge — personality, culture and society (accompanied by the somewhat honorific epithet 'system') — in the new theoretical frame of 'interaction' conditioned by what is called the complementarity of expectations. The system of interaction is analysed in terms of the extent of *conformity* of ego's action with alter's expectations and *vice versa.* 'Interaction makes possible the development of culture on the human level and gives culture its significance in the determination of action'.[42] The systems of interaction 'which have become differentiated to a cultural level' form the central theme of Parsons's magnum opus, *The Social System.*[43]

The key concept of *The Social System* is that of the 'division of labour as developed by Adam Smith and his successor utilitarians'. The social system, conceived as 'a system of instrumentally oriented interaction', is a generalised version of the classical case of exchange, where alter's action is a means to the attainment of ego's goal, and, vice versa, ego is a means of the attainment of alter's. Exchange in this sense may be confined to a highly *ad hoc* particular transaction, but it may become elaborated into a highly organised and durable system of interaction. As this occurs, ego may become specialised in the process of "production" of means of the attainment of the goals of one or a class of alters. Reciprocally, the attainment of his own goals is enmeshed in expectations of (to him) 'instrumentally significant results of the actions of these alters'.[44] Thus, social action resembles the process of exchange, its motivation resembles choice of the means of gratification of needs. The system of interaction resembles the operation of the market. And society is a generalised form of what Smith meant by 'economy', differentiated according to the principle of division of labour.

A Note on Functionalism

Social sciences today have grown largely by disowning the philosophical tradition of the past and borrowing from the natural sciences. Thus, the eighteenth century theory of separation of powers was influenced by Newtonian physics, and Herbert Spencer wrote his *Social Statics* in 1851. Max Weber, on the other hand, is regarded as the Galileo of social sciences. The terms 'structure' and 'function' owe their origin to Newtonian mechanics which, for a long time, dominated physics and biology, and then entered the field of social sciences.

There the theory cropped up first in colonial anthropology through the study of some primitive societies. The biological view of functions as the part which the components of an organism play in supporting it was applied to the analysis of culture of a primitive society. Bronislaw Malinowski defined 'function' as the part an organ plays 'in the social and cultural system'. Radcliffe-Brown defined the function of any recurrent activity as 'the part it plays in the social life as a whole and therefore the contribution it makes to the maintenance of the structural continuity'.[45]

This anthropological version of what the Germans had earlier developed as the organic theory of state/society proved unsuitable for broader sociological purposes, particularly for complex and developed societies. It blurs the distinction between 'interdependence' and 'process'.[46] The quest for such interdependence opened up the 'dynamic' vision of functions. The new concept of stability would imply not that a system was static, but that it was 'going', capable of maintaining its overall integrity by adapting itself to demands for change. In this view, 'function' is the consequence of an action that is relevant to the social structure in terms of the maintenance of its integrity. A social system being a system of interaction among two or more individuals, on a socio-cultural plane, human actions as inputs would produce the changes in the social structure suitable to the needs of its constituents as well as to its own integrity.

The ultimate goal of Parsons's theory of action, it has been stressed, was the 'perfection'of classical mechanics. In fact, the concept of 'system' belongs to the domain of classical mechanics. Robert Merton, Parsons's student, generalised the concept of 'functions'. 'The entire range of sociological data' was subjected, by Merton, to functional analysis.[47] And as the difficulties of such extensive generalisation are only too obvious, Merton restricted the scope of his theories to the middle range. Middle-range theories lie between minor hypotheses and unified general theories and Merton claimed that they could fit even the Marxist theoretical framework.[48]

Merton rejected the concept of 'functional requirement' of social systems, as developed by erstwhile sociologists and anthropologists, that tended to be 'tautological or *ex post facto*', being confined to the conditions for 'survival' of a given system, and thus become a conservative doctrine.[49] Instead, he defined 'functions' as 'those observed consequences which make for the adaptation or adjustment of the system'. 'There is also an empirical possibility of *non-functional* consequences, which are simply irrelevant to the system under consideration'.[50]

'The key concept bridging the gap between statics and dynamics in functional theory is', according to Merton, 'that of tension, contradiction, or discrepancy between the component elements of social and cultural structures. Such strains may be dysfunctional for the social system in its then existing form; theory may also be instrumental in leading to changes in that system...when social mechanisms for controlling them are operating effectively, these strains are kept within such bounds as to limit change of the social structure'.[51]

Conversely, the absence of such mechanisms creates conditions for the arrival of a state of *anomie.* Durkheim, author of the term in sociology, meant by it a condition of relative normlessness in society, a property of the cultural and social crisis. Later sociologists like Maciver and Riesman, however, added to this social aspect of the problem a psychological aspect.[52] Merton includes among deviant behaviours, innovations, rebellion and anomie.[53] Deviance begins 'when the individual has assimilated the cultural emphasis upon the goal without equally internalizing the institutional norms governing ways and means for its attainment'.[54] Anomie, therefore, is the polar opposite of integration, being the 'absence of structured complementarity of the interaction process'.[55]

This new theory of *anomie* serves two purposes. On the one hand, by emphasising that deviant behaviour is as much a product of social structure as conformity, it repudiates the anarchistic hypotheses of Hobbes, Freud and Eric Fromm.[56] On the other hand, by emphasising the psychological aspect of *anomie,* it regards the phenomenon as a personal failure in the form of the contradiction between the cultural goals he adopts and the means he possesses.[57] But the main point about *anomie* is the sociologists' negative perception of it—as normlessness. Its most organised form, revolution, is therefore not a means of structural transformation of society. Stability rather than transition is the 'normal' condition of society. 'As we survey the course of history', Merton writes, 'it seems reasonably clear that all major social structures have in due course been cumulatively modified or abruptly terminated.... But at a given moment of observation, any such social structure may be tolerably well accommodated both to the subjective values of many or most of the population, and to the objective conditions with which we are confronted.' Hence, 'recognising as they must, that social structures are forever changing, functional analysts must nevertheless explore the interdependent and often mutually supporting elements.'[58] In 1951, Talcott Parsons took comfort from the fact that 'Though proclaimed and threatened for a long time this [a communist revolution] has not yet happened in any major industrialized country of the Western world, least of all in the most highly industrialized, the United States'.[59]

If Merton's functional analysis is regarded as an extended version of Parsons's action theory, two significant properties of functionalism emerge. In the first place, Parsons's general theory has restored, to some extent, the interrelation of the sciences of society lost since the break-up of political economy. In the second place, it has brought back the social structure into the frame of the action theory. This has been called 'sociological imperialism' in which 'all economic, political and psychological realities are subsumed under a tautological category called "interactions".[60] The not-so-shockingly original statement that 'This fundamental relationship between need-dispositions of the personality, role-expectations of the social system and internalized-institutionalized value-patterns of the culture, is the fundamental nodal point of the *organization* of system of action',[61] which is apparently the substance of the action theory, will vindicate the judgement *vis-a-vis* the initial premise that 'a social system is the mode of organization of action elements relative to the persistence or ordered processes of change of the interactive patterns of a plurality of individual actions'.[62] Stronger comments have come from liberal sociologists like Stanislav Andreski, who has called it 'promiscuous crypto-conservative', and has added: 'Not surprisingly, as far as I know, no dictator has yet banned the books of the arch-priest of euphemistic sociology, although in most communist countries even Keynes is forbidden'.[63]

Politics as a Synthetic Science

The functionalists' achievement rests in a new kind of integration of the sciences of society, lost since the decay of political economy, on an interdisciplinary plane.[64] The action theory was ordered into these theoretical subsystems : (a) psychology, corresponding to personality, (b) anthropology, corresponding to culture (latent-pattern maintenance and tension-management), (c) economics, sociology and political science corresponding to the social system. In a narrow sense these last three are regarded as the social sciences.[65]

Parsons, however, disfavours the reduction of economic theory in terms of the theory of rational choice as, on the one hand, it is only partly relevant to the explanation of the economic process which is the 'allocation of facilities', and, on the other, is 'within certain limits psychological'. Economics 'as a *social* science is concerned with the phenomena of ratio-nal decisions within an institutionalized system of exchange relationships'. This being, 'within the theory of action,...a highly distinctive complex...the claim of economic theory to autonomy with respect to it seems quite justified'.[66] Economics, as a social science, is concerned with the *adaptive* functions of society.

The traditional concern of sociology is institutionalisation and integration. Parsons is a sociologist; he only contributes a dynamic element to this problem of institutional integration. To him, sociological theory is 'that aspect of the theory of social systems which is concerned with the phenomena of institutionalization of patterns of value-orientation in the social system, with the conditions of that institutionalization and of changes in the patterns, with conditions of conformity with and deviance from a set of such patterns and with motivational processes in so far as they are involved in all of these". No doubt, sociology is at the centre of the *general theory* of the social system.[67]

The case of political science, according to the authors of the manifesto, was 'somewhat different', because of its traditional focus on the philosophical and ethical problems of government. Government was a legitimate field of study. 'But, like economics, its special relevance does not emerge until degrees of differentiation on both theoretical and empirical levels beyond those reached in the...general statement have appeared'. And as 'the processes and structure of government necessarily have highly diffuse functions in social systems', political science was more likely to draw from 'a much wider range of the components of the general theory of action and to find its distinctiveness in the way it combines these components in relation to its special empirical interests, rather than in the technical elaboration of a narrow and sharply focused segment of the theory of action, as is the case with economics'.[68]

Subsequently, Parsons administered a stronger reprimand to political science which he called a 'synthetic science in the social system field, not one built about a distinctively *analytical* conceptual scheme, that is, a strictly iimited set of variables'. The claim of political theory to analytical status was justified by the only formula that it should be treated as a theory of power. But power, in the *political* sense, being 'inherently diffuse as contrasted with the specificity of economic power... a theory of political power must in the nature of the case take into account, *as variables*, most of the variables of the social system'.[69]

Parsons's elaboration of the distinction between political power and economic power is crucial for the later development of political science toward an analytical status. Power is a relational phenomenon, being one's capacity in society to control the action of others, and can be split broadly into economic and political power. The differences between these two types of power are summed up in this way :

> While the structure of economic power is ... lineally quantitative, simply a matter of *more and less*, that of political power is hierarchical; that is, of *higher and lower* levels. The greater power is power *over* the lesser, not merely *more* power *than* the lesser. Political power is relational, not merely in reference, that is, to *n* political exchange partners, but in direct significance.[70]

Obviously, Parsons's view of economic power is based on the neoclassical analysis; it relates to a competitive market and not production relations where power would mean the power of the employer over the employee. Parsons did not take long to revise the hierarchical view of political power. By that time, myth-making in social science had developed as a sophisticated creed obfuscating the reality of social hierarchy.

Politics and Sociology

The obfuscation of social hierarchy had been contingent to the great ideological battle against Marxism. Vilfred Pareto, one of the founders of neo-classical economics, substituted the concept of the 'ruling class' by that of the 'elite'. This polite description could not hide the concentration of economic and political power in societies based on private ownership. Max Weber, therefore, went a step ahead; he sought to separate political and economic power. 'Part of Weber's work may be seen as an attempt to "round out" Marx's economic materialism by political and military materialism. The Weberian approach to political structures closely parallels the Marxian approach to economic structures. Marx constructed economic periods and located major economic classes in them; he related the several social and political factors to the means of production. In political matters Weber looks for the disposition 'over weapons and over means of administration'. To the extent that Weber balanced 'economic determinism' by the autonomy of politics, both the economy and the polity were subsumed in a new sociological imperialism represented by that omnibus term 'interaction'.

Politics was thus given a sociological basis by Max Weber who defined the state as an 'infinity of diffuse and discrete human actions, both active and passive, factually and legally regulated relationships, partly unique and partly recurrent in character, all bound together by an idea, namely the belief in the actual or normative validity of the rules and of the authority relationships of some human beings toward others'.[72] But he acknowledged the role of power as the state successfully 'claims the monopoly of the legitimate use of physical force within a definite territory'.[73] The initial impact of Weber on political theory was the sociological reaction that politics was a theory of power.[74]

There were, however, two problems with the power approach. One was its discomforting association with the nineteenth century force theory, if not with the Marxist theory.[75] David Easton, a functionalist, gave vent to this suspicion when he criticised Lasswell's volume on Politics :

> ... it is devoted to exploring the sources of power held by a political elite. Its focus, therefore, is not on the way values are distributed but on the way the elite, which has power, uses it to acquire the desirable things of society, such as safety, income, deference....

> It centres only on one problem, however crucial it is today : the tendency in mass societies for power to concentrate in the hands of a minority. It assumes that this oligarchic tendency in the political system eternally prevents the diffusion of power beyond the governing group.[76]

V.O. Key asserts that the 'characteristic of democratic orders, or at least of the American democratic order, is a wide dispersion of power.... Moreover, the power-structure tends to be segmented : authority over one question rests here and over another there.'[77] 'As long as we adhere to the notion that power is an empirically separable variable of social stratification', writes Nelson Polsby, 'we must reject these as improper, and search for specific, separate empirical indices by which power can be measured.'[78]

Here arises the second problem. Is power empirically separable from the network of social relations? Parsons and his structural-functionalist colleagues have argued that *political* power, being concerned with the overall problem of order, is not isolable. The only way out of the logical paradox was to eliminate the problem of order from the frame of analysis. It is within the structural-functional framework that David Easton builds up the concept of the 'political system' by identifying the 'significant political variables' and describing their mutual relations[79] only to reassert the autonomy that Parsons and his colleagues denied political science.

An Analytical Theory of Politics

Easton shifts the focus on to 'policy" for the society and defines political science as the science of 'the authoritative allocation of values as it is influenced by the distribution and use of power'.[80] Easton accepts Parsons's stricture that political power is a relational phenomenon and, therefore, analytically not separable. But, 'The interest of political science in power is only educed from its preoccupation with how policy is made and executed'.[81] A policy is authoritative only when the people to whom it is intended to apply, or who are affected by it, consider that they must or ought to obey it. Easton argues that this is a psychological rather than moral explanation[82], and thus shifts the attention of political science from power to consensus, from the elite to the people.

Secondly, he proposes the possibility of a quantitative approach to politics. 'Authoritative allocation of values' sounds like 'allocation of resources' in economics. 'It indicates that even where the state ... does not exist (as among nomadic tribes or non-literate societies), as long as something we call social policy appears, then there are data for political research. The concept of the state as here interpreted refers to special political circumstances; the idea of authoritative allocation of values characterizes a function or web of interrelated activity present in every viable society.'[83] The specific terms of this quantitative approach were spelt out some years later : 'The allocation of values for a society and the relative frequency of compliance with them are the *essential variables* of political life.'[84]

Easton does not rule out power, he only relegates it to a secondary position. His input-output model is, therefore, more tentative. Posing the central question of a functionalist —'How do political systems manage to persist in a world of both stability and change?'—Easton begins by defining the political system as a 'system of behavior imbedded in an environment to the influences of which the political system itself is exposed and in turn reacts'.[85] A transaction or exchange between systems being the gist of the input-output relation, the behaviours of persons in the periphery of the political system are regarded as inputs and 'the decisions and actions of authorities' within the political system as outputs.[86] 'Outputs not only help to influence events in the broader society of which the system is a part, but also, in doing so, they help to determine each succeeding round of inputs that finds its way into the political system. There is a *feedback loop* the identification of which helps us to explain the processes through which the system can cope with the stress.'[87]

Of all social scientists, Easton must be given the highest credit for bringing political theory to the proximity of economic theory in analytical status. If power could not be separated from the ruling class/elite, it would be a constant and evade analysis. But if power could be fused into authority and order into consent, politics could be analysed in terms of input and output.

From this base one logical step forward was the market theory of politics of which Buchanan's individualistic model is illustrative. The model is not necessarily interest-centric. 'As a logical theory of political behavior the model is equally applicable to a world of altruists and egoists, even to a world of saints'.[83] The only theoretical requirement is that the individual goals are distinguishable. Such a model would naturally rule out any 'transcendental public interest'. Public interest as such is worked out by means of a distinction between the day-to-day decision-making and the 'constitutional' decision-making, 'where individuals may be thought of as participating in choices on the set of rules under which subsequent day-to-day decisions are to be made'. This second set of decisions is important. 'The essential element here is the recognition that self-interest at the level of decisions on rules or on institutions that are expected to remain in effect for long time periods, imposes on the individual an attitude and a behavior pattern that are not identical with those which the same self-interest would dictate in particular choices on specific issues.'[89] Buchanan suggests that, while the zero-sum 'pure-conflict' model of the mathematical game theory is applicable to day-to-day politics, the positive-sum model applies to constitutional choice involving the growth of consensus. The model is thus essentially based on the assumption of the voluntary nature of political association. It would virtually rule out power as participation in the "great game of politics" must, on balance, be mutually beneficial to all parties, or else revolution would ensue.

Power and Political Theory

Easton, it appears, was *partly* able to persuade the patriarch of functionalism to grant political science the status of an analytical science. His sociological commitment to integration militated against the purely individualistic assumptions of the market theory. In the volume edited by Easton, Parsons, therefore, outlined a scheme for analytical separation of political power.[90] Starting from the 'key orienting concept' of polity as 'a primary functional subsystem of society, strictly parallel in theoretical status to the economy', concerned, not concretely, but analytically, with all actions in 'collective pursuit of collective goal'.[91] Parsons redefined power as 'a medium of controlling action which, *under certain conditions,* is exchangeable for other such media operating in contexts from which power is excluded' (for example, money and influence).[92] Parsons insisted that the polity, like the economy, is more than a network of simple exchange relationships. As he had analysed the economy in terms of input-output analysis, and as Easton had done it in political theory a little earlier, Parsons applied the input-output model for an analysis of the polity.

Parsons rejects the common (individualistic) belief that democratic association is inherently egalitarian and the power system is inherently hierarchical. Parsons himself subscribed to the hierarchical view of power earlier. In the differentiated context now, he modifies his old stand. For a democratic hierarchy, even if bureaucratically structured, is ultimately based on franchise; and 'franchise is directly a form of power'. The uneven distribution of authority to make binding decisions, in such systems, is explained by the delegation of authority to the leadership in view of the increasing scale, complexity and urgency of collective business. Power 'becomes necessary in giving representatives power vis-a-vis their constituencies— especially the minorities in them who are yet bound by their representatives' votes—and yet giving the outcome of legislative votes binding character for the collectivity as a whole'.

> Legitimation...functions to define what political organization is for and, hence, to define the nature and scope of agencies—collectivities and roles—which perform political functions. Correlative with these structural definitions are both authority and implementation of legitimate responsibilities and access to power and the conditions of its use. In a sufficiently differentiated polity we call this the *constitutional system*—with private as well as public collectivities having constitutions more or less formally specified. Where the political aspect of the social structure is sufficiently differentiated from the others, *all* authority is "rational-legal" in Weber's sense.[93]

The key word in the functionalist approach to the social structure is, therefore, differentiation. Vis à vis the individual, it distinguishes his achievement from his ascriptive status. 'The ascription-achievement variable defines the major axis of differentiation of actors in a social system in their capacity as actors whose own orientations are to be analysed'.[94] In politics, 'Differentiation is marked by the development of legitimised procedures for expressing opposition to current leadership without impugning one's loyalty to the system'.[95]

Such a view of differentiation may be illustrative of the tautology of which Parsons has been notoriously accused of. Opposition to current leadership is differentiated from opposition to the system. Yet Parsons himself acknowledges that there may be 'vested interests' in a society resistant to change.[96] The original model of differentiation presented by Herbert Spencer, a century ago, implied an increasing rate of individuation through which society would achieve a new type of integration. One of the legacies of Spencer was the growth of the pluralist doctrine now popular among some US political scientists like Dahl.[97] Parsons is sceptical of its individualistic implications. 'It may very well be that the recent emphasis on the pluralism of expressive orientations is related to a phase of development of our own culture and of the social sciences within it, and will prove in the long run to be untenable.'[98]

Power thus remains at the centre of political science since the classical period, and Almond takes pride in this heritage.[99] Yet, Almond criticises classical Greek political theory for its stress on 'the interrelations of social stratification with the political system as the basis of political classification and political change, leaving the internal operation of the political process in a relatively unelaborated form'.[100] And Sartori spells out the criticism of Lipset : 'As long as we take for granted that changes are *reflected in*, not *produced by*, the political system itself, we necessarily neglect to ask to what extent conflicts and changes may either be channeled, deflected, and repressed or, vice versa, activated and reinforced, precisely by the operations and operators of the political system.'[101]

Almond provides us with an interesting history of the functional approach in which he shows that it was only in the context of the democratic revolutions of the seventeenth and eighteenth centuries, particularly the American revolution, that political theory arrived near the analytical separation of the social structure and the political process as well as of the structure and the function.[102] This gives us an insight into the process of political theorising itself. It is only in the context of *full* democracy that one can sensibly assume the social/political structure to be products of voluntary action — 'full democracy' encompassing the polity, the economy and the society. Alternatively, functional analysis gets its relevance in a period of transition when an old order is making way for a new one. The ability of eighteenth century Europe to disaggregate the structure and the function was first detected by Marx in the concept of the autonomy of 'civil society' (of the upcoming bourgeoisie) from the control of the feudal state.[103] Later, in the heyday of capitalism, when the bourgeoisie attained hegemony over civil society as well as control over state power, function and the structure were reintegrated. For very obvious reasons, the modern functionalist, in pleading for the autonomy of politics, refuses to view power as springing from the social/economic stratification system.[104] For the same reason, Talcott Parsons considers as innocent a book as Lipset's *Political Man* as the work of an 'undogmatic' Marxist.[105]

The Problem of Change

Almond's school of political development in fact grows out of the theory of separation of powers and reaches into the sociological and communication theory for useful conceptual tools and explicitly differs from the 'systems' approach of Easton and Deutsch that starts from the other end.[106] It turns Easton's conception of authority into 'legitimate use of compulsion' in order to restore a broadened view of Weber's conception of force, and defines the political system as 'the legitimate, order-maintaining or transforming system in the society'.[107] It presents a comparative, rather than historical, scheme of classification of political systems between two broad categories : the intermittent and the differentiated. The actual categories are, however, three : (1) the primitive systems with intermittent political structures, (2) the traditional systems with differentiated governmental-political structures, and (3) the modern systems with differentiated political infrastructures.[108]

There are three different sources of this classification. The 'intermittent', primitive systems with 'no differentiated political roles and no specialized political structure'[109] are derived from anthropology, while the 'traditional' systems are derived from Weber, and the term 'modern' is preferred to Weber's 'rational-legal' in keeping with the spirit of value-free science.'[110] Since its application first in communications research, the term 'modern' has acquired a special value in the social sciences in general and political science in particular.[111] The modern political systems were described as 'those in which there is a specialized political structure consisting of associational interest groups, political parties, and media of communication.' The emergence of a secularised political culture and an awareness of the role of government in changing human conditions are also common features.[112] The political participant develops a set of specific attitudes toward the political input structures, such as parties and interest groups, and toward the role he can play in these structures. In Britain, the Scandinavian countries, the USA and Switzerland, a very large, proportion does reach this level. The attitude, it was hoped, was likely to spread with the spread of literacy.[113]

This faith in literacy, a heritage of the European Enlightenment, emphasised repeatedly by John Stuart Mill and the liberal democratic thinkers after him, is, however, contrasted with the Enlightenment theory of evolution. 'The enlightenment theory of progress towards democracy and the rule of law is giving way to a multilinear theory of political development leading us through a break through the historical and cultural parochialism of the field', writes Almond. 'And we are on the eve of a search for rational-choice theories of political growth—an approach which may make political theory more relevant to public policy.'[114] This pithy statement about the new directions of political science sums up the functionalist conviction, shared by Easton too, that social/political systems tend to persist through adjustment and adaptation. As historical changes are ruled out, social sciences today shed their earlier critical attitude to society and look for a 'rational choice' which is the best bargain in a given situation. By prescribing 'rational choice' in a systematic order, social sciences can evidently hope for 'relevance' to the makers of public policy who are also the funding authorities for the huge amount of empirical research going on in the social sciences today.

A comparison of this faith in the spread of literacy, a heritage of the Enlightenment, with the functionalists' disavowal of the enlightenment theory of evolution and progress may be slightly puzzling unless one notes the functionalist hypothesis that 'the earlier historical experience of political systems as well as the environmental challenges to which they are currently exposed affect their propensities to change and set limits on the ways in which they can change'.[115] In other words, change is chiefly a motivational problem of the actors, and *not inherent* in a social structure.[116] Consequently, 'a general theory of the process of change of social systems is not possible in the present state of knowledge'.[117]

It is now possible to summarise the functionalist theory of action. A social/political system is made of patterned interaction systems and, therefore, *normally* tends to persist. As action is primarily based on motivations and secondarily on the role-expectation of the system, and as motivation is primarily a function of cognition, modern social sciences can at best look forward to a probabilistic theory of social/political change depending upon chance and exogenous factors.

The Social Sciences and Dialectics

Speaking of the ancient Greeks who tried to explain 'the why' of things by logical order, Nicholas Georgescu-Roegen, a Harvard economist, observes that 'Had Logic by chance been applied first to constructing a theoretical science in a different field from geometry—where things neither move nor change, but merely are—the war now fought between logical positivists and realists would have very likely exploded soon after the first *Elements [of Geometry* by Euclid]'.[118] In his survey of the relative development of the natural and the social sciences, Georgescu-Roegen notes that Geometry fitted in the frame of positivistic logic excellently, for it had only one—and a quality-free attribute—length. Mechanics was the next chapter in physics to become a complete theoretical system, and he cautions us that 'what mechanics understands by "space" and "time" is not *location* and *chronological time,* but *indifferent distance* and *indifferent time interval...* The space, the time, and the mass of mechanics all have in modern terminology, a *cardinal* measure'. Consequently, 'even the spectacular progress achieved through theoretical mechanics is confined to a phenomenal domain where the most transparent types of measure suffice'. The situation changed with the advent of thermodynamics when *noncardinal* variables like temperature and chronological time entered the theoretical texture.[119]

Even mechanics is still 'struggling with patchy knowledge not unified into a single theoretical body' for most variables in material structure 'are in essence quantified qualities.'[120] Quantification is possible only when a standardised measure of quality is evolved by the human community concerned. Otherwise, the craze for cardinal measures, developed around self-identical notions, degenerates into what he calls the 'arithmomorphic superstition'. Hence the conclusion that 'thinking, even mathematical thinking, would come to a standstill if confined to self-identical notions.'[121]

What applies to the natural sciences, applies more effectively to the social sciences based largely on metaphorical parallels with the natural sciences. To repeat the common- place: man is more than a machine; he is a living, thinking and creative being. This poses two kinds of problems for the social sciences : first, the standardisation of the norms of human action, and second, the measurement of his special faculties. When the functionalists speak of 'standardized values', they are liable to the mistake, deliberate or otherwise, of confusing it with dominant values which frequently emanate from the holders of power in a society. The concept of 'consensus' is equally liable to confusion if the market situation is considered in isolation from the relations of production which ultimately govern the market.

Georgescu-Roegen regrets that 'today there is little, if any, inducement to study change unless it concerns a measurable attribute',[122] even though qualitative change poses the greatest challenge to scientific activity. Even in physics, which for long ignored qualitative change, thermodynamics seeks to reestablish the theory of generation and annihilation of atoms, implying that change is not only locomotion.[123] Qualitative changes have never ceased to be the central theme of the life sciences. But social scientists, misled by the success of physics, have tended to believe that science cannot study change. The conclusion is inescapable that 'qualitative change eludes arithmomorphic schematization.'[124] It is here that dialectical concepts gain relevance in the sphere of the social sciences.

Dialectics is a logical method like positivism, and it was developed to a high degree, at the philosophical level, by Hegel. Positivism tends to regard dialectics as loose thought, even though dialectics does not deny the usefulness of the positivist method.[125]

Like positivism, dialectics comes in science only after its dissociation from the world of ideas. Science can only be materialistic and on this assumption there is hardly any difference between dialectics and scientific positivism. It is on the nature of matter, on the other hand, that dialectics and positivism differ. Society being included in this broad category of 'matter', social sciences reflect the difference between the two approaches.

Marxism

Inspite of sharp differences among social scientists, dialectical social science is now standardised as Marxism. Very appropriately, therefore, the positivist social sciences are at war with Marxism. Talcott Parsons notes it as 'a striking fact' that *general* orientations in the field of social theory 'have, in recent years, tended increasingly to polarize between a nondogmatic and non-political "Marxian" position and one which in the broadest sense may be called one or another version of the theory of action.'[126] And Lipset, whom Parsons considers to be one of the nondogmatic Marxists, interprets this differentiation as follows :

> What Parsons believes, of course, is that sociological analysis may be divided between those who place a primary stress on values as the key source of action, and those who emphasize the significance of interests. The former orientation, stemming from Max Weber, is pitted against the latter, which flows from Karl Marx.[127]

Whereas the distinction made by Parsons is no doubt critical, its reduction into a conflict between value and interest may appear somewhat simplistic. Parsons himself acknowledged the 'massive structuring of interests' in society, noted by Marx, as 'real'.[128] Parsons's (and the action theorists') emphasis on goal-gratification as the primary motivational factor may include interest-orientation. The issue of interest pertains to the early debate of the behaviourists. Parsons substituted the entire concept of behaviour by the concept of role.

Nor does the difference stand on the voluntaristic bias of Parsons's action theory and the allegedly 'deterministic' character of the Marxian theory. In the whole strand of sociological thought from Weber to Parsons, the social structure is either taken as 'given' (as in the case of Weber) or enters the theoretical frame of action as a conditioner (as in Parsons). The allegation that Marx accorded a deterministic primacy to social structure is, on the other hand, misconceived. Marx unmistakably asserted that the social structure is the result of human action. Criticising *'all* hitherto existing materialism', Marx wrote in 1845 that 'The materialistic doctrine that men are products of circumstances and upbringing, and that, therefore, changed men are products of other circumstances and changed upbringing, forgets that it is men that change circumstances and that the educator needs educating.'[129]

In 1859 Marx wrote that, in the social production of their life, 'men enter' into definite relations. Yet such relations are 'indispensable and independent of their will.'[130] Social relations are 'given' in the sense that they place individuals in respective positions and constrain their freedom to operate. Yet, it is for men 'to change'[131] such relations, and the entire communist *movement* is a programme for action along that line. Here arises the first of the basic differences between functionalism and the Marxist *theory* of action. The functionalist assumption that men generally conform to the existing norms makes it possible to circumscribe the scope of action and consequently to analyse it with the pretensions of mechanics. In Marxism, action, being fundamentally oriented to changing the given social system, can, on the other hand, be hardly predicted within the same mechanistic framework of precision.

Marx admitted this limitation. 'In considering such transformations a distinction should always be made between the material transformation of the economic conditions of production, which can be determined with the precision of natural science, and the legal, political, religious, aesthetic or philosophic—in short, ideological—forms in which men become conscious of this conflict and fight it out. Just as our opinion of an individual is not based on what he thinks of himself, so can we not judge a period of such transformation by its own consciousness; on the contrary, this consciousness must be explained rather from the contradictions of material life, from the existing conflict between the social productive forces and the relations of production.'[132]

This leads to the other difference between the Marxist and the Western social sciences of today. It lies in their respective *views* of the social structure. In the Marxist view, there is a fundamental contradiction within the system of production relations that constitute the *ultimate basis* of social relations and leads to its crisis, if not collapse. 'The production relation', a mainstay of classical political economy, is simply absent in neo-classical economic theory and, hence, in the other social sciences in the West. The Western social sciences today take satisfaction from the fact that *normally,* i.e., in terms of statistical frequency, social/political systems tend to survive and seek to analyse the mechanism of this survival. This is a positivistic choice of the Western social sciences today.

But when the Western social sciences ignore the question of production relations, which lead to the problem of distribution in the classical sense, there is obviously an *ideological* choice that affects their scientific potential. It leads to the assumptions that every society is *normally* capable of maintaining its integrity by adapting itself to the changing demands of its constituents and that there is no *inherent* reason why a social structure must, in ihe long run, face a crisis.[133] This prevents them from explaining historical change resulting from class contradiction in any elaborate and systematic form. It is symptomatic of this theoretical shortcoming that Parsons's exhaustive work, *The Social System,* running beyond 550 pages, has just three pages devoted to revolutionary upheavals, and this ignores the socialist transformation of Eastern Europe (outside the USSR) and China, treating Soviet Communism and Nazism at par.[134]

The point needs to be traced from the *scientific* angle. Historical changes can be analysed not in terms of frequency, but in terms of their qualitative significance. And yet, by the time Parsons's book was published, one-third of the globe had experienced socialist transformation. The socialist system had already stabilised itself beyond doubt. On the other hand, the Nazi experience was short-lived. In sheer quantitative terms (with reference to time as well as space), the socialist revolution could not be considered an aberration. The later attempt of the political development school to categorise the USSR as 'radical totalitarian', in terms of the absence of political subsystem autonomy, is poor compensation for this deficiency.[135] In any case, it does not explain the socialist revolution. Consequently, the action theory's claim to 'uni-versalistic' and 'dynamic' status appears pretentious.[136]

Conclusion

The case of this paper is the need for a closer examination of the specific contributions of the two alternative theories of society. A more 'scientific' social science would need to examine to what extent the 'vested interests' can be *entrenched* in society in an exploitative relation—in the Marxist sense—explaining 'the presence in the population of sufficiently intense, widely spread and properly distributed alienative motivational elements'.[137] This may need the shedding of the Weberian confidence in the process of rationalisation 'as a general directional factor in the change of social systems'.[138] That faith is not in keeping with the social scientific opposition to evolutionism and is even subject to varying interpretations. This faith is only more useful to the Western social sciences, concerned as they are with institutional integrity rather than Spencer's model of individuation[139] or Marx's model of dialectics. For Weber made rationalisation situation-specific. And Parsons himself has shown that in the West inequality has been functionally rationalised in terms of equality of opportunity.[140]

By the same token, Marxists may benefit through a utilisation of the specificity of the action theory. If their central purpose is social transformation, the intricate mechanics of the survival of a social system are very significant points of enquiry. Hitherto, progress in Marxian theory has been chiefly confined to two aspects of the problem : the structural and the (revolutionary) organisational. Yet there are diverse schools of thought in those respects. Every class system may inevitably come to a crisis. But why does not every such crisis lead to a revolutionary transformation ? One answer is imperialism which saved Western capitalism at a critical stage of history. But all class societies simply do not become imperialistic. Fascism is an alternative for capitalism in crisis. This is a field of investigation which can be specifically approached with some psychological orientation, concentrating to a greater extent than hitherto on problems of ideology and consciousness and the institutionalisation of beliefs in society, within the broad framework of structural enquiry.

1978

NOTES AND REFERENCES

1. See Nicholas Georgescu-Roegen, *Analytical Economics : Issues and Problems* (Cambridge, Mass. : Harvard University Press, 1967), pp. 12-14.
2. Scott Greer, 'Sociology and Political Science' in Seymour Martin Lipset, ed., *Politics and the Social Sciences* (New Delhi : Wiley Eastern, 1972), pp. 49-64, at p. 51.
3. Eric Roll, *A History of Economic Thought* (London : Faber and Faber, 1966), p. 92.
4. See Greer, op. cit., p. 51.
5. *Ibid.*, p. 52.
6. *Ibid.*
7. Roll, op. cit., p. 20.
8. *Ibid.*, p. 371.
9. Graham Wallas, 'Human Nature in Politics' (1908), extracted in Heinz Eulau, S. J. Eldersveld and Morris Janowitz. eds.. *Political Behavior: A Reader in Theory and Research* (New Delhi: Amerind, 1968), pp. 9-11, at p. 9.

9a. K. Marx, *Capital,* Moscow: Progress Publishers, Vol. 1, 1954, 1974, pp. 84-5, 716.

10. Roll, op. cit., p. 141.
11. *Ibid.*, pp. 396-97.
12. This changing mood of the non-Marxist economists has been appropriately caught by Sweezy in the changing definitions of Economics as the science of investigation into 'the nature and causes of the wealth of nations' (Adam Smith), 'the laws which regulate the distribution of the produce of the earth' (Ricardo), 'man's action in the ordinary business of life' (Marshall), 'price and its causes and corollaries' (Davenport), 'human behaviour as a relationship between end and scarce means which have alternative uses' (Lionel Robbins). See Paul M. Sweezy, *The Theory of Capitalist Development : Principles of Marxian Political Economy* (London : Dennis Dobson, 1946), p. 12.
13. Stanislav Andreski, *Social Sciences as Sorcery* (London: Andre Deutsch, 1972), p. 144.
14. Roll, op. cit., p. 372.
15. Andreski, op. cit., p. 144.
16. See Julien Freund, *The Sociology of Max Weber* (London : Alien Lane, 1968), p. 88.
17. For summaries of the behavioural and the psychoanalytical schools of psychology, see Robert S. Woodworth, *Contemporary Schools of Psychology* (London: Methuen, 1960) chs. 3 and 4; and C.E.M. Joad, *Guide to Modern Thought* (London : Faber & Faber, 1942), p. 3.

18. Wallas, op. cit., p. 9.
19. Arthur F. Bentley, 'The Process of Government—A Study of Pressures' (1908), extracts in Eulau et. al, op. cit., pp. 14-24, at p. 14.
20. Giovanni Sartori, 'From Sociology of Politics to Political Sociology' in Lipset. op. cit., pp. 66-100, at p. 71.
21. *Ibid.*
22. Charles A. Beard, *An Economic interpretation of the Constitution of the USA* (1913; New York: Macmillan, 1961), see particularly pp. vi and 14-15.
23. See Richard Jensen, 'History and the Political Scientist' in Lipslt, op. cit., pp. 1-28, at pp. 5-6.
24. Richard LaPiere, *Collective Behavior* (New York : McGraw-Hill, 1938), pp. 55-56.
25. Robert K. Merton, *Social Theory and Social Structure* (New Delhi : Amerind, 1972), p. 175.
26. Talcott Parsons, *The Social System* (Glencoe, Ill : Free Press, 1951), pp. 544-45.
27. David Faston, *Tne Political System* (1963 ; Calcutta : Scientific Book Agency, 1972), chapter 8.
28. Eulau *et al.*, op. cit., 'Introduction', p. 3.
29. Robert A. Dahl, 'The Behavioral Approach in Political Science : Epitaph of a Successful Protest Movement', *American Political Science Review,* 59 (1961), pp. 763-72.
30. Heinz Eulau, *The Behavioral Persuasion in Politics* (1963; New Delhi: Vakil, Feffer and Simons, 1970).
31. Talcott Parsons, *The Structure of Social Action* (New Delhi: Amerind, 1974), p. 11.
32. This handy summary is provided in T. Parsons and E.A. Shils, eds., *Toward a General Theory of Action : Theoretical Foundations for the Social Sciences* (New York : Harper & Row, 1962), p. 53.
33. Parsons, op. cit., p. 732.
34. *Ibid.*, Preface to the Second Edition (1949), p. D.
35. A. Einstein and L. Infeld, *The Evolution of Physics* (New York : Simon & Schuster, 1938).
36. Parsons and Shils, *op. cit.*, p. 51 and the Preface.
37. Talcott Parsons, *The Social System*, p. 20.
38. Parsons and Shils, op. cit., p. 242.
39. Parsons, op. cit., pp. 21-22.
40. Harald Mey, *Field Theory : A Study of its Application in the Social Sciences*, tr. Douglas Scott (London: Routledge and Kegan Paul, 1972), p. 90.
41. Parsons and Shils, op. cit., p. 52.

42. *Ibid.*, pp. 15-17.
43. Parsons, op. cit., p. 5.
44. *Ibid.*, p. 70.
45. See Robert K. Merton, *Social Theory and Social Structure*, p. 76.
46. *Ibid.*,
47. *Ibid.*, p. 104.
48. *Ibid.*, pp. 39-44.
49. *Ibid.*, p. 106.
50. *Ibid.*, p. 105.
51. *Ibid.*, p. 176.
52. *Ibid.*, pp. 215-16.
53. *Ibid.*, p. 218, and Parsons, *The Social System*, p. 294.
54. Merton, op. cit., p. 195.
55. Parsons, op. cit., p. 39.
56. Merton, op. cit., p. 175.
57. *Ibid.*, p. 211.
58. Merton, op. cit., pp. 94-95.
59. Parsons, op. cit., p. 520.
60. Irving Louis Horowitz, *Foundations of Political Sociology* (New York: Harper and Row, 1972), p. xvii.
61. Parsons, op. cit., p. 540.
62. *Ibid.*, p. 24.
63. Andreski, op. cit., p. 153.
64. It may be pertinent here to draw a distinction between the 'interdisciplinary' and the 'multi-disciplinary' method. The multi-disciplinary approach sprang from the acknowledgement of the autonomy of the disciplines and the need for marshalling of the knowledge of *different* disciplines in addressing particular problems. The 'inter-disciplinary' approach addresses different disciplines from one central point of reference : the theory of action.
65. Parsons, op. cit., pp. 545-52. See also Talcott Parsons and Neil J. Smelser, *Economy and Society: A Study in the Integration of Economics and Social Theory* (Glencoe, Ill : Free Press, 1956), pp. 52-3.
66. Parsons, op. cit., pp. 548-50. Autonomy notwithstanding, Economics was hardly accorded the status of a special theory (see Parsons and Smelser, op. cit., p. 28). Parsons chose to enter directly into the internal controversies of economics while rejecting the psychological atomism of the extremist utilitarians, but approving of the more moderate views of Pareto and Hicks. He stressed that 'the goal of the economy is not

simply the production of income for the utility of an aggregate of individuals. It is the maximization of production relative to the whole complex of institutionalized value-systems and functions of the society and its sub-systems'. Parsons and Smelser, op. cit., pp. 22-23.

67. Parsons, op. cit., p. 552. Sec also the Preface, p. vii.

68. Parsons and Shils, op. cit., p. 29.

69. Parsons, op. cit., pp. 550-51. Note the difference of emphasis on the status of political science : 'somewhat different' (in Parsons and Shils, op. cit.,) and 'wholly different' in (Parsons, op. cit.).

70. *Ibid.*, p. 126.

71. H. H. Gerth and C. Wright Mills, 'Introduction' in Gerth and Mills, eds. and trs.. *From Max Weber : Essays in Sociology* (London : Routledge and Kegan Paul, 1964), p. 47.

72. E. A. Shils and H. A. Finch, eds., *Max Weber on the Methodology of Social Sciences* (Glencoe, Ill: Free Press 1949), p. 99.

73. Max Weber, 'Politics as a Vocation', in Gerth and Mills, op. cit., p. 78.

74. *Ibid.* Also see George E.G. Catlin, *A Study of the Principles of Politics* (New York: Macmillan, 1930); *Systematic Politics* (London : George Allen & Unwin, 1962); and H. D. Lasswell, *Politics : Who Gets What, When, How* (New York: McGraw-Hill, 1936).

75. Catlin, of course, emphasised that this analysis is 'more fundamental than the Marxist', in as much as it assigns a certain *primacy* to social control. *Systematic Politics*, p. 79.

76. David Easton, *The Political System : An Inquiry into the State of Political Science* (1953 ; Calcutta : Scientific Book Agency, 1971), pp. 120-21.

77. V.O. Key, *Politics, Parties and Pressure Groups* (New York; Crowell-Collier, 1945), pp. 4-5.

78. Nelson Polsby. *Community Power and Political Theory* (New Haven Conn.: Yale University Press, I963), p. 104.

79. Easton, op. cit., p. 61.

80. *Ibid.*, p. 143.

81. *Ibid.*, p. 144.

82. *Ibid.*, p. 132.

83. *Ibid.*, p. 143.

84. David Easton, 'Categories of Systems Analysis of Politics' in David Easton, ed., *Varieties of Political Theory* (Englewood Cliffs, N. J. : Prentice-Hall, 1966), pp. 143-54, at p. 148. This essay summarises Easton, *A Framework of Political Analysis* (Englewood Cliffs, N. J. : Prentice-Hall, 1965), and is a revised version of Easton, *A Systems Analysis of Political Life* (New York : John Wiley, 1965).

85. *Ibid.*, pp. 143-44.
86. *Ibid.*, pp. 150-51.
87. *Ibid.*, p. 152. Easton owes part of this theoretical sophistication to Deutsch's communications theory of politics. Karl W. Deutsch, *The Nerves of Government* (New York : Free Press, 1963).
88. James M. Buchanan, 'An Individualistic Theory of Political Process' in Easton, Varieties of Political Theory, at p. 28. For a summary of the development of the market bargaining theory, see Ithiel de Sola Pool, 'The Public and the Policy' in Ithiel de Sola Pool, ed., *Contemporary Political Science: Toward Empirical Theory* (New York : McGraw-Hill, 1967), pp. 22-52, at p. 37.
89. *Ibid.*, p. 29.
90. Talcott Parsons, 'The Political Aspect of Social Structure and Process' in Easton. ed., *Varieties of Political Theory*, pp. 71-112.
91. *Ibid.*, pp. 71-72.
92. *Ibid.*, pp. 85-88. Emphasis added in order to show the qualified nature of Parsons's sanction.
93. *Ibid.*, p. 82.
94. Parsons, *The Social System*, p. 96.
95. Parsons, 'The Political Aspect', p. 85.
96. Parsons, *The Social System*, p. 491.
97. See Robert A. Dahl, *Pluralist Democracy in the United States : Conflict and Consent* (1967; Calcutta: Scientific Bock Agency, 1969), particularly pp. 3-24.
98. Parsons, op. cit., p. 501.
99. Gabriel A. Almond, 'Political Theory and Political Science' in Ithiel de Sola Pool, op. cit., pp. 1-21, at p. 18.
100. *Ibid.*, p. 5.
101. Giovanni Sartori, 'From Sociology of Politics to Political Sociology' in Lipset, ed. *Politics and the Social Sciences*, pp. 65-100, at p. 89.
102. Almond, op. cit., p. 6.
103. Karl Marx, 'The German Ideology', Chapter I, in Marx and Engels, *Selected Works* (Moscow : Progress Publishers, 1973), Vol. 1, p. 76.
104. See Robert A. Dahl. 'The Evaluation of Political Systems' in Ithiel de Sola Pool, op. cit., pp. 166-91, at pp. 188-89.
105. See Seymour Martin Lipset, *Political Man: The Social Bases of Politics* (New York : Doubleday, Anchor edition, 1963), p. xxi.
106. Almond and Powell, op. cit., p. 12, fn. 10.
107. Gabriel A. Almond, 'Introduction : A Functional Approach to Comparative Politics' in Gabriel A. Almond and James S. Coleman, eds., *The Politics of Developing Areas (Princeton:* Princeton University Press, 1966), pp. 3-64, at p. 6.

108. For details, see Almond and Powell, op. cit., p. 217.

109. *Ibid.*, p. 43.

110. *Ibid.*, pp. 44-47.

111. Daniel Lerner, *The Passing of Traditional Society* (Glencoe, Ill, Free Press, 1958) ; Lucien W. Pye, ed., *Communications and Political Development* (Princeton : Princeton University Press, 1963}; David E. Apter, *Political Modernization* (Chicago : University of Chicago Press, 1965). For a critique of the theory of modernization in Western social sciences, see *Daedalus*, Winter 1973.

112. Almond and Powell, op. cit., p. 255.

113. *Ibid.*, pp. 58-59.

114. Gabriel A. Almond's presidential speech at the American Political Science Conference, 1966, 'Political Theory and Political Science' in Ithiel de Sola Pool, ed., op. cit., pp. 1-21, at pp. 14-15.

115. *Ibid.*, p. 215 ; cf. Parsons, *The Social System*, p. 491.

116. Parsons, *The Social System*, op. cit., p. 493.

117. *Ibid.*, p. 486.

118. Georgescu-Roegen, op. cit., p. 10.

119. *Ibid.*, p. 48.

120. *Ibid.*, p. 49.

121. *Ibid.*, p. 44.

122. *Ibid.*, p. 42.

123. *Ibid.*, p. 30.

124. *Ibid.*, p. 31.

125. *Ibid.*, pp. 27-28.

126. Talcott Parsons, 'The Point of View of the Author', in Max Black, ed., *The Social Theories* of *Talcott Parsons* (Englewood-Cliffs, N.J.: Prentice-Hall, 1961), p. 362.

127. Seymour Martin Lipset, *Political Man : The Social Bases of Politics*, p. xx.

128. Talcott Parsons, *Essays in Sociological Theory* (1948; Indian edition, New Delhi : Light and Life, 1975), p. 323.

129. Karl Marx,'Theses on Feuerbach', no. III, in Karl Marx and Frederick Engels, *Selected Works*, Vol. I (Moscow : Progress Publishers, 1973), p. 13.

130. Marx, 'Preface to a Contribution to the Critique of Political Economy', *ibid.*, p: 503.

131. Marx. Theses on Feuerbach', No. XI, *Ibid.*, p. 15.

132. Marx, op. cit., p. 504.

133. There is, however, a rather late realisation among the political development theorists that such crises do actually appear, and Ithiel de Sola Pool ('Foreword' in Ithiel de Sola Pool, op. cit., pp. x-xi) denies that contemporary political science is non-normative. Although Parsons is satisfied that revolutionary change can hardly occur in the industrialised countries of the West, the Marxists see the potential for such change and explain the political/ economic stability of the West in terms of the benefits of economic imperialism.
134. Parsons, *The Social System,* pp. 520-22.
135. Almond and Powell, op. cit., p. 217.
136. Parsons deals more elaborately with the repercussions of change introduced by scientific and technological advance. But, like the general orientation of this theory of the social system towards conditions in the United States, the orientation of this treatment also tends towards the same country. See Parsons, op. cit., pp. 505-18.
137. *ibid,* p. 520-521.
138. *ibid.,* p. 499.
139. For a summary of Spencer, see Barnes, 'Herbert Spencer and the Evolutionary Defence of Individualism' in Harry Elmer Barnes, ed., *An Introduction to the History of Sociology* (abridged edition, Chicago : University of Chicago Press, 1967), pp. 81-108, particularly, pp. 93-94.
140. Talcott Parsons, 'Equality and Inequality in Modern Society or Social Stratification Revisited' in Edward O. Laumann, ed., *Social Stratification: Research and Theory for the 1970s* (Indianapolis: Bobbs-Merryl, 1970), pp. 13-72, at pp. 14-16.

2

The Raja and the Raj : Conflict and Collaboration

The title of this article may sound anachronistic to those who believe that British rule in India was established in 1600, when the East India Company obtained the British Royal Charter.[1] For the title of 'Raja' was conferred on Rammohun Roy by Emperor Akbar II, in 1830, while sending Rammohun as his ambassador to the British emperor to protest against the arbitrary behaviour of the East India Company and the Company did not recognize the title.[2] This paper intends to examine the issue in course of its general argument that Rammohun should be considered at least as much a man of transition as a pioneer of a new era. Metaphorically, one may say that a man of transition has one leg each in the old and the new era; a pioneer has just left the old one.

Contradictions of Rammohun's Age

Tagore called Rammohun the founder of a new Bengal,[3] inaugurator of the modern age.[4] Susobhan Sarkar called him the central figure at the starting point of the Bengal Renaissance (exactly, the years 1814-33, from the time when Rammohun settled down in Calcutta till the time of his death in England).[5] The blurb of his book traces the Bengal Renaissance to the late eighteenth century, the time of the consolidation of the British power in Bengal. Sarkar, however, would "only smile" at the "mystic idea that British conquest was the instrument of providence for India's uplift".[6]

Sarkar's article, originally published in 1946, was not the first to use the term 'Renaissance'. In 1910, F.B. Bradley-Birt had written : "Among the famous men of Bengal in the nineteenth century, no name deserves a more honoured place than that of Rammohun Roy. At once the pioneer of the great Renaissance that was slowly dawning in Bengal and the first representative of India to the British people, he opened up to his countrymen new paths of progress and reform."[7]

"The impact of British Rule, bourgeois economy and modern western culture was felt first in Bengal and produced an awakening known usually as the Bengal Renaissance," wrote Sarkar. "For about a century, Bengal's conscious awareness of the changing modern world was more developed than, and ahead of, that of the rest of India. The role played by Bengal in the modern awakening of India is thus comparable to the position occupied by Italy in the story of the European Renaissance."[8]

It is possible to discern a subtle contradiction between this statement and the skepticism of Sarkar (noted earlier) about British rule believed by some to be a "providential instrument of India's uplift", for the earlier comment hints at a dialectical relationship between the rulers and the ruled while the latter suggests a somewhat linear evolution of the Renaissance out of the British rule. The contradictions that are cited in both Tagore and Sarkar were at the social and religious levels of the Indians. Rammohun's arguments with the Christian missionaries can by no means be cited as evidence of such contradictions.

Rammohan and the Christian Missionaries

It is well known that the Christian missionaries were no darlings of the East India Company, which was ruling India during Rammohun's time. The missions were admitted into the Company's territory only after the passage of the Charter Act in 1813 and acquired a firmer ground twenty years later. Rammohun's main battles with the Christian missions were fought between 1820 and 1823 through his *Precepts of Jesus* (1820), the three *Appeals to the Christian Public*, written within the next three years, and the pages of his *Brahmanical Magazine* (1821-23), wherein he protested against "encroachment upon the rights of (this country's) poor, timid and humble inhabitants" by proselytising Christian missionaries through ridiculing the native religions and material inducement to the converts.[9]

Such activities would make Rammohun the darling of the East India Company. Yet, according to the young, India-born US scholar, Robertson, Rammohun's interrupted services to the East

India Company covered a total period of only three years and eight months.[10]

On the other hand, Rammohun collaborated with the Christian missionaries in their intellectual and constructive undertakings. He assisted the Serampore mission in certain translations of the Gospel, set up the Unitarian Committee in 1821 and ran its congregation service, school and printing press, and supported Duff's fight against "godless education".[11] Christianity appealed to his intellect rather than his faith as did Islam. His faith was in Vedantic monism within the framework of the Brahminical society. While advocating inter-caste marriage, he retained his sacred thread ensuring his top place in the *Varna* hierarchy.

The Problem about 'Renaissance'

In general historical literature, there seems to be a tendency to encapsulate in 'Renaissance' the whole concept of progress. Consequentially it was, indeed, so. In its essence, however, 'Renaissance' means *rebirth.* In Europe, it meant rediscovery of her past which, although it grew within the precincts of the Christian church, was, in fact, a rediscovery of her pagan past. Rammohun rediscovered the monistic past in the Indian tradition, as enshrined in the *Upanishads*, not the *Vedas* which were polytheistic. This rediscovery was confined to an extremely limited section of the Bengali elite which gathered at the Atmiya Sabha. It is a different matter that, in the subsequent phase of the 'Indian Renaissance', thinkers like Dayananda obliterated the difference between the *Vedas* and the *Upanishads.* The literary creativity of Rammohun is, of course, comparable to that of the European Renaissance. The credit for ushering in a "moral revolution", "an era of inquiry and investigation", and the establishment of the concept of "freedom and equality", which S.N. Mukherjee rightly grants to Rammohun, belongs to the age of Enlightenment and not to the Renaissance.[12] Even the concept of 'nationhood', which Rammohun is believed to have fathered among the Indians, belongs to the age of Enlightenment. The Renaissance created hundreds of sovereign states in Europe, not nations.[12A]

Rammohun and the British Empires

His relation with the Raj at the political level was even more problematic. Rammohun worked in collaboration with the British administration in the fields of social reform and spread of modern education. His letter to Lord Amherst on 11 December 1823 became the precursor of the educational policies of Bentinck and Macaulay.[13] He supported the Permanent Settlement of Cornwallis ensuring the stability of the *zamindars'* right over land and wanted its extension to the relation between the *zamindars* and the cultivators. He welcomed British investment in India in the indigo plantations, overlooking its two contradictory implications : (1) the East India Company was a trading company and not an investing firm, and (2) the indigo planters turned out to be not only oppressive towards the cultivators, but they also clashed with the *zamindars* in several cases. While the Permanent Settlement of the land with the *zamindars* might be consistent with the East India Company's general philosophy of non-interference in the Indians' internal affairs, investment in indigo was not, unless one remembers the compulsions of the Company in the first two decades of the nineteenth century forcing the Company to allow private investment.[14]

Rammohun's closeness to Islam and its followers is well-documented. Robertson observes that "Rammohun was proud of his family's service for three generations under the Mughals" and cites his undertaking Akbar II's assignment to "the court of Directors of the East India Company" for "an increased pension" in London in 1830.[15] In his *Appeal to the King in Council,* Rammohun recalled that "under the former Muhammedan rulers, the natives of this country enjoyed every political privilege in common with Mussalmans". Recording that "under the British rule, the natives of India have entirely lost this political consequence", Rammohun, however, acknowledged that "Your Majesty's faithful subjects were consoled by the more secure enjoyment of those civil and political rights which had been so often violated by the rapacity and the intolerance of the Mussalman".[16]

R.C. Majumdar cited this statement as historical evidence of Hindu-Muslim hostility in pre-British India and treated it as an example of "how the Hindus in India acclaimed the establishment of British rule as a divine dispensation for their deliverance from the tyrannies of Muslim rule. Leaders like Raja Rammohun Roy gave public expression to this view".[17]

This certainly is an imputation which Rammohun did not

deserve, for he was precisely speaking of the fair treatment of the Hindus by the Muslim rulers at the *administrative* level. Majumdar, however, goes beyond this imputation by seeking to correct Rammohun. "The blessings of the Muslim rule, mentioned by the Raja, may be true of only a short period of Muslim rule, roughly extending from the middle of the sixteenth to the close of the seventeenth century A.D."[18] Majumdar's dearest thesis is not exactly proved. But Rammohun's observation remains puzzling.

It can, of course, be argued that Rammohun was making the first political demand of the British India elite, namely, freedom of the press and was called upon to cite the political-administrative fairness of the Muslim rulers. It may even be argued that Rammohun was anticipating an elite level Hindu-Muslim unity under the new dispensation, simultaneously distancing himself from the life of the common people. His advocacy of the rights of the cultivators in land shows his concern for the common people at the economic level.[19] He was not actively engaged in the amelioration of the plight of the common people in the way he engaged in opposing the *sati*, a vice of the Hindu upper castes. He could afford to ignore the unity of the folk-level culture in rural India between the Hindus and the Muslims. The observation is surely elitist though not clearly communal. This elitist outlook is well explicated by the summary of Rammohun's political view of the British empire :

> He argued that, since 1712 until the emergence of the Company as a political power, there was no effective political force in India. Akbar II, the last but one 'representative of the imperial throne of Timur', enjoyed only the empty title of 'king of Delhi' without royal prerogative or power. Ranjit Singh's power was confined to north-western India only. The new middle classes were no doubt a significant social and economic force in Bengal, but they lacked cohesion to become an effective political force and had no influence outside the province. The British were in the circumstances the only effective political force in the country and ... had used that position to maintain orderly relations of exchange and to protect the 'lives, religion and property' of the individuals... But

> he emphatically asserted that sovereignty must not be in the office of the Governor-General or in his subordinate officers but in the King-in-Parliament, who was the supreme legislative power in the country.[20]

The ambivalence of Rammohun's attitude to the empire suggested by this pithy summary of Rammohun's political thinking is made explicit by a short quotation from his own writing presented by Mukherjee in the same article:

> Though it is impossible for a thinking man not to feel the evils of political subjection and dependence on foreign people, yet when we reflect on the advantages which we have derived from our connection with Great Britain, we may be reconciled to the present state of things which promises permanent benefits to our posterity.[21]

One point is clear : Rammohun did not consider the Mughal rule 'foreign' as he did the English rule. His acceptance of the title *of Raja* from Akbar II and holding his brief in London establish not only his linkage with the pre-British political regime but also his moral sympathy for it. He made probably one mistake : he gives an impression as if it was open to the Indian people to accept or to reject British rule. Maharaja Ranjit Singh's reputed comment — *"sab lal ho jayega"* — perhaps presents a greater awareness of the reality. On his part, Rammohun was an advocate of British colonization, i.e., settlement and investment, a policy disapproved by the East India Company. Rammohun was in favour of the rule of the British King-in-Parliament, rather than of the Governor-General who was an employee of the East India Company. Rammohun was opposed to the Company as many British liberals were.

Rammohun and the Mughal Empire

Rammohun is said to have cherished the desire to visit Europe and America since at least 1823.[22] But he actually set sail on 17 November 1830 with a commission of the "King in Delhi" and a title of Raja conferred by him. The purpose of the mission was to convey the grievances of one sovereign to another against a chartered company under the sovereignty of the latter. Bentinck refused to recognize this status of Rammohun and, instead, issued him a private introduction. On his arrival in London, Rammohun could not hand over this letter to the British King. He ended up submitting written evidence to the British Parliamentary Committee on Indian Affairs.[23] Rammohun, however, did what he could best do in the circumstances. He circulated to influential Englishmen a printed statement corresponding in substance to the letter of the Emperor. As a result, the Court of Directors of the East India Company raised the 'stipend' of the imperial family from Rs. 12 lakh to Rs. 15 lakh per annum, leaving it to the Emperor to distribute the additional Rs. 3 lakh to other members of his family as he thought just and proper.[24]

Rammohun's was not the first mission to England from the Emperor at Delhi. Sixty-five years before him, another Indian, Mirza Iteshamuddin, had been sent by Emperor Shah Alam with a somewhat similar request and was treated with plain deception. This happened close on the heels of the Treaty of Allahabad, after which Robert Clive, during his second term, gave the Mughal Emperor an assurance that the Company would station two contingents of its army at the disposal of Shah Alam. Very soon the Emperor was told that this could be done only after obtaining the sanction of the British Parliament. He promised to send Major Swinton with a letter from Major Carnac, the British Officer signatory to the Treaty of Allahabad, containing the request and proposed that an emissary of the Emperor should accompany him. On the day the Mirza was to depart by a ship, Swinton did not arrive and the former was told that it was only because the gifts to be carried had not arrived. Clive promised to come himself with the gifts and the letter by the next ship. Clive did arrive in London but did not contact the Mirza, who returned to India frustrated.[25]

The Traditional Character of Rammohun's Age

By the time of Rammohun's entry into the socio-political scene of Bengal, political power had effectively passed from the Emperor at Delhi to the East India Company and the British Parliament had put effective control over the East India Company. In fact, Rammohun's socio-political life at Calcutta and at London was sandwiched by the two critical Charter Acts of 1813 and 1833. In 1813 the Company lost its trading monopoly in India[26] and in 1833 it lost its trading right and was instituted as the representative of the British Government. By that time the *tribute of Rs. 26 lakh* had been reduced to a "stipend of Rs.12 lakh". In 1857 the British called it a pension.[26]

Rammohun, one feels, banked too much on the internal contradiction of the British empire and hoped that an enlightened rule of law of the British King-in-Parliament, colonization of India and English education would improve India's fate. In effect, India got an economic colonization by the British under the British rule, of course, along with a liberal and scientific education. Whether the benefits of education and science would have been available to the Indians without British rule is a speculative question and belongs to the domain of polemics.

Rammohun's departure to London was shrouded in a conspiracy uglier than the one that had visited Mirza Iteshamuddin. According to Rammohun's own admission, he was "one of the humblest of the subjects of His Britannic Majesty" and was moved by the "indigent condition of the illustrious House of Tymoor" in taking its complaint to the British Royalty.[26] When the Delhi ruler conferred the title of Raja on him, Rammohun sought Bentinck's "sanction for the adoption of the title" and was declined recognition of the title. However, the Governor-General did not forbid him to use the title, for the British government, in 1827, had acknowledged the Delhi ruler's power to grant titles to his "servants".[27] Expectedly, the Governor-General denied the charge of Akbar II, the denial being backed up by a letter, obviously obtained from the heir apparent to Akbar II, complaining that the latter had lost his sense due to age and was illegally favouring his second son for succession, and that Rammohun had forged a conspiracy with some officers of the royal court against him and the Company.

Even at this twilight hour of India's political independence, intrigues played the usual role it had played in the court politics. Rammohun could only chastize the heir apparent : "Those who do not comprehend their own good or evil cannot comprehend the good or evil of others."[28]

It can be argued that Rammohun's title and status were declined by Bentinck because of the Delhi ruler's claim to parity with the ruler of Britain and the use of the term 'tribute'. Although the East India Company, which was grabbing territorial power in India was, in turn, being grabbed by the British government, by

1830 the East India Company and the British government had united in their objective to grab India. Rammohun, however, was aware of the inherent contradiction in the British imperial design. His brief was to secure financial relief to the Delhi ruler and not to fight for his sovereignty, which in any case was a fiction. Interestingly, his friends in England were the liberals, who were critical of the East India Company. Rammohun made his appeal to this liberal imperialist section of the British elite. On the other hand, he made it clear to the Company that, in case they did not heed the Delhi ruler's demand, he would be forced to meet the British king.

It will be belittling Rammohun to call him an "archetypal Bengali intellectual of the early nineteenth century". But Rammohun certainly reflected their existential dilemma. In quite a few letters, Rammohun gave out the impression that he did not regard the establishment of British rule in India as legitimate even though it was inexorable and, probably, beneficial. His numerous assertions as a loyal subject of the British Crown are technically inconsistent with his claim to be a servant of the Delhi Emperor unless one takes into account two facts: (*i*) the fluidity of the legal status of the British power at the time, and (*ii*) a certain faith in the fairness of the liberal British opinion on the part of Rammohun and the emerging Bengali elite of his time.

1999

NOTES AND REFERENCES

1. For instance, A.B. Keith, *A Constitutional History of India 1600-1935*, Methuen, London, 1937, andA. G. Banerjee, *A Constitutional History of India*, Vol. 1, 1600-1858, Macmillan, Delhi, 1977.
2. Bruce Carlisle Robertson, *Raja Rammohun Roy : The Father of Modern India*, Oxford University Press, 1995, p. 45.
3. Rabindranath Thakur (Tagore), *'Rammohan Prasanga'* (in Bengali), *Rabindra Rachanabali*, Birth-Centenary ed., Government of West Bengal, Vol. 11, Pravandha (B.S. 1368, A.D. 1961), p. 429).
4. 'Rammohun Roy' (in English), *ibid.*, p. 436.
5. Susobhan Sarkar, *Bengal Renaissance and Other Essays*, People's Publishing House, New Delhi, 1970, p. 4.
6. *Ibid.*, p. 135.
7. FD. Bradley-Birt, *Eminent Bengalis in the Nineteenth Century* (1910), reprint, Inter-India Publications, New Delhi, 1985, p. 1.

8. Sarkar, *op.cit.*, p. 3.
9. *Ibid.*, pp. 7-8.
10. Robertson, *op. cit.*, p. 22.
11. Sarkar, *op. cit.*, p. 8.
12. S.N. Mukherjee, 'The Social Implications of the Political Thought of Raja Rammohun Roy', in R.S. Sharma, in collaboration with Vivekananda Jha (ed.), *Indian Society : Historical Probings in Memory of D.D. Kosambi*, People's Publishing House, New Delhi, 1974, pp. 356-89.

12A. See Delisle Burns, *Political Ideals*, Chapter VI, "Renaissance Sovereignty", 1914, World Press, 1960.

13. Sarkar, *op. cit.* p. 10.
14. R.C. Majumdar (General Editor), *The History and Culture of the Indian People : British Paramountcy and Indian Renaissance*, Part 1, Bharatiya Vidya Bhavan, Bombay, 1963, pp. 1097-98.
15. Robertson, *op.cit.*, p.11. There are two controversial points about this statement. Rammohun had been sent by Akbar II with a letter to King George IV and not the Court of Directors of EIC. Further, the letter did not speak of a 'pension'.
16. R.C. Majumdar (gen. ed.) *op.cit.*, Part II, pp. 11-12.
17. *Ibid.*, p. 418.
18. *Ibid.*, p. 12.
19. Sarkar, *op.cit.*, p. 13.
20. S.N. Mukherjee, *op.cit.*, p. 380.
21. *Ibid.*, p. 385.
22. "A letter of introduction by a friend" of Rammohun to Jeremy Bentham quoted in F.B. Bradley-Birt, p. 29. The letter went on to say: "It is no small compliment to such a man that even a Governor-General like the present who, though a man of the most honest intentions, suspects everybody and trusts nobody, and who knows that Rammohun Roy greatly disapproves of many of the Acts of Government, should have shown him so much respect as to furnish him with introductions to friends of rank and political influence in England" *(ibid.*, p. 30).
23. R.C. Majumdar, *British Paramountcy*, etc., Part II, p. 518.
24. R.C. Majumdar, *op.cit.*, Part I, p. 19. The increase remained on paper only.
25. Shibani Kinkar Chaube, "*Vilat Pherat Pratham Bangali: Mirza Iteshamuddin*", (in Bengali), *Antarjatik*, February-March, 1962.
26. Association of this year with what Marx called "the glorious Wars of Liberation" in Europe may be an interesting angle of study of Rammohun Roy (see, K. Marx and F. Engels, *Selected Works*, Vol.1, Progress, Moscow, 1969, p. 39).

26A. In 1773 Warren Hastings stopped the payment of the tribute. During the second Maratha War Lord Lake secured from Holkar "the person of the Emperor" (Edward Thompson and G.T. Garratt, *Rise and Fulfilment of British Rule in India,* second edition, Central Book Depot, Allahabad, 1962, p. 220). Wellesley carved out a "small kingdom" surrounding Delhi for the Emperor and continued to call him "His Majesty". The British Commissioner would be responsible for the administration and revenue collection of this territory in His Majesty's name. Rs. 12 lakh out of this revenue would go to the "Emperor" *(ibid.,* p. 22). The British Resident at Delhi, on ceremonial occasions, presented His Majesty with the Governor-General's *nazar* and the seal of the Governor-General bore a phrase describing him as the servant of the Emperor (Majumdar, *British Paramountcy,* Part I, p. 17). After the passage of the Charter Act, 1813, Marquess of Hastings abolished both the practices in order to extinguish "the fiction of Mughal government" *(ibid).* Shah Alam's successor, Akbar II, complained that the "tribute" paid to him and his family was insufficient (Thompson and Garratt, *op.cit.,* p. 249). In fact, the revenue collection from the area west of the Yamuna, in Rammohan's language the "Crownland", had increased. Rammohan's own correspondence, however, mentions "stipend".

27. See J.K. Majumdar, *Raja Rammohun Roy and the Last Mughals: A Selection from Official Records,* 1803-1859, London 1939.

28. *Ibid.,* p. 214.

3

Personalistic Ethics in Gandhi's Political Philosophy

For the purpose of this paper 'Philosophy' is defined as the system for conduct of life. It is noted that individual philosophies are subsystems of older philosophies or their variants. The universalization of such philosophies, however, depends upon its internal strength, the character of the milieu and the extent of reciprocity between the two.

Gandhi has written a great deal to enunciate and explicate his theory. Gandhi's action-packed life broadly conforms to his ideology though some incongruities can be traced there as arising out of dictates of circumstances.

The core of Gandhi's philosophy—*satyaagraha*—is a systen of personal ethics that could be summed up as right conduct. Gandhi believed that Indians were subjected to continuous British rule owing to their own fault, that is to say, their love for the lures of the Englishmen's civilization. Without cooperation of the Indians the British could not rule India. Therefore, Gandhi's strategy was non-cooperation with the British rulers.

Gandhi hated the English 'civilization', not Englishmen. For the Indian society the Gandhian prescription was toleration of communities which he called *ahimsa*. The alternative institutional framework for Indians prescribed by Gandhi was based upon the indigenous strength of the Indian community rather than imitation of the West.

Thus Gandhi offers a complete theoretical system though its components may be controversial. One great theoretical weakness of the Gandhian system is that, beyond toleration, it hardly offers a formula for interpersonal collaboration that may cement communal or national unity. Collective action is based on the leadership principle rather than interdependence of the members of the group.

This weakness is exposed, time and again, in the Gandhian saga of freedom struggle, as for example, when Gandhi started the non-cooperation movement almost single-handed, combined it with the Khilafat, and suspended it, all of a sudden, unilaterally, in the event of the Chauri Chaura violence. From jail, leaders such as C.R. Das, Motilal Nehru, Lajpat Rai, Subhas Chandra Bose and Jawaharlal Nehru[1] sent out their strong protests to Gandhi when he thus withdrew his non-cooperation movement.[2] The noted Indo-British communist intellectual, R.P. Dutt, wrote in 1948:

> Given this understanding that it was not a strategy intended to lead to the victory of independence, but to find the means in the midst of a formidable revolutionary wave to maintain the leadership of the mass movement and restraint upon it, it was a skilful strategy.[3]

M. N. Roy, in his communist phase, shared, more or less, the same opinion.[4] Subhas Chandra Bose was more understanding :

> There is something in Mahatma Gandhi which appeals to the mass of the Indian people. Born in another country he might have been a complete misfit ... In India it is different Wherever he may go, even the poorest of the poor feels that he is the product of the Indian soil—bone of his bone, flesh of his flesh... When he talks to them about Swaraj, he does not dilate upon the virtues of provincial autonomy or federation, he reminds them of the glories of Ram Rajya and they understand. And when he talks of conquering through love and ahimsa, they are reminded of Buddha and Mahavira, and they accept them.[5]

Three Strands of Freedom Movement

The milieu in which philosophers who were children of the freedom movement operated was the Indian social complex. All of them belonged to the same age, vastly constituted by Gandhi himself.

The pre-Gandhian national movement was broadly divided into two strands : the moderate and the extremist, with a revolutionary wing of the extremist strand. It included M. N. Roy (an alias of Narendranath Bhattacharyya) and other early revolutionaries who toyed with the idea of revolution with arms aid from Germany. Overstreet and Windmiller's history of

Communism in India opens with the cryptic observation that in 1915 M. N. Roy left India in pursuit of his revolutionary goals and Gandhi reached India— finally—to revolutionize her people.

But Gandhi did not only revolutionize the Indian masses, he brought these teeming millions into the mainstream of national movement. In 1915 Subhas Chandra Bose was yet to join the movement. He subsequently joined the Indian National Congress under Gandhi's spell and parted company with him in 1940, but remained a critical admirer of him throughout his life. M. N. Roy went to Russia, became a communist leader of international ranking and finally relinquished communism to end up being a frustrated 'radical humanist'.

Not that Gandhi's personal success was outstanding. Gandhi left the Congress in 1934-35, was disgusted with it in 1947 and was murdered by an Indian less than a year after the Independence of India. On the other hand, the Congress never disowned him formally, always used his moral authority during the freedom struggle and capitalized on his name to stick to power.

The Making of a Mahatma

Gandhi chose to call his philosophy 'satyagraha'—the pursuit of truth which is the quintessence of human existence. Analysts have found in him both Western and Indian influences. Guy Wint links his passion for Utopias with the English and American philanthropists of the 19th century. Individualism, iconoclasm, the cult of austerity, the emphasis on self-discipline—these were not of course unknown to India, but in Gandhi they took the form common to English puritanism. He derived his faith in suffering from the Bible. His faith in non-violence was a Jain, rather than an Indian, element. His method of gaining his way by spectacular fasts and organization of life in Ashram as well as his ambiguous attitude to caste were regarded to have been drawn from the Indian traditaton.[6]

Nirmal Kumar Bose could readily think of two *samskaras* that found expression in Gandhi's universal ideas : one derived from ancient Hindu culture and the other, apparently, from Christianity. To quote Bose, Gandhi's 'predilection for forms or institutions which have endured through ages, in other words, the recognition of permanency as a quality of Truth, has obviously been derived from his traditional social equipment. This has led him to a mild form of conservatism, but which has the redeeming feature of being always subjected to the final tests of reason and universal morality. Inspite of this, the thin strain of conservatism makes Gandhi a shade more receptive of old ideas than of those which have not yet been tested by the hand of time.

The other *samskara* which may have resulted from a reaction in his own life against childhood's married experiences, or from his early Christian associations, is his concept of sin and the special attitude which he bears towards sensual purity.[7]

Personalistic Ethics

Gandhi has been regarded by many as a sublime despot, although a skilful strategist. Everyone connected with him reports that he was not only religious, but also introvert ; in times of crisis he was practically incommunicable, sitting with his spinning wheel and with his face down.

One gets a bit of Gandhi's mental fabric in *Hind Swaraj* which was written as early as 1908 when Gandhi was involved in South African politics. There are reasons for treating *Hind Swaraj* to be as much a mirror of Gandhi's mind as a blueprint for India[8] if only because it was his first complete political thesis.

In this book, Gandhi first pays his compliments to Alan Octavian Hume and William Wedderburn, the two Englishmen responsible for the birth of Congress, and the moderate Indian leaders. He explicitly states that he is not so much opposed to the Englishmen as he is to English rule which has degenerated even Englishmen. He not only calls the British Parliament a sterile prostitute and condemns the newspapers as an evil influence upon the people, but regards modern comfort-oriented civilization as a disease. Then he regards as the cause of India's subjection and continued subordination to England the greed of the Indians. 'We like their commerce, they please us by their subtle methods and get what they want from us.'[9]

Among the evil influences of civilization Gandhi characteristically picked up the railways, lawyers and doctors. Before the introduction of the railways, Indians had 'natural segregation'.[10] Formerly people could travel to holy places only with difficulty. So the good people alone went there. Now the rogues also go there. The railways have fast spread evil. The English could not have ruled the country without lawyers and law courts. Instead of settling the disputes between persons the lawyers aggravate them and thrive on them.

Most characteristic of Gandhi, however, was his condemnation of the doctors who offer remedy to diseases. Diseases occur because men indulge in vices. Had there been no doctors, men would not have indulged in vices and would have behaved properly.

The whole argument is not only moral, it is personalistic. The 'unity' of India resulting from natural segregation before the introduction of the railways was really similarity and mutual coexistence. It can be argued that this is not the scientific conception of a nation, members of which interact with, rather than tolerate, each other. This toleration is the keynote of his formula for communal harmony.

The Political Philosophy of Gandhi

Gandhi himself was opposed to cow slaughter. But he would rather appeal to the Muslims at their feet to desist from cow slaughter than take a Muslim life. This philosophy of toleration induced him to accept Lord Morley's formula of separate electorate for the Muslims, if they so desired.[11] The philosophy of toleration was, however, not a fetish or creed in itself with Gandhi. It was part of a broader philosophical system called '*ahimsa*', and defined by him as real love. In essence, this real love would teach us to hate wrong but not the wrong-doer. It would plead with the wrong-doer to give up his wrong practice rather than take revenge on him. The pursuit of this *ahimsa* needs on the part of its practitioner an indomitable moral courage that enables him to suffer in the cause of truth.

To Gandhi, attainment of this moral quality is tantamount to the attainment of 'swaraj' or home-rule. In Gandhi's own language :

1. Real home rule is self-rule or self-control.
2. The way to it is passive resistance, that is 'soul' force or 'love' force.
3. In order to exert this force, Swadeshi in every sense is necessary.

4. What we want to do should be done, not because we object to the English or because we want to retaliate but because it is our duty to do so. Thus, supposing that the English remove salt-tax, restore our money, give highest posts to Indians, withdraw the English troops, we shall certainly not use their machine-made goods, nor use the English language, nor many of their industries. I bear no enmity towards the English, but I do towards their civilization.[12]

Gandhi turns *swaraj* into an individualistic concept :

> It is 'swaraj' when we *learn* to rule ourselves. It is, therefore, in the palm of our hands. The Swaraj that I wish to picture is such that, after we have once realized it, we shall endeavour to the end of our life-time to *persuade* others to do likewise. But each one for himself. One drowning man will never save another. Slaves ourselves, it would be a mere pretension to think of freeing others.[13]

I underline the two words 'learn' and 'persuade' to show that *swaraj,* for Gandhi, is a personal faculty and not an external condition. In fact, to Gandhi, 'swaraj' is the instrument to end the vices of Western civilization manifest in British rule. Gandhi would accept the Englishman in India when he is freed from his vices and has been sufficiently 'Indianized'. Thus Gandhi's philosophy is individualistic in the sense that it is a guide to individual action. The defect of this philosophical system lies in the absence of a *theory* of collective action. Gandhi banks entirely on common action through individual examples.

Commonality, it may be stressed, is different from communality that rests on a perception of complimentarity and interdependence.[14] Viewed from this angle Gandhi's '*ahimsa*' does not necessarily mean real love. It is this dificiency which led G.D.H. Cole to comment on *Hind Swaraj* that though Gandhi was as near as a man could be to Swaraj in a personal sense, 'he has never solved to his own satisfaction, the other problem — that of finding terms of collaboration that could span the gulf between man and man, between acting alone and helping others to act in accordance with their lights, which involves acting with them used as one of them — being at once one's self and someone else, someone one's self can and must regard and criticize and attempt to value.'[14]

Gandhi's Style

Gandhi's style of work would vindicate this statement. Gandhi regarded his humiliation on the Natal railways during the South African sojourn (1893) as 'the most creative experience' in his life.[15] Since his South African experiences, Nehru wrote, 'he had a fixed basis of all his ideas and his mind was hardly an open mind.'[16] During the Boer War Gandhi collected a batch of volunteers to work in the British ambulance corps and wanted that the subjects must accommodate themselves and accord their support to the acts of the state.

During World War I he appealed to the Indians to join the British Indian army and collaborate in the war effort. In an interview with Louis Fischer in 1942 Gandhi explained his stand: 'I had just returned from South Africa. I had not yet found my feet. I was not sure of my ground.'[17]

In India Gandhi's first political agitation was in defence of the indigo share-croppers of Champaran in 1917. The plight of the share-croppers convinced Gandhi of the need to urge for the departure of the British.[18] Next he intervened in the strike at the Sarabhai Textile Mills. His maiden fast on the occasion moved the heart of the friendly owners, confirming his faith in the change of the opponent's heart through self-suffering. In 1918 he started agitation against the Rowlatt Act and gave it up in the midst of violence confessing 'Himalayan blunder'. He took over the leadership of the nationalist movement in India in 1920, coalesced it with the Khilafatists and started the non-cooperation movement. Gandhi assured the country of Swaraj within a year. As Swaraj was elusive, the AICC, in November 1921, resolved upon 'mass satyagraha'. Gandhi, however, chose to launch it on a limited scale in Bardoli. When violence broke in Chauri Chaura, he withdrew the movement.

Gandhi's coalition with the Khilafatists has been the greatest point held out against Gandhi. It hardly brought about a lasting union of the two major communities of India. The movement lost its moral strength when the people of Turkey themselves overthrew the Caliphate. After Gandhi withdrew the movement on the dictate of his 'inner voice' a series of communal riots occurred in the country.

In 1923 Gandhi relaxed his non-cooperation to the extent of allowing the Congress Swarajists to enter the legislature but forbidding them to assume office. The Swarajists could not proceed far and, in the wake of the Simon Commission Report, Gandhi launched the civil disobedience movement. Qualitatively, the CD (civil disobedience) movement was more advanced than the NC (non-cooperation) movement. The NC movement meant merely non-collaboration with the evils of British rule (civilization). The CD movement was a programme of action of resistance to British rule. It enthused the Indian people more than the NC movement, but was soon reduced into a sort of 'individual satyagraha'. The movement fizzled out. Gandhi left the Congress for ever when it decided to accept office in 1934. Gandhi led the 1942 'Quit India' movement from outside the Congress.

Conclusion

Gandhi's expositions in his profuse writings, from *Hind Swaraj* onward, and his style of work give out the following philosophy, of which his political philosophy was a central component.

The outstanding feature that emerges is Gandhi as an intense individual with profound faith in personal ethics. To Gandhi, an individual is required to observe right action irrespective of public approval. For a practising politician this almost total neglect of public appreciation or otherwise is an apparent paradox unless one remembers that Gandhi expected others to follow him.

The second point about Gandhi's philosophy is his profound conviction that one gets nothing without a price. This frank approach to life may be traced to his Bania background, but it was thoroughly honest. Given the colonial situation of the country, this gave him a faith in self-sacrifice.

The most positive element in this philosophy was self-reliance accompanied by self-discipline. Gandhi hated the civilization of the West which had robbed India of her rich moral content. Among other things Gandhi was opposed to the elaborate political institutions that the British had been creating to strengthen their rule and secure the active participation of the Indians. Gandhi knew for certain that without the collaboration of Indians British rule could by no means be entrenched in India. Hence the call to leave government services, legal professions and government-run educational institutions. The NC movement went down to even the village level challenging the establishment of the Union Board.[19]

It is misleading to depict Gandhi as a pure anarchist. Gandhi was far from it. He had a definite set of alternatives of the institutions and values he was challenging. To the tyranny of Lancashire industry Gandhi's reply was Indian textile, hand-woven or machine-made. To the British official education Gandhi's answer was 'national' and 'basic' education which would be production-oriented rather than office-oriented. To the Union Board Gandhi's reply was the traditional *panchayat*. The idea of a panchayati raj was an answer to the Western system of parliamentary democracy.

It is possible to differ on the merits and demerits of the Gandhian system. It is impossible to consider it less than a complete *theoretical* system. Practically, its significance was profound in the anti-imperialist struggle of India. Gandhi's firm conviction that it was impossible to fight the British rule within its own institutional framework was shared by terrorists. But Gandhi's emphasis on mass involvement in the freedom struggle as its main strength was a totally new phenomenon in India.

1993

NOTES AND REFERENCES

1. Jawaharlal Nehru, *An Autobiography*, London, Bodley Head, 1958, p. 514.
2. Subhas Chandra Bose. *The Indian Struggle, 1920-1942*, Bombay, Asia Publishing House, 1964.
3. R.P. Dutt, *India Today*, Bombay, People's Publishing House, 1948, p. 341.
4. *See* the controversy between Nirmal Kumar Bose and V.G. Kulkarni on M. N. Roy's attack on Satyagraha in Nirmal Kumar Bose, *Studies in Gandhism*, Calcutta, The Indian Associated Publishing House, 1947, pp. 316-36.
5. Subhas Chandra Bose, *op. cit.*, p. 73.
6. Guy Wint, *Spotlight on Asia*, Penguin, 1955, p. 69.
7. Nirmal Kumar Bose, *Studies in Gandhism*, p. 339.
8. In the preface to the 1938 edition to the *Hind Swaraj or Indian Home Rule*, Mahadev Desai wrote apologetically : 'I must confess that in "the

urgency of his vision" Gandhiji used rather crude language about machinery, which, if he were revising the book, he would himself alter'. Gandhi corrected him : 'After the stormy thirty years through which I have since passed, I have seen nothing to make me alter the views expounded in it', Shriman Narayan (General Editor), *The Selected Works of Mahatma Gandhi*, Ahmedabad, Navajivan, 1968, Vol. 4.

9. *Ibid.*, p. 126.
10. *Ibid.*, p. 131.
11. *Ibid.*, p. 141.
12. *Ibid.*, p. 201.
13. *Ibid.*, p. 155.
14. *Ibid.*, p. 14.
15. See Louis Fischer, *The Life of Mahatma Gandhi*, Bombay, Bharatiya Vidya Bhavan, 1959, Vol. 1, p. 39.
16. Nehru, *op. cit.*, p. 516.
17. Louis Fischer, *op. cit.*, p. 156.
18. *Ibid.*, p. 167.
19. See Hitesh Ranjan Sanyal, 'Dakshin-Paschim Banglaye Jatiyatavadi Andolan' (in Bengali), *Chaturanga*, 38th year, Kartik-Pous, 1383 B.S.

4

The Indian Constitution Through Half A Century

When Aristotle discussed 150 constitutions of the Hellenic cities to write *Politics,* he meant by 'constitution' a description of the system of government of a polity.[1] The meaning of 'constitution' remains more or less the same today, i.e., a set of positive laws that determine the structure and ways of government and the status of citizens. When, however, we speak of 'constitutionalism', we combine this statement of positive law with a political norm. We mean that such a set of positive laws, written or unwritten, are followed by the government, precluding arbitrary rule. The absence of arbitrariness is the guarantee of the rights of the people. In fact, such rights act as limits to state power.

When John Locke wanted a limited government—a monarchy circumscribed by the advice of the legislature[2]— he laid down the basis of constitutionalism that became an article of faith with political liberalism. But there is a subtle theoretical contradiction between the 'constitutionalism' of Locke and the pure democracy envisaged by Rousseau whose 'general will' is the unlimited sovereign[3]. British parliamentary democracy sought to reconcile the contradiction by setting up the King/Queen in Parliament as the sovereign and by universalizing the franchise. The USA declared the 'people' as sovereign who 'ordain and establish' the constitution— the supreme law of the land[4]. Republican India followed the US model, but set up a parliamentary government within a federal set-up—not quite a novel experiment, as the USSR had already done that.

By this definition India may be said to have had a constitution even before independence, in the form of the Government of India Acts of 1919 and 1935. However, it certainly did not have constitutionalism. The Acts were grants of the British Parliament and consequences of devolution of power from the Crown. They did not flow from the people. The new constitution of 1950 altered this frame of reference by vesting the authority of the constitution in the people of India[5].

A bird's-eye view of the Indian Constitution will present the following picture. India's parliamentary system is different from that of Britain in being a republic and in providing for a statutory system of fundamental rights. It is different from the US system in not only being parliamentary but also being a highly centralized federation. There are other special features distinguishing the Indian Constitution from both these models, e.g., the Directive Principles of State Policy borrowed from the Irish constitutional model; the Fifth Schedule, vaguely resembling the old Scottish pattern of government in the United Kingdom; the Sixth Schedule, modelled on the autonomous governments in the USSR; and the Finance Commission, modelled on the Australian federal system (The Commonwealth Grants Commission). Certain special institutions were set up in order to deal with some special problems, e.g., the Commission on Scheduled Castes and Scheduled Tribes by the Constituent Assembly and Commission on Linguistic Minorities by the Parliament.

Such a complex constitutional structure was bound to contain some structural contradictions which were manifested from time to time in periodic 'crises' like the 1959 supersession of the Kerala government, the series of supersessions of state governments between 1967 and 1969, the infamous emergency of 1975 and ministerial instability at the Centre occasioning three general elections in three years. Yet such 'crises' could not destroy the overall stability of the Indian political system. On the other hand, there are signs of stability appearing in the states' politics. The confrontation between the legislature and the executive, the hallmark of Indian politics in the late sixties and early seventies of the last century, has all but disappeared. The judiciary has shifted its attention from property to freedom and is even passing judgements on questions of social justice.

Over-Reliance on the Centre

Not that the makers of the Indian Constitution were unaware of a possibility of change in the power balance and the consequent tensions. The series of communal riots, accompanied by Communist uprisings in parts of the country immediately after independence, made the leaders of the Assembly hesitant about granting unfettered personal/political freedom. Personal liberty was granted subject to preventive detention[6]. Three rigorous kinds of emergency, one of which (financial emergency) has not yet been applied, were provided for[7]. Article 365 further provided that the failure of a State government to comply with a directive issued by the Centre under any provision of the Constitution would entitle it to supersession and to be brought under President's rule. There was of course an over-reliance on the Centre. But, even about the Centre, the possibility of change was not ruled out. As Dr Ambedkar put it succinctly on the status of the Constituent Assembly:

> The Constituent Assembly in making a constitution has no partisan motive. Beyond securing a good and workable constitution it has no axe to grind. In considering the articles of the constitution it has no eye on getting through a particular measure. The future parliament, if it met as a constituent assembly, its members will be acting as partisans seeking to carry amendments to the constitution to facilitate the passing of party measures which they have failed to get through parliament by reason of some article of the constitution which has acted as an obstacle in their way[8].

Ambedkar, in later years, complained of the 'brute majority' of the Congress in the Constituent Assembly. On its floor, however, he paid warm compliments to its strength and role:

> The task of the Constituent Assembly would have been a very difficult one if the Constituent Assembly had been merely a motley crowd, a tessellated pavement without cement, a black stone here and a white stone there in which each member or each group was a law unto itself.... This possibility of chaos was reduced to nil by the existence of the Congress Party inside the Assembly, which brought into its proceedings a sense of order and discipline. It is because of the discipline of the Congress Party that the Drafting Committee was able to pilot the constitution in the Assembly with the sure knowledge as

> to the fate of each Article and each Amendment. The Congress Party is, therefore, entitled to all the credit for the smooth sailing of the Constitution in the Assembly[9].

Another point Ambedkar made strongly was that a Constitution is a political document and does not commit itself to any particular socio-economic ideology—a point that came out of the criticism of the Constitution by the Congress radicals[10]. However, several leaders of the Assembly hoped that the Constitution would open avenues for socio-economic progress.

In 1973, this writer contended that the Indian Constitution is a liberal-democratic document with a bias for property but orientation for welfare[11]. This contention went against the rather platitudinous view that the Constitution is a charter of social revolution[12]. However, two criticisms, not quite new ones, deserve to be answered. One, the Constituent Assembly was not elected through universal adult franchise and was not representative enough to reflect the aspirations of the people or the spirit of Indian civilization. The answer is that none of the classical democratic constitutions, that have survived the test of time, were framed by assemblies elected through universal adult franchise. The point is not about how such assemblies were constituted, but what their visions were. This vision cannot be backward, it has to be forward. A polity, which seeks to live by past traditions, does not need a constitution! In tribal societies, they go to the old men for learning about their past and seeking their advice on the future.

Misinformed Criticism

The second criticism—of relatively recent origin—is actually misinformed. Quotations have been made from speeches of Assembly leaders like Jawaharlal Nehru to the effect that they had acknowledged the limitations imposed on the body by the British Government and, therefore, they promised to summon another Constituent Assembly after India gained sovereignty. The fact is that such statements were made before the partition of India, when the Muslim League members were absent[13]. After Partition was announced, the Muslim League members in the Indian part joined the Constituent Assembly of India and the British Government stopped interfering with the work of the

Assembly. During the final reading of the Constitution no one raised any objection to the status of the Assembly. Several members expressed the hope that the Constitution would not need an amendment in several years to come. No one demanded a 'free' constituent assembly and no one promised it. Of course, the Constitution was amended several times after that. But such amendments were well within the competence granted by the Constitution itself.

That the 'people of India', on 26 November 1949, adopted, enacted and gave to themselves a Constitution establishing a sovereign, democratic republic, is of great legal implication. Whereas 'democracy' is largely a political concept, sovereignty is a subject of international law and republicanism belongs to the domain of municipal law. By now it is well accepted that membership of the United Nations Organization and the various functional associations, such as the Commonwealth of Nations, does not affect the country's sovereignty. Democracy is a matter of substance rather than law. But universal adult franchise, more or less effectively made use of over thirteen times, has distinguished India among all the post-colonial states.

The implication of republicanism is manifold. Historically, it meant India's refusal to accept a dominion status—something that was actually bestowed by the Indian Independence Act, 1947. Secondly, India had this Constitution framed by its own representative assembly rather than it being enacted by British Parliament, as in the cases of Britain's White colonies (Canada, Australia, etc.). The Constitution of India was authenticated by the chairman of the Constituent Assembly himself. Even the assent of the Governor-General was not taken. The Governor-General was replaced by an indirectly elected President without any 'discretionary' power. All vestiges of monarchy were abolished, not only at the Centre but also in the states, 554 princely states were merged into this republican structure.

Absence of 'Prerogative' of Executive

A consequence of this republicanism is the absence of any kind of 'prerogative' of the executive. Any 'discretionary' power has, of necessity, to be expressly conferred by the Constitution or delegated by the people or their representative body. The

British Queen retains the power of appointment/dismissal of the Council of Ministers as well as to refuse dissolution of the House of Commons as a prerogative. The Indian President has the power of appointment/dismissal of a Council of Ministers by virtue of Article 75 of the Constitution. The President has the further power of asking his Council of Ministers once to reconsider its advice (Article 75). Beyond these the Indian President is as powerless as the British Queen is. The Governors of the Indian states enjoy the same powers with regard to the states' executive affairs (Article 163). But there is apparently a drafting anomaly that makes unlimited discretionary power available to the Governors.

Can the President of India or, for that matter, a state Governor decline to grant dissolution advised by a Council of Ministers? Such a refusal leads to the resignation/ dismissal of the Council of Ministers and, probably, a fresh election. In either case the President/Governor undertakes a political responsibility, liable to be controversial. A Governor may escape responsibility by advising President's rule in a state. The President has no such option. He has, therefore, to do as his Council of Ministers advises him to do. That is, if he does not replace it. Such replacement is occasioned by the resignation or dismissal of the Council of Ministers. The Council of Ministers usually resigns when it loses confidence of the House of the People (Lok Sabha). If, on the other hand, the Lok Sabha is not in session at the time this loss of confidence of the members occurs, the President has a problem. Sessions of the Houses of Parliament are summoned by the President only on the advice of the Council of Ministers. If the President feels that the Council of Ministers has lost the confidence of the majority of the members of the Lok Sabha, at a time it is not in session, he may ask his Council of Ministers to be advised to summon the Lok Sabha. In case the Council of Ministers refuses to oblige him, he has the right to withdraw his pleasure from the Council of Ministers. In other words, he may dismiss it.

While a vote of no-confidence is a time-honoured convention in parliamentary democracy, a vote of confidence is a more recent phenomenon. British parliamentarians are rather fastidious about their autonomy and do not like to run to the Crown to decide what can be decided on the floor of the House of Commons. In India, however, inter-party confidence with regard to parliamentary norms is rather weak. The state Governors and, subsequently, the President have come under increasing pressure to intervene in inter-party tussles for power. The chronic political instability, arising chiefly out of party splits and changing alliances, has often compelled state Governors and the President to appoint Chief Ministers and Prime Ministers, without being adequately able to ascertain their legislative backing. They have felt compelled to ask the appointees to seek a vote of confidence on their assumption of office. This practice has generated some controversy in political circles. The legislative experience with a confidence vote has not been quite happy. On the other hand, the Law Commission's recommendation to restrict the number of no-confidence motions is apparently against the principle of ministerial responsibility. The Constitution says that the Council of Ministers *shall* be responsible to the concerned House. Legally it means must always be so. The right of the legislature to express no-confidence in a Council of Ministers can by no means be taken away even for a limited period of two years as suggested by the Law Commission.

Governor's Discretion

It is necessary to discuss the provisions of Section 50 of the Government of India Act, 1935, to understand the anomaly in Article 163 of the Constitution of India about the discretion of the Governor. Under the 1935 Act, the Governor had three kinds of powers: (1) powers exercised with the aid and advice of the Council of Ministers, (2) powers exercised in his discretion, and (3) powers exercised in his individual judgment in the case of certain special responsibilities. Whereas 'discretion' meant freedom from the obligation to accept ministerial advice, 'individual judgment' meant that the Governor would consult

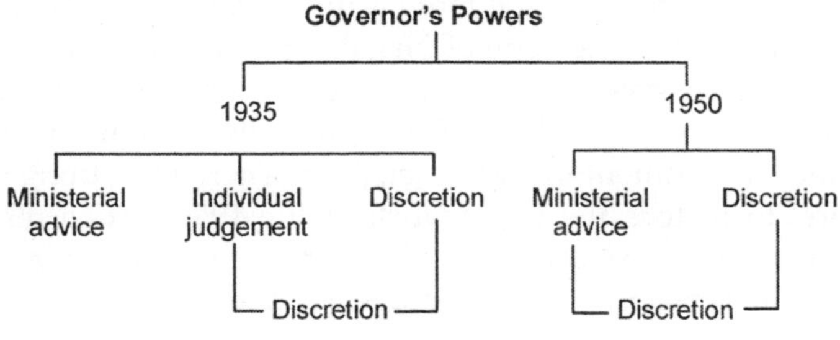

the Council of Ministers but would not be bound by its advice. On the question whether a matter fell within the sphere of a Governor's discretion or individual judgment, the Governor had the discretion to decide.

The Constituent Assembly, however, retained the Governor's discretion, but abolished individual judgment. Thus, the Constitution, in clause (1) of Article 163, provides that there shall be a Council of Ministers to aid and advise the Governor, except when he is required by the Constitution to act in his discretion. But clause (2) of the same Article provides, that the question whether a matter fell within the discretion of the Governor or not could be decided by the Governor in his discretion. As a result, the Governor can decide that anything under the sun is within his discretion.

This anomaly has put in limbo Dr Ambedkar's assurance in the Constituent Assembly that the Governor would strictly follow the rule that discretion would be applied only when the Constitution required it[14]. Governors have used their discretion while acting as Chancellors of state universities, in meeting government officials independently, in reserving bills passed by state legislatures for the President's assent and in making 'reports' on the states' affairs to the Union Government. Of these reports the one on constitutional breakdown alone unquestionably belongs to the domain of discretion. Considering the fact that the federal autonomy of the Indian states largely depends upon the freedom of the states' Councils of Ministers to conduct their states' affairs without interference by the Governor, who is but an agent of the Union Government, the Governors have come under great suspicion.

Special Responsibilities in Northeastern States

The dilemma has become more acute because of the fact that, since the creation of the state of Nagaland in 1963, Governors in the northeastern states have been assigned a number of special responsibilities to be discharged in their individual judgment as under the Government of India Act, 1935. There is a strong case, therefore, to restore the framework of the 1935 Act to restrict the domain of discretion to specified areas. As it happens, the Indian Constitution originally assigned only two fields of discretion to the Governor of Assam alone—within the Sixth Schedule. One of them disappeared with the creation of Arunachal Pradesh as a state[15].

A related controversy, involving the State governments, is Article 356, by which the Central government may declare a constitutional breakdown in a State following the report of the State government or its own satisfaction. The problem is complicated by Article 365, which provides that the failure of a State government to comply with a Union government directive under any provision of the Constitution may imply a constitutional breakdown, which gives the Union government unlimited authority to decide on the necessity of a constitutional breakdown. Another factor that has occasioned rampant use of Article 356 is the Governors' unwillingness to take responsibility. Whenever party volatility leads to ministerial instability, the Governor, instead of making an honest effort to form an alternative government, recommends President's rule, thus passing the buck to the Centre. The Supreme Court judgment in the Bommai case, laying down that the court has the power to examine the relevance of a Governor's report for the satisfaction of the President (i.e., the Union government) to the effect that a constitutional breakdown has occurred in a state, has but partly mitigated the irregularity.

Recently focus has been thrown on ministerial stability at the Centre as well as at the States. The Law Commission has recommended: (1) constructive vote of no-confidence, by which the Opposition, before moving a motion of no-confidence, should elect its leader capable of taking over the reins of government, in case the government falls, and (2) ban on a motion of no-confidence for two years, once such a motion is defeated in a House.

This is a thoroughly misconceived idea of ministerial responsibility which assumes that, once a Council of Ministers is installed in office, it has no more responsibility to prove that it continues to enjoy the confidence of the House. It is the burden of the Opposition to prove that it has an alternative leader capable of commanding the support of the House. Drawn to the extreme, this argument may also imply that a Council of Ministers, once in office, may never have to prove its majority support. What is, however, quite possible for a Council of Ministers is to engineer a fraudulent no-confidence motion in the House, get it defeated and stay in office for two years without interruption. The burden of proving the constant support of the legislature to a Council of Ministers belongs to the latter. The burden of proving the loss of confidence is not on the Opposition which, of course, has the liberty to prove it any time.

Right to Seek Dissolution of House

The stability argument often derives its support from the presidential system in the USA and the semi-presidential systems in continental Europe. A presidential system is based not on responsibility but representativeness. There is in fact a subtle theoretical contradiction between the two principles. A representative body or office-holder cannot be held responsible, in the sense of being replaceable, on a daily basis, to its electorate. Both the US President and the members of the Congress are elected and, therefore, enjoy fixed tenures. Even the members of the Indian Parliament are elected by and not responsible to the electorate. The Lok Sabha may be dissolved; its members may not be recalled. In a mass democracy like India recall is absurd except probably at the local government level. The only guarantee of ministerial stability in a parliamentary democracy, even in the United Kingdom, is the right of the Council of Ministers to seek dissolution of the House, to which they are responsible, to deter the members from indulging in fickleness. That is, so long as a vote of no-confidence has not been passed against it.

It is essential to remember that, had the USA been not a rigorously-defined federation and had there been no strict separation of powers at the Centre, the US President could well be a dictator. As it happens, the Indian federation is highly centralized and there is no separation of powers in a parliamentary democracy. Indian democracy cannot afford to be presidential. Nor can it have two elected chief executives—a President and a Prime Minister. A clash of personalities, in such a situation, could make government impossible. India, therefore, chose an elected President and an appointed Prime Minister responsible to an elected legislature.

The West German model, cited by the supporters of the notion of constructive no-confidence, actually lays down that the

President nominates the Prime Minister and puts his nomination to vote in the German lower House (Bundestag). If the person nominated by the President is not acceptable to the Bundestag, that House will have to elect a Prime Minister (Chancellor) with a majority of the votes in the House within 14 days. If no Chancellor is elected within that period, a new election shall take place without delay, in which the person receiving the largest number of votes may be chosen. If the chosen person is not acceptable to the President, he may dissolve the House[16].

This virtually amounts to the election of the 'Federal Government' by the Bundestag, leaving only a small leeway for the Federal President to choose the Chancellor. Further, as the Chancellor has had the confidence of the Bundestag before assuming office, a vote of no-confidence is allowed to be moved only after the Bundestag has elected an alternative Chancellor. Even then, if the Chancellor ever loses the confidence of the majority of the members of the Bundestag, (s)he may ask for dissolution of the House within 21 days. The right of dissolution will, however, lapse as soon as the Bundestag elects a Federal Chancellor by a majority of its members[17]. The German system, therefore, does not provide for a foolproof system of stability. In India, on the other hand, the system is of appointment of the Prime Minister by the President. The German model cannot be adopted without changing this basic feature. Besides, the system may be disastrous for democracy in India. Given the political volatility of India today, a President may be able to handpick a Prime Minister and the two may manage to be in power through any number of devious means.

A theory advanced by certain well-intentioned people that the vote of constructive no-confidence can be introduced without amending the Constitution, but by simply changing the rules of the House, has no logical foundation. The change will need amendment of the powers and position of the President and the Council of Ministers. If the change is envisaged for the states, there will be further complications.

A Negative View of Citizens' Rights

Constitutionalism is a concept predicated upon restraining the powers of government from encroaching upon the rights of the people. This is of course a negative view of rights as against state power, implying a contradiction between authoritarianism and natural rights. The Magna Carta of 1215 reflected this contradiction for the first time in history by seeking to curtail the taxing power of a King by a Parliament and the coercive power of the same by the rule of law defined by the courts. Subsequently, the Parliament appropriated the King's powers. The judiciary was left with the rule of law, subject to the law of the Parliament. The first ten amendments of the US Constitution, on the other hand, cut out the spheres of citizens' rights against the state and the courts took over the guardianship of those rights. The rights of the US citizens are, therefore, framed in a negative language.

The trend towards a welfare state that developed at the beginning of the twentieth century, particularly after World War I, changed the perspective on rights. The state gradually emerged as the source of rights rather than its antagonist. The precondition of such a role of the state is of course the establishment of democracy, for an authoritarian state, however benevolent, does not guarantee rights. It merely doles out favour. But this is not a sufficient condition. In order to grant positive rights, the state must have the capability to do so. Thus, the Constitution of the USSR granted all rights—including the right to employment—to all its citizens, because it had socialized all means of production. The USSR could guarantee free secondary education to all its citizens, but not free higher education. No liberal democratic constitution can grant such rights because they do not control the means of production.

The fundamental rights of the citizens, guaranteed in Part III of the Indian Constitution, were drafted in a negative language and set against the state, i.e., the executive and the legislature[18], and gave the power of adjudication to the courts. The positive rights were set out in Part IV as Directive Principles of State Policy, which were not judicially enforceable but politically mandatory. The failure of a government to implement them will be punished by the people. Hence, the formal distinction between 'justiciable' and 'non-justiciable' rights. The Indian courts cannot grant rights, they can forbid the state to violate them. The 25th amendment to the Indian Constitution (1971), of course, provided that if the state passed a legislation expressly for giving effect to any of the Directive Principles of State Policy, such legislation would not be void on ground of its conflict with the rights to equality before law (Article 14), freedom (Article 19) and property (Article 31) or any of them. By the 44th amendment property was removed from the Part on Fundamental Rights to the Part on Finance, Property, Contracts and Suits (Part XII), as Article 300A. Property remains a right all the same, subject to 'authority of law'.

It is not that rights of Indian citizens are derived solely from Part III of the Constitution. Thus, though franchise is not a fundamental right, no citizen can be made ineligible from being included in the electoral roll, or claim to be included in a special electoral roll on grounds of race, religion, caste or sex (Article 325).

Certain Judicial Directives Incongruous

The point that needs to be made is that welfare measures are provided for in the Constitution as permission to the government as far as law is concerned, for example, Articles 15(4) and 16(4) relating to the welfare of the Scheduled Castes, the Scheduled Tribes and other backward classes. The recent trend of 'judicial activism', directing the state to take such actions as closure of factories, is incongruous with this view of rights. Can a court compel the state to provide compulsory primary education to all children or employment to all workers retrenched by a closed factory? These are matters of state policy. No court takes responsibility for such actions, however benevolent they might be. They should probably not issue such directives.

By the same token, a constitutional amendment cannot remove illiteracy, unemployment or poverty, unless there is a systemic change. Liberal democracies have hitherto conceived rights essentially as freedom from the state's action, not as obligations of the state. Constitutional amendments can increase or decrease rights, they cannot affect welfare. Thus, the first, the fourth, the 24th, the 25th and the 44th amendments reduced the right to property enabling the government to adopt land reform and certain other measures. They did not by themselves establish equal ownership of land or removal of poverty. On the other hand, the 38th, the 39th and the 42nd amendments substantially reduced personal/political freedom, which were restored by the 43rd and the 44th amendments.

The overall trend of the judiciary is quite interesting. In the fifties and the sixties of the last century, the judiciary generally presented a liberal-conservative view of itself by upholding preventive detention legislations and opposing the curtailment of the right to property by the state. After the Emergency and the 44th amendment, however, it has followed the opposite course. It has given up on the question of the right to property, but has tried to expand the domain of personal/political freedom.

The 'basic features' theory has a chequered history. In the Golaknath case (1967), the Supreme Court laid down that the fundamental rights in Part III are not open to amendment. In the Keshavananda Bharati case (1973), the Supreme Court laid down that the basic features of the Constitution are not open to amendment, but that the right to property is not a basic feature. For the first time in India's history, the Supreme Court invalidated a part of the 25th amendment which militated against the principle of judicial review, held by the Supreme Court as a basic feature of the Constitution. In the Bommai case, the court held that secularism is another basic feature. In the P V Narasimha Rao vs CBI case the Supreme Court held that parliamentary democracy is a basic feature too. The 'basic features' theory has generated some controversy from time to time. The total impact of this innovation has proved salutary.

2000

NOTES AND REFERENCES

1. 'A Constitution is the arrangement of magistracies, especially the highest of them all. The government is everywhere the sovereign in the state and the constitution is the government.' Aristotle, *Politics*, The Modern Library, pp. 136-37.
2. 'Absolute arbitrary power, or governing without settled standing laws, can neither of them consist with the ends of society and government.' John Locke, 'Treatises of Government, II', Section 137, quoted by W A Dunning, *A History of Political Theories: From Luther to Montesquieu*, Allahabad, Central Book Depot, 1966, p. 358.
3. See W I Dunning, *A History of Political Theories: From Rousseau to Spencer*, Allahabad, Central Book Depot, 1966, pp. 29-30.
4. The Preamble and Article VI, para 2, the Constitution of the United States of America.

5. Preamble to the Constitution of India.
6. Article 22, Clause 4 of the Constitution of India.
7. Articles 352-360, ibid.
8. *The Constituent Assembly Debates* (CAD), New Delhi, Manager of Publications, The Government of India, Vol. VII, pp. 43-44.
9. CAD, Vol. XI, p. 974.
10. See K T Shah's observation, CAD, Vol. VII, p. 345.
11. Shibani Kinkar Chaube, *Constituent Assembly of India: Springboard of Revolution*, New Delhi, People's Publishing House, 1973.
12. Granville Austin, *The Indian Constitution: Cornerstone of a Nation*, Oxford University Press, 1966.
13. See Shibani Kinkar Chaube, op cit, p. 52.
14. CAD, Vol. VIII, p. 501.
15. The remaining discretion relates to the settlement of disputes between a state government and a District Council on the share of revenue on licensing of mineral extraction.
16. Article 63, *Basic Law for the Federal Republic of Germany*, promulgated by the Parliamentary Council on 23 May 1949 as amended up to 16 July 1998, Bonn, Press and Information Office of the Federal Government, 1998.
17. Article 67, ibid.
18. Articles 12 and 13 of the Constitution of India.

5

Basic Structure, Judicial Review and Supreme Court Limits of the Privileges and Powers of the Indian Parliament

At the beginning of the year (2007) the Supreme Court of India delivered two benchmark judgements on two consecutive days. On January 10 the Court, by a decision of 4 - 1, upheld the right of Parliament to expel an erring member, a judgement that was hailed by some leading jurists of the country, including the Lok Sabha Speaker, as 'statesmanly.' By its sheer ethical strength the judgement secured the acquiescence of the Bharatiya Janata Party which had submitted a note of dissent through its representative in the parliamentary committee set up by the Speaker to examine the cash for query scam and make a report. On the next day the Court passed a unanimous verdict holding that the legislations included in the Ninth Schedule to the Constitution are subject to judicial review. This second judgement has produced a mixed reaction, particularly among the political parties, with the Chief Minister of Tamil Nadu calling for a revision of the Constitution.

The first case *[Raja Ram Pal v. The Hon'ble Speaker, Lok Sabha & Others: Writ Petition (Civil) No. 3 of 2006 (Under Article 32 of the Constitution of India)]* arose out of the challenge of 11 former MPs (nine of the Lok Sabha and two of the Rajya Sabha) who were expelled from Parliament in December 2005 in the infamous cash for query episode. The ground of the challenge was broadly threefold: that the decisions of the two Houses of the Parliament were taken in a hurry and even prejudice; that Parliament had no power to expel any member and that the expulsion deprived the MPs' constituencies of the right to representation. The first of the arguments was bolstered up by interpreting the announcement of the Lok Sabha Speaker that the guilty would be punished and by alleging that the persons concerned were not given a proper hearing. The second argument was that Articles 101 and 102 that deal with disqualification of members do not allow expulsion. The third argument was: In a democracy could an elected member of a Parliament be expelled?

To the Supreme Court there appeared to be neither hurry nor a prejudice in the two Houses' decision. The expulsion followed a perfectly legitimate enquiry and opportunity of hearing. The Speaker's words had been torn out of context and did not imply any prejudice. As to the second argument expulsion was not disqualification; it did not carry the attendant disqualification to contest another election immediately; and it was under Article 105, relating to the powers and privileges of Parliament, that the expulsion had been ordered. By the same token the constituencies of the expelled MPs were not denied representation, as the voters were free to re-elect them. The decisions were almost unanimous in the Houses. They were valid.

While delivering the judgement, however, the Court made a somewhat superfluous assertion that the Constitution is supreme and the Court's power of review of parliamentary decisions was unquestionable. Superfluous, because no one really challenged this power in the case and it was established long ago. Even in the *A.K. Gopalan v. The State of Madras* case of 1950 *(AIR 1950 SC 27)* the Supreme Court exercised the power of judicial review but held that the power should be used with 'judicial restraint' and no limitation on the legislature should be imposed by any consideration outside the express provisions of the Constitution.

The significance of this assertion rests in the Court answering the Union of India's argument that proceedings in the Houses of Parliament were outside the scope of judicial review by virtue of Articles 105 and 122. The Court, therefore, held 'beyond the pale of all doubts that neither Parliament nor State Legislatures in India can assert power to provide for or regulate their own constitution in the manner claimed by the House of Commons in the United Kingdom' (See *Raja Ram Pal,* original print: pp. 32 & 144).

The next day, in the case of *L.R. Coelhoe (Dead) by LRs v. The State of Tamil Nadu (Civil Appeal Nos 1344-1345 of 1976)*, a nine-judge Special Bench, constituted on reference from a five-judge Constitution Bench *[I.R. Coelho (Dead) by LRs v. State of Tamil Nadu]* of the Supreme Court in 1999 to consider a set of plaints against the Ninth Schedule, decided unanimously that inclusion of any law in the Schedule did not protect it from judicial review. At the background of the original case there were two legislations: (1) The Gudalur Janmam Estates (Abolition and Conversion into Ryotwari) Act, 1969 of Tamil Nadu that was struck down by the Supreme Court in Balmadies Plantations Ltd & Anr. *V*. The State of Tamil Nadu because that was not found to be a measure of agrarian reform protected by Article 31A of the Constitution; and (2) The West Bengal Land Holding Revenue Act, 1979, Section 2A of which was struck down by the same Court as being arbitrary and, therefore, unconstitutional. The first Act was included in the Ninth Schedule by the Thirty-fourth Amendment Act, 1974 and the second Act in its entirety was included there by the Sixty-Sixth Amendment Act, 1990. After declaring the vulnerability of every law included in the Ninth Schedule after the *Keshavananda* judgement (1973) the Special Bench referred the specific plaints to a three-judge bench for decision in the light of its 11 January decision.

Even this was not novel for, in the Keshavananda case *(Keshavanda Bharati v.The State of Kerala: AIR 1973 SC 1463)*, the Supreme Court had invalidated a part of the 25th amendment to the Constitution passed in 1971 *vis a vis* Article 3IB and, in 1975, in the Minerva Mills case the Court invalidated another part of the 25th Amendment *vis a vis* clauses 4 and 5 of Article 368. However, the Supreme Court upheld the 29th Amendment Act, 1972, the main ground of the case, that had included two land reform legislations of Kerala in the Ninth Schedule: (1) The Kerala Land Reforms (Amendment) Act, 1969 and (2) The Kerala Land Reforms Amendment Act, 1971.

In the *Keshavananda* case the Supreme Court had laid down two essential principles: (1) All Articles of the Constitution are subject to the Parliament's power of amendment; but (2) the basic structure of the Constitution cannot be amended to the extent of its loss of identity. The phrase 'basic structure' does find a place in the earlier judgements too but alternately with the word(s) 'basic features,' 'foundation' and 'framework'. Subsequent to

Keshavananda it appears in the *Waman Rao* case, the *Indira Gandhi* case and the *Minerva Mills* case. From time to time the features of the basic structure were elaborated. But the basic structure itself was never precisely defined. Occasionally, the Preamble was pointed out for its outlines. The problem arises out of the fact that the authority of the Preamble has not been consistently acknowledged by the Court, and the Preamble itself has been amended. The 'basic structure,' therefore, remains a subject of debate. In 1995, for instance, L.K. Advani announced that parliamentary democracy is not basic structure of the Indian Constitution. In 1994 SC said parliamentary democracy is a basic feature of this Indian Constitution.

The roots of the problem go down to the origin of the Constitution. During the making of the Constitution a great deal of debate took place on the question of rights - specifically on two aspects, namely, right to personal liberty and right to property. There was, on the one hand, extreme sensitivity about security and, on the other, urgent commitment to the abolition of zamindari and implementation of land reform. While providing for the right to freedom and the right to life and personal liberty the Constituent Assembly qualified them by 'reasonable restrictions' to the extent of constitutionalizing preventive detention. The right to property was also granted 'save by authority of law, and subject to acquisition for public purposes with compensation' (Article 31, clauses 1 & 3). A number of political activists were then in preventive detention, laws of censor were strict in certain states and a number of cases were pending in state High Courts over zamindari abolition.

In *A.K.Gopalan v. The State of Madras (AIR 1950 SC 27)* the Supreme Court held that 'procedure established by law' just meant that a law passed by proper procedure in legislatures is valid enough thus reopening the famous debate on 'the due process'. It took the view that judicial review in the Indian Constitution is present but restricted. Judicial review is inherent in a written Constitution. Article 13(2), that prohibited legislation contrary to the Fundamental Rights in Part III, was put merely by way of abundant caution.

Our Constitution, unlike the English Constitution, recognizes the Court's supremacy over the legislative authority, but such

> supremacy is a very limited one, for it is confined to the field where the legislative power is circumscribed by limitations put upon it by the Constitution itself. Within this restricted field the court may, on a scrutiny of the law made by the legislature, *declare it void if it is found to have transgressed the constitutional limitations.* But our Constitution, unlike the American Constitution, does not recognize the absolute supremacy of the Supreme Court over the legislative authority in all respects. For, outside the restricted field of constitutional limitation, Parliament and State legislatures are supreme in their respective legislative fields and in that wider field there is no scope for the courts in India to play the role of the Supreme Court of the United States. It is well for us to constantly remember the basic limitation on our power (p. 106; emphasis added).

Yet the Supreme Court, in that very first year of the Republic (in *Gopalan*), applied judicial review in invalidating a part of the Preventive Detention Act, 1950, as it then stood (section 14) and the whole of the Madras Maintenance of Public Order Act, 1949 *(Romesh Thappar v. The State of Madras: AIR 1950 SC 124)*, on the ground of transgression of constitutional limitation. The latter judgement led to the expansion of limitation on the right to freedom of speech and expression through section 3 of the First Amendment Act, 1951. In 1952 Chief Justice Patanjali Shastri declared that the Indian Constitution 'contains express provisions for judicial review of legislation as to its conformity with the Constitution' *[The State of Madras v. V.G. Row: 1952 SCJ 257]*. While the power of judicial review remained constantly in focus even after this, the debate on the 'procedure established by law' in the Indian Constitution (compared to the 'due process of law' in the US Constitution) reappeared in the *Maneka Gandhi v. Union of India* case *(AIR 1978 SC 597)*. In that case the Supreme Court bench of seven judges held that procedure established by law had to be reasonable and not violative of Article 14 as the fundamental rights guaranteed by Part III of the Constitution were distinct and mutually exclusive rights. The spirit of 'due process' was back. As chief justice Y.K. Sabherwal put it in his 11 January 2007 judgement, '*A.K. Gopalan* was no longer good law' (original judgement, p. 21).

Right to property had a more chequered history. The High Court of Patna in *Kameshwar Prasad v. The State of Bihar (AIR 1951 Patna 91)* held that a Bihar legislation relating to land reform was unconstitutional while the High Courts of Allahabad and Nagpur upheld the validity of the corresponding legislations passed in their states. The aggrieved parties filed appeal at the Supreme Court. Certain zamindars had also approached the Supreme Court under Article 32 of the Constitution. It was at this stage that Parliament amended the Constitution for the first time adding Articles 31A, 31B and the Ninth Schedule for the purpose of validating land reform to the immunity from Article 13(2) that prohibits laws violative of the fundamental rights of the citizens. In *Sri Shankari Prasad Singh Deo v. The Union of India (AIR 1951 SC 458)* the Supreme Court upheld the first amendment opining that it was not affected by Article 13(2) as it had been done under the constituent power of Parliament vested by Article 368. 'The makers of the Constitution must be taken to have intended Parliament to follow the procedure so far as it may be applicable consistently with the express provisions of Article 368, when *they entrusted to it the power of amending the Constitution'* (p. 458). The decision was reiterated in *Sajjan Singh v. The State of Rajasthan (AIR 1965 SC 1648)* that had arisen out of a challenge to the addition of the Acts to the Ninth Schedule by the Constitution Seventeenth Amendment Act, 1964.

The *Shankari Prsad* judgement acknowledged that the power of amendment was entrusted to Parliament. The power of amendment by Parliament under Article 368 was a constituent power and was not subject to the limitation of Article 13(2) under which 'law' has to be understood as rules and regulations made in exercise of ordinary legislative power. The judgement pointed out that the provisos to Article 368, that made exception for the amendments that required the ratification by half the state legislatures did not include the Fundamental Rights. Therefore, the Court, would not exclude the Fundamental Rights from the amending powers unless the effect of an amendment on Article 226 (writ-issuing power of the State High Courts) was direct and not incidental, and in significant order. In such cases different considerations could arise.

Hidayatullah, J, while agreeing to the order passed by Gajendragadkar, CJ for himself and two other judges, disagreed with the view on the exclusion of fundamental rights from the provisos to Article 368(1) as it would reduce the fundamental rights to 'playthings' of a special majority. He was in favour of immunizing the fundamental rights, barring probably the right to property, from the amending power of Parliament. (He felt that land reform, with compensation, would have been possible even under Article 19(l)(f) as the right to property was originally qualified). It was Mudholkar, J who held that the citizens have a right to know if the 'basic features' of the Constitution would endure for all time or they are no more enduring than the 'implemental and subordinate provisions of the Constitution' (*ibid.* pp. 865-66). Though he also concurred with the majority judgement in upholding the validity of the Constitution Fourth Amendment Act, his question went beyond the domain of positive law, if not into the domain of politics.

Land reform led to altogether three major amendments: the 1st, the 4th, and the 17th and seven minor ones: the 29th, the 34th, the 39th, the 40th, the 47th, the 66th and the 78th. The 4th and the other subsequent amendments, however, went beyond the scope of land reform and dealt with broader questions of property. On the other hand, land reform constituted only a minor part of the Ninth Schedule amendments since the Fortieth Amendment Act, 1976. The right to property as such went through two drastic amendments: the 42nd and the 44th. Each of these amendments was governed by ideology and, therefore, belonged to the domain of politics. The Supreme Court has so far desisted from challenging such amendments. In the *Waman Rao* case *(AIR 1981 SC 281)* it went to the extent of asserting that land reform strengthens the basic structure of the Constitution. Yet, it laid down that amendments to the Ninth Schedule made on or after 24th April 1973 by which the Ninth Schedule was amended from time to time by inclusion of various Acts and regulations therein were open to challenge on the ground that they, or any one of them, are beyond the constituent power of Parliament since they damage the basic or essential features of the Constitution or its basic structure.

There appears to have been a judicial acquiescence, even if reluctant, in the land reform legislations and consequent amendments. Expansion of Parliament's power into the sphere of property received its first challenge in *I.C. Golak Nath v. The State of Punjab & Ors (AIR 1967 SC 1643)* the Supreme Court confronted the dilemma while reversing the two previous judgements 6-5. It did not address itself to the question of basic feature, but held that amendment is 'law' within the meaning of Article 13 as the amendment procedure of the Indian Constitution was different from that in the United States Constitution. The Indian amendment procedure required the assent of the President of India while the US amendment did not require it. By means of prospective overruling the Court declared that Parliament would have no power to amend the Fundamental Rights contained in Part III, which had a transcendental character, in future. Coming at the beginning of Indira Gandhi's socialism, the judgement set up a controversy in India, leading to two quick amendments (24th & 25th) in 1971, the first declaring that amendments under Article 368 could not be challenged (clause 4 of Article 13 and clause 4 of Article 368 being added) and the second laying down that laws made in order to give effect to the directive principles of state policy embodied in Part IV could not be challenged on the ground that they violate Article 14 or 19. These amendments created more problems than they solved.

In the normal circumstances amendment of (addition of clause 4 to) Article 13 and of (addition of clause 3 to) Article 368 (with identical effect) would have been enough. However, the 25th amendment went to the extent of asserting in the new Article 31C that no law containing a declaration that it is for giving effect to such policy shall be called in question in any court on the ground that it does not give effect to such policy. This, in effect, sought to take away such legislations from the sphere of judicial scrutiny the validity of the declaration. The Supreme Court hit back in the *Keshavananda* judgement that laid down the rule that the basic structure of the Constitution may not be amended and that judicial review is a feature of this basic structure.

Though *Keshavananda* is usually regarded as a benchmark judgement, and though the Supreme Court in the Coelhoe case set store by it, the former contained ambiguities lending it to varying interpretations. There were altogether nine judgements delivered by 11 judges. During the *Indira Gandhi* case Ray, CJ cited the judgement in the following way:

> The Constitution 29th Amendment Act was considered by this Court in *Keshavananda Bharati's* case. The 29th Amendment Act inserted in the Ninth Schedule to the Constitution entries 65 and 66 being the Kerala Land Reforms Act, 1969 and the Kerala Land Reforms Act, 1971. *This Court unanimously upheld the validity of the 29th Amendment Act....* The view of seven judges in *Keshavananda Bharati's* case is that Article 31-B is a constitutional device to place the specified statutes in the Schedule beyond any attack that infringe Part III of the Constitution. *The 29th Amendment Act is affirmed in Keshavananda Bharati's case (supra) by majority of seven against six.*

Mercifully, Sabherwal, CJ has himself underlined the two sentences in the above quotation. It only highlights the contradiction between the two statements. In the same *Indira Gandhi's* case Khanna, J had to record that:

> There was a controversy during the course of arguments on the point as to whether I have laid down in my judgment in *Keshavananda Bharati's* case that fundamental rights are not a part of the basic structure of the Constitution. As this controversy cropped up a number of times, it seems apposite that before I conclude I should deal with the contention advanced by learned Solicitor General that according tc my judgment in that case no fundamental right is part of the basic structure of the Constitution. I find it difficult to read anything in that judgment to justify such a conclusion. What has been laid down in that judgment is that no article of the Constitution is immune from the amendatory process because of the fact that it relates to a fundamental right and is contained in Part III of the Constitution....
>
> .... The above observation clearly militates against the contention that according to my judgment fundamental rights are not a part of the basic structure of the Constitution. I also dealt with the matter at length to show

> that the right to property was not a part of the basic structure of the Constitution. This would have been wholly unnecessary if none of the fundamental rights was a part of the basic structure of the Constitution (Quoted ibid, pp. 62-63).

The Supreme Court, now, tried to set the record straight. 'Six learned judges (Ray, Palekar, Mathew, Beg, Dwivedi and Chandrachud, JJ) who upheld the validity of the 29th Amendment did not subscribe to the basic structure doctrine. The other six learned judges (Chief Justice Sikri, Shelat, Grover, Hegde, Mukherjee and Reddy, JJ) upheld the 29th Amendment subject to it passing the test of basic structure doctrine. The 13th learned judge (Khanna, J), though subscribed to basic structure doctrine, upheld the 29th Amendment agreeing with the six learned Judges who did not subscribe to the basic structure doctrine,' (pp. 56-57).

Put differently, this summary would show that seven judges held that the basic structure of the Constitution cannot be amended and six judges disagreed. And those who disagreed were joined by one judge (Khanna, J) in holding that the 29th Amendment was valid. According to Sabherwal, CJ who wrote the judgement of 11 January, 'there is no mention of the test that is to be applied to the legislations inserted in the Ninth Schedule' (p. 59). But two of the six judges who held that all parts/Articles could be amended joined the seven judges, who held that the basic structure may not be changed, in signing the summary of the judgement overruling the *Golak Nath* judgement but announcing that Article 368 does not enable Parliament to amend the basic structure or framework of the Constitution, and that the 24th Amendment, the 29th Amendment and sections 2(a) and 2(b) of the 25th Amendment Acts are valid. While upholding the first part of Section 3 of the 25th Amendment Act, that formed Article 31C, however, the ruling declared void the second part of the Section that said that 'and no law containing a declaration that it is for giving effect to such [Directive Principles of State] policy shall be called in question in any Court on the ground that it does not give effect to such policy' in the same Article. This was because the part excluded judicial review that the Court held to be a basic feature of the Constitution.

The *Coelhoe* judgement, however, sidestepped a broader point that Khanna had suggested in his above-quoted explanation: the point of property as such being not a part of the basic structure. If this explanation would be available in the *Keshavananda* judgement, it would have made the entire right to property amendable. Technically, it was not a part of the *Keshavananda* judgement. On the other hand, by making every inclusion in the Ninth Schedule subject to judicial review, the *Coelhoe* judgement made Article 31-B vulnerable because that Article had granted Parliament unquestionable power to insert any law in the Ninth Schedule beyond the authority of Article 32. This, in effect, kills Article 31-B without declaring it void.

The *Keshavananda* verdict was a unique judicial review - that of a constitutional amendment. That it was repeated successively was partly the Government's own undoing. During the pendency of Indira Gandhi's appeal against the Allahabad High Court judgement on her election in the Supreme Court, and during the Emergency, Parliament passed the 39th Amendment Act inserting Article 329A that immunized the election of the President, the Vice-President, the Prime Minister and the Speaker of the Lok Sabha to Parliament, clauses 4 and 5 specifically ruling out judicial intervention. In *Smt. Indira Nehru Gandhi v. Raj Narain (AIR 1975 SC* 2259) the Supreme Court declared void clauses 4 and 5 of Article 329A as violative of the basic structure of the Constitution. By the 44th amendment Article 329A was altogether scrapped. In *Minerva Mills & Others v. The Union of India & Ors (AIR 1980 SC* 1789) the Court declared void clauses 4 and 5 of Article 368 that had been incorporated by the 42nd amendment by the Emergency Government of Indira Gandhi but was retained by the Janata Party Government in the 44th amendment intended to eliminate the Emergency 'excesses.' Those two clauses were:

> (4) No amendment of this Constitution (including the provisions of Part III) made or purporting to have been made under this Article [whether before or after the commencement of section 55 of the Constitution (Forty-second Amendment) Act], shall be called in question in any court on any ground.
>
> (5) For the removal of doubts, it is hereby declared that there shall be no limitation whatever on the constituent

> power of Parliament to amend by way of addition, variation or repeal the provisions of this Constitution under this Article.

Obviously, these two clauses had been inserted by the 42nd amendment in order to revive the ruling in the *Sankari Prasad* case that had been nullified in *Golak Nath* and *Keshavananda*. In *Minerva Mills* this nullification was endorsed. In *Kihoto Hollohan v. Zachillhu [1992 Supp (2) SCC 651]* the Court struck down paragraph 7 of the Tenth Schedule as it ousted judicial review of the Speakers' decision on disqualification of members. Parliament was denied the constituent power. Now comes the *Coelhoe* judgement effectively nullifying Article 31-B.

The indiscriminate way the words like 'basic structure,' 'basic features', 'framework', and 'foundation' have been tossed about poses some semantic and logical problems. Consider this quotation from Chief Justice Y.K. Sabherwal's presentation of the majority judgement in *Coelhoe* that:

> The separation of powers between Legislature, Executive and the Judiciary constitutes basic structure, has been found in ***Keshavananda Bharati's case*** by the majority. Later it was reiterated in ***Indira Gandhi's case.*** A large number of judgments have reiterated that the separation of powers is one of the basic features of the Constitution (p. 43).

A structure implies institution(s), an object or a set of interrelated objects; a feature its attribute. It is imperative for a scientist who discovers a structure to at once describe it fully. Identification of its features may legitimately take time, but it will certainly be wrong to add up certain features to make a structure. A foundation is a vertical concept, a framework horizontal. Both these terms are contextual and vague. From the days of Aristotle a constitution has meant a description of the structure of government and the way of its working. A *limited* government refers to its attribute, an ideology about government, and judicial review has been derived from that premise. The 10th January verdict of the Supreme Court in *Raja Ram Pal* summarizes the *Keshavananda* verdict in a better way:

> ... this Court found some basic features of the Constitution that include, besides supremacy of the Constitution, the

republican and democratic form of Government, and the separation of powers between the Legislature, the Executive and the Judiciary (p. 22).

In the 11 January decision it uses the phrase 'basic structure' with reference to the same preceding judgement. In the *Keshavananda* ruling the basic structure was not defined; only, certain features were identified by individual judges. In practical terms, however, one feature appears to have been asserted repeatedly since the *Gopalan* judgement. That is the feature of judicial review. The various efforts from Amendment 39 to Amendment 42 were aimed at curbing this power of the Supreme Court and the High Courts; and they were all struck off. The Supreme Court's emphasis on Articles 14 (equality), 19 (freedom) and 21 (life) in the *Coelhoe* case would have made a better sense if they were viewed as 'basic features.' A Constitution essentially lays down the rules of government; rights set limit to the powers of the government. The Supreme Court said as much in a recent judgement *(M. Nagaraj & Ors v. The Union of India & Ors, 2006,* quoted in Sabherwal's judgement itself at p. 41). 'Individuals possess basic human rights independently of any constitution by reason of the basic fact that they are members of the human race.' It may be recalled that the world's first written constitution, the Constitution of the USA, was originally framed as a body of just seven articles concerning government. The fundamental rights of the US citizens were later incorporated through ten amendments as several states had misgivings about the new federal government that was created in 1789 (It took two years for the US Constitution, framed in 1787, to be ratified by the states due to such misgivings).

A Constitution *is* the basic structure of a polity. It lays down how the country will be governed. In a broader sense it is possible to conceive of the Constitution as a structure of dialectical relationship between the power of the government and rights of the people. To create a 'basic structure' of the Constitution is, *prima facie,* to distinguish it from the 'implemental and subordinate' provisions in Mudholkar's way. This is a source of possible subjectivity and arbitrariness. Even Article 368 is no proper guide. It grades Chapters, Articles and Schedules in terms of rigidity. It is difficult to agree that rigidity alone is the indicator of 'basalness.' For example, secularism has long been acknowledged as a basic feature of the Constitution. Yet its lever, Article 25, may be amended by a mere majority of two-thirds of the members present and voting in the two Houses of Parliament without the requirement of ratification by the majority of state legislatures. The same thing may be said about Articles 14, 19 and 21 by which the Court in the present case has set store. In fact, in *Sajjan Singh* Hidayatullah, J had first suggested that right to property is a qualified right. He repeated it in the *Golak Nath* case. (A side story of this evolution of concepts is that in the first *Searchlight* case of 1959, Subba Rao, J floated the idea of rights being 'transcendental' in a minority judgement. As CJ in *Golak Nath* he revived that, only temporarily.) Right to property was altogether removed from Part III of the Constitution by the 44th Amendment Act by a Government that had replaced Indira Gandhi's. Can the 44th amendment be challenged now?

Further, the way the *Coelhoe* judgement draws upon the theory of separation of powers in the above quotation is questionable. In page 45 of the same judgement it is claimed that 'Even before the basic structure doctrine became part of Constitutional law, the importance of the separation of powers on our system of government was recognized by this Court in *Special Reference No. 1 of 1964 [(1965) 1 SCR 413].'* As early as 1951 *In Re Delhi Laws Act, 1912, (A.I.R. 1951 SC 332)* the Supreme Court held that separation of powers is not an essential part of the Constitution. The *Coelhoe* judgement itself quotes the judgement in the *Special Reference* thus:

> .. .whether or not there is distinct and rigid separation of powers under the Indian Constitution there is no doubt that the Constitution has entrusted to the Judicature in this country the task of construing the provisions of the Constitution and of safeguarding the fundamental rights of the citizens (p. 29).

Separation of powers is indeed an instrument of limited government as conceived by Montesquieu who thought it existed in the British system of constitutional monarchy. He read too much into Locke's writings. Locke was a votary of limited government but his position on separation of powers was at best ambiguous. In Britain limited government stands on the executive's responsibility to the legislature and not on separation of powers. The same is true about India. It may be added that a certain kind of judicial review does exist in Britain. The understanding that I have is that most of the earlier judgements of the Supreme Court built their argument on limited government and judicial review on the ground of India having a written constitution and a federal state.

This is not the first time that the Ninth Schedule has drawn judicial scrutiny. Ever since *Indira Gandhi's* case the Court has ruled against indiscriminate inclusion in the Ninth Schedule. This is the first time that the Ninth Schedule as such has lost its authority. 'Every insertion into the Ninth Schedule does not restrict Part III review, it completely excludes Part III at will,' said the Court (p. 83). '[L]aws included in the Ninth Schedule do not become part of the Constitution, they derive their validity on account of the exercise undertaken by the Parliament to include them in the Ninth Schedule. That exercise has to be tested every time it is undertaken' (p. 93).

An examination of 284 Acts included in the Ninth Schedule so far will show that three politically charged Acts have been excluded from the Schedule through amendments. The rest, barring one [The Tamil Nadu Backward Classes, Scheduled Castes and Scheduled Tribes (Reservation of Seats in Educational Institutions, and Appointments or Posts in Services under the State) Act (Tamil Nadu Act 45 of 1994)], relate to right to property, mostly agrarian, but also to mining, forest, industry, transport and urban land. Will all of them be open to judicial scrutiny? We have argued that, in the unlikely event of Khanna, J's explanation delivered during *Indira Gandhi* on his judgement in *Keshavananda* being counted as part of the *Keshavananda* judgement, right to property as such would be excluded from judicial review. The right to property has been amended so many times before and after 1973, finally being eliminated from Part III of the Constitution by the 44th amendment that reopening all the Acts included in the Ninth Schedule will amount to opening the Pandora's box. On the other hand, the overworked Supreme Court may take satisfaction from the fact that the Ninth Schedule has saved it a lot of work.

There remains the ultimate question: what is the basic structure of the Indian Constitution? Right from the days of *Gopalan* the Supreme Court has insisted that Indian Constitution provides for a limited Government. The legislature, the executive, and the judiciary all work on the basis of this premise dictated by India's constitutionalism. In *Raja Ram Pal* the Court declared that the

Indian Parliament is not self-composed in the British way; it is the product of the Constitution and must work within the limits set by the Constitution. Besides this there is hardly any unanimity on the basic structure. *Golak Nath* made the chapter on Fundamental Rights immutable; *Keshavananda* laid down that all parts of the Constitution are amendable, though not the basic structure.

It may be pointed out that the Indian Constitution nowhere says that it is the supreme body of laws. That is read by the Supreme Court, and quite legitimately. So is the theory of limited government that may stand even without separation of powers. In its preoccupation with the concept of a limited government, however, the Supreme Court appears to have trivialized the question of representation. If limited government is the essence of constitutionalism, the essence of democracy is representation. In *Raja Ram Pal* it would have been enough for the Court to answer the argument of deprivation of representation to the erring MPs by pointing out, as it actually did, that their constituents still have the right to re-elect them. After all, the life of the Lok Sabha may at any moment be terminated by dissolution by the President. Instead, the Court produced a questionable dissertation.

> While it is true that the right to vote and be represented is integral to our democratic process, it must be remembered that it is not an absolute right. There are certain limitations to the right to vote and be represented. For example, a citizen cannot claim the right to vote and be represented by a person who is disqualified by law or the right to be represented by a candidate he votes for, even if he fails to win the election.

With great respect, it may be submitted that the implication of representation goes beyond the question of winning an election or winning a majority in a general election. The legitimacy of the Opposition attests to that. Over and above that, in every election some bonafide citizens fail to be enrolled as voters and a large number of voters do not vote. There is no writ available against such failures anywhere in the democratic world. Hence, franchise is not a fundamental right. That does not derogate from the value of representation for, essentially, representation is a political question. No court should be approached for it; no court should entertain a petition on it.

The Supreme Court being a court of records, a great deal of consistency is required from their authors. The judges, the most illustrious legal professionals of the country, must be doing their jobs with great competence. Yet slips occur due to the pressure of work and other factors. Y.V. Chandrachud, after his retirement as chief justice, gave some indication of how such slips may occur.

> *Keshavananda Bharati's* case ....was a marathon case, the arguments having lasted for about 70 working days, four-and-a-half hour each day, which occupied the court's time for five months. Those five months were full of excitement and unusual happenings which culminated in a majority judgement of 7-6.... What constitutes the basic structure of the Constitution did not fall to be decided in that case and was not, therefore, decided ....
>
> I believe that in *Keshavananda Bharati's,* we could have condensed our performance to half its length without impairing the value of our findings and the wisdom of our observations. But the court worked under an unusual pressure - the pressure of time, not of external politics and the deadline was set by the impending retirement of Chief Justice Sikri on 24 April 1973. Evolving the largest agreement among the 13 learned men of law became an elusive affair, resulting in the undesirable consequence of each for himself *(Sardar Patel Memorial Lectures 1987: The Basics of the Indian Constitution: Its Search for Social Justice and the Role of Judges.* Y.V. Chandrachud: GOI, Publications Division, 1989, pp. 17-18).

Political Science down to the nineteen fifties was seeped in studies of ideas and institutions including Constitutions. With the onslaught of behavioural studies in the sixties Constitutions became downgraded with the result that jurists took over the field exclusively. A Constitution is as much about politics as about positive law. It is politics encased in positive law. May I, therefore, appeal for the revival of constitutional studies in Political Science without, of course, neglect of behavioural studies?

2007

6

The Supreme Court, Federalism and Secularism in India

ABSTRACT

The recent judgement of the Supreme Court on a number of supersessions of state governments and dissolutions of state legislatures under article 356 may prove to be the most significant judgement on the constitutional principles ever laid down in independent India. Besides laying down important rules for application of the governmental power, it has prescribed rules of behaviour for political parties. The Court asserted its power to examine the relevance of the material on the basis of which a presidential "satisfaction" is reached and also its power to revoke a proclamation and revive a dissolved legislature. While the proclamations in Nagaland, Karnataka and Meghalaya were found unsustainable, those on Madhya Pradesh, Himachal Pradesh and Rajasthan were upheld. The Court also disapproved of the mixing of religion with politics.

Civil Appeal No. 3645 of 1989 (S.R. Bommai & Others versus Union of India & Others) with TC (C) Nos. 5, 7, 8, 9/93, CA Nos. 193, 194/ 1989, 1692, 1692 A-C/93, 4627-30/93 & IA No. 4 in C.A. No. 1692/93[1] may well go down in history as the most significant judgement passed by the apex court of India since the promulgation of the Indian Constitution. The significant judgements earlier passed related mainly to questions of fundamental rights, that is, of citizen-government relation even though in the *Keshavananda Bharati* case[2] the Supreme Court came out with the profound ruling that the basic structure of the Constitution cannot be amended. The present set of cases relates to the nature of the state itself.

It is interesting to note at this stage that the profound ruling on "basic structure" was incidental to a judgement on fundamental rights. The Supreme Court, in the *Keshavananda Bharati* case, did not spell out the components of the basic structure. Some subsequent judgements of the Court, however, laid down that judicial review itself was a part of the basic structure. The present case lays down another element of the basic structure.

Background

A number of disputes were involved in the present judgement. The first was a challenge to dissolution of the Nagaland legislature in 1988 in which the Gauhati High Court ruled that a Governor recommending President's rule could not claim immunity under Article 361 and the material on the basis of which a President's rule is recommended is subject to judicial scrutiny. However, as there was some difference in the two-judge bench, on the extent to which the court could question the material for the President's satisfaction under Article 74(2), the matter was referred to a third judge. The matter was finally transferred to the Supreme Court when it took up the Karnataka case.

As in Nagaland, in Karnataka, President's Rule was imposed after floor crossings and the act was challenged. As in the Gauhati High Court, in the Karnataka High Court the proclamation was held to be subject to judicial review. But the Court upheld the action of the President because the Governor's *bona fides* had not been challenged. The material supplied by him had to be treated as relevant and reasonable. S.R. Bommai, the deposed Chief Minister, appealed to the Supreme Court.

The case of Meghalaya had come directly to the Supreme Court. It concerned the fall of a state government through floor crossing with the blessings of the then Speaker. In August 1989 a constitution bench of the Supreme Court invalidated an order of the Speaker but the Speaker paid no heed to it. Finally, in 1991, the President's Rule was imposed.

During the pendency of these disputes the dismissals of the three BJP-run state governments of Madhya Pradesh, Himachal Pradesh and Rajasthan took place following the demolition of the Babari Masjid and a chain of communal riots in the country. There was no judicial dispute in Uttar Pradesh because the BJP government there had resigned before being dismissed. On the other hand, the Madhya Pradesh High Court declared the supersession invalid. The Union of India appealed to the Supreme Court against this judgement of the Madhya Pradesh High Court while appeals were made directly to the Supreme Court on the two cases of Rajasthan and Himachal Pradesh.

The other point that needs to be remembered is that none of these cases involve the simple dismissal of councils of ministers under Article 164. Such cases have not yet been settled by the Supreme Court but a judgement of the Calcutta High Court in *Mahavir Prasad versus Prafulla Chandra*[3] in 1969 has not yet been revised in any High Court. That judgement gave unquestionable discretion to the state Governor with regard to his pleasure to retain a council of ministers in office. The present cases relate to the dissolution of state legislature under Article 356 read with Article 174. The other Article involved is Art. 365 which deals with the effect of failure of state governments to comply with or to give effect to directions given by the Union.

Finally, all dismissals of state cabinets and dissolutions of state legislatures are largely political decisions. The ultimate remedy of any perceived misuse of power has to be sought through an appeal to the electorate. The scope of judicial intervention is limited. In the present cases the judges of the Supreme Court refused to enter the political arena. Even in the first three cases where the Supreme Court declared the Presidential intervention invalid there could be no action as elections had already taken place. The judgement, thus, in effect, is prospective.

In another sense, too, the judgement is prospective. It has laid down some definite norms of behaviour. It has told the Union Government to behave. It has told political parties to behave.

The Federal Problem

President's rule, occurring a hundred times since 1950,[4] has been the greatest irritant in the Union-State relation in India. The President, in the context, means the Union government as the President, according to Article 74(1), acts on the advice of his council of ministers. According to clause (2) of the same Article the question if, and if so what, advice was tendered by the council of ministers, however, "shall not be enquired into in any court." Such an advice is a political matter and can only be interrogated in the Parliament to which the council of ministers is accountable.

This accountability is strengthened, in the matter of President's rule, by Article 356 (3) which lays down that a proclamation shall lapse after two months unless it is approved by resolutions in both the Houses of Parliament. However, if the President dissolves the state Legislative Assembly meanwhile, the damage will be irreparable except through another election.

At least three major committees have dealt with this problem: the Administrative Reforms Commission, the Rajamannar Committee and the Sarkaria Commission. No tangible solution has emanated except by way of the suggestions that the Governors should be men of stature and impartial attitude and that President's rule should be applied with great restraint, in exceptional circumstances. All the judges in the present case shared these convictions. On the other hand, the Supreme Court has made positive progress on the legal front.

As the judges decided not to enter into a political question, the Union of India, on its part, did not oppose judicial review of a proclamation. The arena of conflict was thus restricted.

A nine-judge bench passed six separate judgements: P.B. Sawant, J. for himself and Kuldeep Singh, J., B.P. Jeevan Reddy, J. for himself and S.C. Agrawal, J., J.S. Verma, J., for himself and Yogeshwar Dayal, J., K. Ramaswamy, J., S. Ratnaval Pandian, J., and A.M. Ahmadi, J. The six separate judgements were the result more of the elaborative stresses than of substantial disagreement though there were minor disagreements. The common points that emerge are as follows.

The application of President's rule is subject to the President's satisfaction that a situation has arisen when the government in a state cannot be carried on according to the provisions of the constitution. The President reaches this "satisfaction" on the basis of Governor's report or "otherwise." It is the "otherwise" which makes the Presidential satisfaction virtually unjusticiable. In any case, the advice of the cabinet that constitutes the President's "satisfaction" has to be based on some material. The Supreme Court, for the first time, declared that the *relevance* of the material on the basis of which the advice is tendered can be scrutinised by the Court although its correctness or worth may not.

However, there are differences on the above point. Ahmadi, J. holds that the Court can interdict a proclamation only when a *mala fide* is proved. Verma and Singh, JJ. hold that, though the proclamation may be judged objectively when it is related to Art. 365 (failure of the state government to comply with the directives of the Union), the term "otherwise" lets in several imponderables not liable to judicial scrutiny. Ramaswamy, J. thinks that the decision can be tested on legal mala fide and high irrationality. If *high irrationality* is approximated to irrelevance, the difference would boil down to that between *irrelevance* and *mala fide.*

The operational significance of the judgement is two-fold: *(a)* The Court can invalidate a proclamation. It may revive a legislature and even issue a stay order on the holding of an election seeking to short-circuit a judicial scrutiny, *(b)* A proclamation shall not immediately result in dissolution. The President may only suspend a state legislature pending the approval of the proclamation by Parliament. But a Parliamentary approval shall not preclude a judicial nullification of a proclamation.

These formulations per Sawant and Reddy, JJ. have not been agreed to by Ramaswamy, J., while others have expressed their agreement generally. According to Ramaswamy there is no express provision in the Constitution to revive an Assembly dissolved by a Presidential proclamation or to reinduct a removed government at the state. Stay cannot be granted of the operation of the Presidential proclamation till both Houses of Parliament approve the Presidential proclamation. The suspension without dissolution of the Legislative Assembly of the state also creates functional disharmony leading to constitutional crisis. The grant of stay of elections to the legislative assembly, occasioned pursuant to the Presidential proclamation, also creates constitutional crisis. Ramaswamy, therefore, held that "the courts should not issue such directions leaving it to the Parliament to amend the Constitution if need be."

Thus the Supreme Court has established the questionability of the Presidential proclamation on the basis of relevance of the material on the basis of which the presidential satisfaction was reached. The relevance may even be partial. There is a clear suggestion that the lack of relevance would prove *mala fide.* The Court also laid down remedies. There is no dissent among the judges on principle. There are only some doubts among a minority of the judges on the practicability of the judgement. Five of the nine judges declared the proclamations on Nagaland, Karnataka and Meghalaya unconstitutional but could not pass any remedial order as fresh elections had already taken place in those states. Three others did the same for Meghalaya while one judge refused to intervene.

On the dismissal of the three BJP-run governments there was no difference. Even the five judges who wanted to limit the power of proclamation were convinced that the Centre had reason enough. The BJP's case was that it was faithfully implementing the central directives and, in fact, controlled communal violence better than in the Congress-run states. The centre was only vindictive in superseding the governments of Madhya Pradesh, Himachal Pradesh and Rajasthan.

The Union Government's case had virtually been summarised in the white paper. It cited the BJP's oft-repeated commitments to the construction of a *mandir,* its *Yatras* and its active role in the demolition of the *masjid* (the "disputed structure") along with the fact that two of the Chief Ministers were members of RSS, then a banned organisation. The Court held that the Union government was justified in doubting the *bona fides* and capability of the BJP governments in enforcing the ban on the RSS and controlling communal tension. The fact that the ban on the RSS was *subsequently* invalidated is irrelevant. It was on the question of *bona fides*/credentials of the BJP that the Supreme Court's unanimous decision on secularism was pronounced.

The Question of Secularism

The Supreme Court clearly saw the demolition of the Babari Masjid as an act of deliberate and organised violence to the Constitution of India, a basic feature of which is secularism. (Some judges called it "a part of the basic structure"). This verdict, read with the *Keshavananda* case ruling, would mean that secularism cannot be abandoned even by an amendment.

The judges quoted Mahatma Gandhi, Jawaharlal Nehru, S. Radhakrishnan and M.C. Setalvad, besides a host of other judgements of the Supreme Court to define secularism. Secularism in India is not identical with the Western notion of complete separation of State and religion. Secularism in India means that the state will not associate itself directly with any religious faith but give freedom to all religious functions. This spirit, implicit in Articles 14, 15, 16, 25, 26 and 27, was made explicit by the 42nd Amendment through insertion of the word *secular* in the Preamble. (One may add that, had it not been so, the 42nd Amendment would attract the Keshavananda case ruling passed only three years ago).

B.P. Jeevan Reddy, J. took up the argument of Shri Ram Jethmalani, counsel for the petitioners, that secularism is a "vacuous word" or a "phantom concept." He turned down Shri Jethmalani's argument that India was partitioned on the basis of religion and that areas having majority Muslim population were constituted into a new entity — Pakistan — which immediately proceeded to proclaim itself as an Islamic Republic. (Shri Jethmalani may be faulted on two counts: *(a)* There is nothing in the Indian Independence Act suggesting the creation of Pakistan as a Muslim-majority Dominion, *(b)* Jethmalani was seeking judicial confirmation of a political objective). Reddy, on the other hand, pointed out:

> It is equally a fact that even after partition, India contained a sizeable population of minorities. They comprised not less than 10 to 12 per cent of the population. Inspired by Indian tradition of tolerance and fraternity, for whose sake the greatest son of India, Mahatma Gandhi, laid down his life and seeking to redeem the promise of religious neutrality held forth by the Congress party, the founding fathers proceeded to create a state secular in its outlook and egalitarian in its action. They could not have countenanced the idea of treating the minorities as second-class citizens. On the contrary, the dominant thinking appears to be that the majority community, Hindus, must be secular and thereby help the minorities to become secular.

If this is not a clear condemnation of the BJP's politics, Reddy's Conclusion no. 10 certainly is:

> In matters of state, religion has no place. No political party can simultaneously be a religious party. Politics, and religion cannot be mixed. Any state government which

> pursues unsecular policies or unsecular course of action acts contrary to the Constitutional mandate and renders itself amenable to action under Article 356.

This judgement, incidentally, will go a long way in solving the Rao government's dilemma with regard to separation of religion and politics — a legislation on which was unsuccessfully sought to be pushed through in 1993. A constitutional amendment may no more be necessary but an amendment of the Representation of the People Act will be, in order to give effect to the imperatives of the judgement. It will be necessary to set up the authority that will invalidate the registration of a political party indulging in the use of religion for political gains and contributing to communal disharmony.

There is another long-term impact of the judgement. As Ahmadi, J. pointed out, Article 27 of the Indian Constitution provides that no person shall be compelled to pay any taxes, the proceeds of which are specifically appropriated in payment of expenses for the promotion or maintenance of any particular religion or religious denomination. According to Ahmadi, J.:

> This is an important article which prohibits the exercise of the State's taxation power if the proceeds thereof are intended to be appropriated in payment of expenses for the promotion and maintenance of any particular religion or religious denomination. That means that State's revenue cannot be utilized for the promotion or maintenance of any particular religion or religious group.

This would mean that all kinds of state assistance toward construction and maintenance of temples/mosques/churches/monasteries/synagogues and religious performances must stop forthwith. But secular activities connected therewith shall fall well within the ambit of State's power and responsibilities. There will be another exception. With the merger of the former princely state of Travancore certain financial obligations of the state were taken over by the Government of India. After reorganisation of states they devolved upon the state governments of Kerala and Tamil Nadu. As per Art. 290A some funds are, therefore, charged upon the Consolidated Funds of Kerala and Tamil Nadu.[5]

1994

NOTES AND REFERENCES

1. *Judgments Today*, 2, No. 8, 21 March 1994.
2. *All India Reporter (AIR)* 1973, SC 1461.
3. *AIR* 1969, Calcutta 198, paras 41, 42, 50.
4. Pandian, J. recorded 82 instances of President's Rule in states and 13 instances of the same in Union territories upto 1991.
5. Inserted by the Constitution (Seventh Amendment) Act, 1956, s. 19.

NOTES AND REFERENCES

[illegible]

7

Nation Building and Ethno-Cultural Tensions in South Asia

The concepts of nation and nation building have of late come under attack. While the globalizers point to the emergence of the European Union to demonstrate the futility of nationalism, the cultural fundamentalists seek to impart homogeneity/integrity to a nation on a cultural - particularly a religious-cultural - plank, and the post-modernists emphasize the sanctity of the small community. The emphasis on territorial nationalism - with a view to consolidating and strengthening political independence and socio-economic progress of a people - has, as a result, been considerably diluted.

Nationalism in Europe

Since the appearance of nationalism in Europe there have been two parallel streams in its flow. In the 1770s J.G. Herder[1] looked for linguistic and cultural affinity to identify *volkstum*, literally meaning 'peopleness' but subsequently being identified with 'national character' among the population of some 300 German states created by the Treaty of Westphalia in 1648. On the other hand, in 1789, when the States-General declared that sovereignty in France vests in the French nation, less than 50% of the people of France spoke the French language.[2] No one had heard of religious nationalism in Europe as nationalism appeared after the Reformation.

Reaction to the Napoleonic conquests gave a thrust to the anti-imperialistic content of the nationalist agenda but could not fully overcome the dynastic pull on political identities so that the Vienna settlement (1815) merely strengthened the Austrian hegemony over Europe. The only democratic achievement at Vienna lay in re-establishing multi-lingual and multi-religious Swiss confederacy.

Never before the *Resorgimento* in Italy was there a union of cultural nationalism - that had developed mainly on the German soil - and territorial nationalism based on citizenship rights and democracy. Neither Italy, nor any other European state, however, could perfectly match territorial and cultural nationalism. This discrepancy led to two world wars.

Third World Nationalism

Because of long colonial rule and the popular character of the anti-colonial struggles third world nationalism had a broadly democratic character. Indeed there existed hidden and open inequality within this nationalism. At the same time this nationalism was subjected to regional, religious, linguistic and ethnic pulls giving the anti-colonial struggles a generally federal character. Such pulls were, in several cases, overlapping and, in several others, cross-cutting making the broad unity possible. After the disappearance of political colonialism, as the common focus of anti-imperialist struggles, the broad unity of the particularistic forces has naturally weakened.

Anti-colonial struggles everywhere need popular support and, therefore, had to have a democratic character though, of necessity, under elite leadership. Anti-colonial movements spoke of a nation in the French Revolutionary sense as the Indian National Congress founded in 1885 did. The cultural contours of this nationhood were not clearly drawn and the nation was defined roughly by the limits of the colonial territorial authority. When the demands of political identity appeared, religious, linguistic, regional and even continental affinities were asserted or sought to be built. Thus West Asia grew through the Wahabi and the Khilafat movements, with their leaven in the Faraizi movement reaching as far as eastern India in the nineteenth century. Indo-China, on the other hand, split itself into three separate regions (Cambodia, Laos and Vietnam), while the African people sought to build their unity on a continental basis.

In British India the first attempt at administrative reorganization, on religious basis, in 1905 was frontally challenged on the ground of language demonstrating the intensity of a cross-cutting cleavage within the cultural frame. Though the 1905 Bengal partition was undone. India was finally partitioned on religious basis in 1947 and the partitioned India has been successively reorganized on linguistic basis since 1953.

The fundamental problem of nation building in post-colonial South Asia, thus, is a contradiction between the territorial boundaries and the ethno-cultural affinities. An ancient, subcontinental civilization built, layer after layer, by continuous migration of populations and their cultures, pre-colonial South Asia housed numerous states and communities of varying sizes who never had a conception of territorial power and were governed more by social than by political orders. The colonial masters initially disre-garded these ethno-cultural specificities and, later, were unable to adjust their territorial power perfectly to the needs of such specificities. They, rather, sought to make use of the diversities to weaken the aspirations for nationhood that began to grow in their territories.

Given this complex background an ethno-culturally homogeneous state, far less a theocratic state, is hardly possible in South Asia unless the state government is controlled by a particular, religious denomination that hierachizes citizenship on ethno-cultural criteria or resorts to open ethnic cleansing. Such a strategy usually boomerangs on 'the majority' which becomes victims of authoritarianism because without scrapping universal franchise and disregarding world opinion the goals cannot be achieved. Pakistan and Bhutan are the saddest examples of this dilemma though the tendencies are discernible in the more liberal states too. On the other hand, the current trends forebode the increasing assertion of the hitherto marginal groups with various demands for autonomy.

Secularism

In these circumstances the advisable policy would be a cultural *laissez faire* of which secularism is a component. Secularism is a much abused term today, particularly in India. While certain political parties and groups make a mysterious distinction between 'pseudo-secularism' and 'genuine secularism', liberal political opinion in India has built up another mysterious theory that 'our secularism' is different from the 'western secularism' as Indians are very much religious. This view has been endorsed even in a number of judicial pronouncements at the highest level with the result that secularism in India has been identified with tolerance or, in the Sanskrit cliche - **sarva dharma samabhava** (equal respect for all religions) - a socially laudable, personally impracticable and politically unsuitable principle.[3] There can be no 'secular society' in the world because (1) 'secular' means non-religious, mundane, profane, and *not* tolerant, and (2) there is no society which is non-religious though there may be some atheists in it. Religion is an integral part of the society not only in India but throughout the world also.

Secularism is a term that attaches to an institution of society concerned with a mundane affair and not the whole society. A football club or an industrial enterprise is secular, a prayer meeting is not. A society contains both the kinds of organization. A member of each organization in a society is likely to have his/her private religious belief. Many of them are likely to practise religion in association with others. But when they go to play football or work at the assembly line they forget their religious commitments. Similarly, the state is an institution mainly concerned with worldly affairs. It does not need to have a religious function. In fact, there is a strong case that states should not take part in religious affairs.

While the Reformation in Europe ended the control of the Church over the state in Germany, it reversed the control in England where the Anglican Church was brought under the authority of the Crown. Generally, however, in western Europe the state washed its hands of religious affair. It was the first amendment to the Constitution of the United States of America which brought about a complete separation of the church and the state. The Constitution of India, initially, did not declare the Indian state secular. But Article 25 made a clear distinction between the religious and the secular activities of the religious institutions and provided for state control over secular activities of such organizations. The Indian Constitution granted religious freedom to all persons (ibid.) and prohibited taxation for the specific purpose of supporting any particular religion (Art. 27), but it fell short of prohibiting state expenditure for religious purposes. Patronization of all religious communities has displeased all religious communities who are accusing the state of discrimination.

Political Geography of South Asia

Though South Asia is a geographic concept, it fits better with political geography than with natural geography. It consists - in the SAARC framework - of Britain's Indian empire with its satellites but minus Aden and Burma (separated from British India in 1937). On the eve of transfer of power this imperial system comprised British India consisting of Governors' and Chief Commissioners' provinces, 566 princely states; two tribal areas (in the far northeast and the far northwest of British India) under the authority of the Governor-General of India, the three together constituting 'India'; Ceylon (ruled from 1796 to 1802 as part of the Madras Presidency and later as a crown colony); Nepal, Bhutan and Sikkim, controlled from British India as vassals; and the Maldives controlled similarly from Ceylon (Sri Lanka).

British India, the 566 princely states and the two tribal areas comprised the territory that was later split into India, Pakistan and Bangladesh. The Maldives became independent in 1965 and a republic in 1968. Sikkim had a democratic revolution and joined India in 1974. Nepal had an anti-Rana revolution in 1950, established a constitutional monarchy that became real in the 1990s and gradually became independent of Indian control. Bhutan had become a monarchy in 1907. After 1947 it also became gradually independent of Indian control.

Ethno-cultural Divisions in South Asia

Except for the Maldives, which has an ethnic and historical linkage with Sri Lanka (former Ceylon) and is wholly Muslim, all the South Asian countries have strong ethno-cultural divisions. The cross-cutting cleavage between religion and language has given India a mosaic appearance, an appearance which was shared, to a lesser extent, by Pakistan until its split in 1971. Religious minorities in Pakistan today - barring the Shias - are insignificant as linguistic minorities in Bangladesh are. Ethno-cultural diversities are positively related with the size of the population and the territory of a state.

During the nineteenth century British connections substantially affected the ethno-cultural composition of the Himalayan states. First they lost territories to British India. After 1857 some territories were restored to Nepal. Then there was a multi-directional process of migration from India to Nepal and from Nepal to India, Bhutan and Sikkim. Demands for civil and political rights of the immigrants became the basis of democratic movements in Bhutan and Sikkim.

Impact of Migration

In Bhutan and Sri Lanka linguistic and religious divisions largely coincide due to immigration. In Sri Lanka, whereas the migration of labour force during the colonial period was effectively contained after independence through citizenship laws, the pre-colonial migrants are a claimant to political rights. In Bhutan (or, for that matter, Sikkim) the minority problem is, essentially a legacy of British colonialism. Migrations between India and Pakistan and between India and Bangladesh, have been of religious character while migrations between Bangladesh and Pakistan were of linguistic character.

A certain amount of regionalization is inherent in all migrations. Thus while the old Tamil migrants preponderate in the northern and the eastern districts of Sri Lanka, the late Tamil immigrants were settled in the central region as labourers. The Terai area of Nepal contains a large number of Indo-Gangetic population. No immigrant is allowed to settle above 5,000 feet altitude in Bhutan. The bulk of the population from West Pakistan were settled in eastern Punjab, Delhi and its neighbourhood while the bulk of the refugees from East Pakistan were settled in West Bengal and its neighbouring states. Muslim refugees from India to West Pakistan were largely settled in Sind while those to East Pakistan preferred the border districts.

Ethno-Cultural Tensions

South Asia has experienced three kinds of migration of people: (1) Natural migration in the pre-colonial period in quest of land or occupation; (2) settlement, contract or indenture in the colonial period; and (3) refugee movement among post-colonial states where natural migration, to a much lesser extent, does continue. During the age of the politics of scarcity such migrations have, in no small measure, contributed to intra-state and inter-state ethnic conflicts.

Interestingly, while religion and religion-mixed-with-language have divided the South Asian communities, language alone has had a salutary effect in inter-state relations as in the case of Bengali (shared between India and Bangladesh), Punjabi and Urdu (shared between India and Pakistan), and Hindi (close to Nepali). In the intra-state relations, however, language has produced tension almost comparable to that produced by religion. Tamil in Sri Lanka, Urdu in India and Bangladesh and Nepali in Bhutan are causes of suspicion, if not open conflict. Languages confined within state borders have produced riots and the successive reorganization of states. The implication of this analysis is as follows. If a substantial minority in a nation state shares the religion or/and language of a neighbouring nation state, it is suspected by the majority in its own state. This formulation will apply even to the 'Bihari Muslims' in Bangladesh if Pakistan is regarded as her 'historical neighbour'.

The ethno-cultural mismatch with the political boundaries, a product of colonial rule, is the single most important cause of political unrest in South Asia. Thus, in 1902, the Durand Line was drawn between British India and Afghanistan. Neither the Afghans reconciled themselves to it, nor the British could administer the whole territory upto the Durand Line till 1947. It was only after the rise of the Taliban that Pakistan could make the people of the erstwhile North-West Frontier Tribal Area participate in its elections. A huge hilly region between the British Indian districts and Manipur on the one hand and the Irawaddy valley of Myanmar was never properly administered. British India and Burma were separated in 1937 on the basis of a notional border along the Patkai range of mountains which, after 1947, became an international border. In 1947 a still greater dislocation of the hitherto prevalent political alignment took place. The entire tribal population of northeast India was divested of their traditional ethno-cultural linkages and economic accesses. The hills of Myanmar became the paradise of arms smugglers, bootleggers and drag dealers. The disoriented tribal people respond only by clamouring for autonomy from this chaos.

Minority Behaviour

A major reason of cross-cutting between religion and language is that the so-called 'great religions' have wider spread than language. Linguistic division is more easily regionalized than religious division though there are identifiable regions dominated by religious groups. Wherever linguistic and/or religious divisions are regionalized federation has been a useful strategy to keep the various groups together. Wherever a minority is spread out and mixed only an effective system of civil and political rights can maintain harmony. In such a system the demand for civil autonomy of the minorities grows over the questions of cultural and educational rights and personal law.

Minority behaviour in politics is, thus, essentially democratic in character. In politics they act as special interest groups a manifestation of this tendency being the so-called 'vote bank'. The minority movements are essentially defensive and, according to circumstances, either conservative or radical. The rise of the so-called 'fundamentalism' of the religious variety among the minorities is an example of the conservative line of response while the support to the communists by the minorities in Sri Lanka, Burma, India, Pakistan and Bangladesh is an example of the radical option. Comparatively, the minority trust in the liberal leadership is in decline.

The Leadership's Role

In the first flush of freedom the liberal leaders of the South Asian countries took a position accommodative of the minorities. The Indian leaders adopted a constitution which abolished the political status of the minorities but granted them personal and group rights. In his address to the Constituent Assembly of Pakistan M.A. Jinnah promised equal citizenship to people of all faiths. Solomon Bandarnaike offered assurances to the Tamil minorities in respect of Ceylon. Sheikh Mujibur Rehman obtained the unanimous support of the religious minorities of Bangladesh. King Jigme Dorjée Wangchuk of Bhutan encouraged the Nepalese-speaking southern Bhutanese to participate in Bhutan's government and administration and even their intermarriage with the Drukpas.

The initial liberal approach to the minorities was subjected to violent attack from the orthodox sections of the majority community culminating in the assassinations of Mahatma Gandhi, Liaqat Ali, Solomon Bandarnaike, Jigme Dorji and Sheikh Mujibur Rehman by their co-religionists. Growing majoritarianism with economic scarcity resulted in increased communal tension.

Minorities became the soft targets of the disgruntled sections of the majority communities.

When the liberal leadership of the Third World countries in general and South Asian countries in particular had taken up the task of nation building, they had before them the democratic view of a nation, based on the concept of citizenship cutting across religious, linguistic and ethnic groupings. They set before themselves the task of growth with justice ignoring, perhaps, a number of pitfalls. In many cases they failed, in some cases they succumbed to the forces of reaction at home and abroad, in some they became martyrs. India has proved one thing. A democratic nation is the only bastion from which neo-colonialism can be fought.

2002

NOTES AND REFERENCES

1. For Herder's political thought see P.M. Barnard, *Herder's Social and Political Thought,* Oxford, Clarendon Press, 1965, and I. Berlin, Vico and Herder, London, Hosrath Press, 1976.
2. F. Hobsbaym, *Nations and Nationalism since 1780: Programme, Myth, Reality,* Cambridge University Press, Second Edition, 1992, p. 60.
3. This confusion prevailed even in the Supreme Court judgement in the famous Bommai case in which, except the dissenting judgement of Ahmadi, J. no one recommended complete separation of religion and state. See *S.R. Bommai and others v The Union of India and others, Judgements Today,* Vol. 2, No. 8, 21 March 1994. See also S.K. Chaube, "Communalism and Secularism in India", *Fifty Years of India's Freedom.* Indian Academy of Social Sciences, 1997, pp. 177-85.

8

The Ethnic Problem in India : A Historical Perspective

The Semantic Problem

One of the professional hazards of the social scientist of today is semantic. Because of the value-load he inevitably bears, the social scientist is liable to be misunderstood at every point he uses a jargon unless its contextual meaning accompanies it. 'People', 'race', 'nation' and 'ethnic groups' are some such words that can be ascribed different meanings in different places.

Thus a political scientist means by a 'people' more than a collectivity of persons. The word 'race' has fallen into disuse, except in the physical anthropologists' parlance, after world war II. Political scientists hardly agree on the definition of a nation.

The word 'ethnic group' is in fashion today,[1] yet, as early as in 1890 H.H. Risley pointed out that in this category 'the race basis is palpable and acknowledged'.[2] 'Ethnics' in the US vocabulary is only a euphemism for 'minorities', particularly the non-white, and is used handy in denying them legal rights in a country of immigrants.[3]

Risley's Categories

Risley's own thinking was not well-known for scientific precision; he dichotomized the entire Hindu population of northern India 'racially' into two types—the Aryan and the Dravidian disregarding Maxmuller's warning against the confusion which might arise from using philological terms to denote ethnological conclusions. But Risley had a thesis— a political one for that—which admirably served the purpose of *divide et impera.* It was this: The Aryans preserved their racial characteristics, mainly to preserve their superior status, by means of endogamy, 'and finally, that within the last few years it has helped to unite the most advanced classes of the Indian people in an organized effort to win for themselves the characteristic Aryan boon of representative institutions'.[5]

If Risley's categories were marked by a lack of precision, his insights had great bearings upon future political development in India. Risley noted a vast difference between the cultural and educational levels of the 'Aryans' and the 'Dravidians' although 'property' especially property in land, and the power which masses of men can exert when they move together, are not so concentrated in the hands of the more advanced race, nor are they distributed according to intellectual attainments:[6] In effect, Risley disfavoured a representative government in India which, if it took the shape of an intellectual oligarchy, with franchise based on literacy, 'would leave the landed interests practically unrepresented,' and if it were based on a wider franchise, might 'give undue leverage to the caste organization'.[7]

Risley was in the midst of a controversy created by the demand of the Indian National Congress in the wake of the Ripon Reforms. The Ripon Reforms (1882) had initiated a large-scale local self-government scheme which Risley, expectedly, endorsed full-throatedly. By 1890 talks were on to introduce limited representation at provinces.

The Divide and Rule

Risley's intellectual master was W.W. Hunter who, in 1868, published *A Comparative Dictionary of Non-Aryan Languages*[8] with a view to promoting among the British administrators greater understanding of the tribal population of India. In the political dissertation pre-fixed to the *Dictionary* Hunter accused the British administrators of having uselessly flirted with the Aryan population. Now that the hitherto flattered classes were growing disloyal, Hunter advocated a shift of policy towards the non-Aryan population. Hunter's *The Indian Musalmans,*[9] published in 1870, is widely believed to have encouraged the British policy of *divide at impera* with regard to the so-called 'communal question'.[10]

To say this is not to suggest that the British invented the communal or the tribal question or even easteism. It is not even true that the British government was made aware of these rifts in the Indian society by W.W. Hunter or H.H. Risley. It was, on the contrary, that the British officials first became aware of such rifts and made good use of them. The British intellectuals later came up to justify and bolster such policy. The Rising of the Indian Sepoys of the East India Company in 1857 was unanimously ascribed by the British officials to the fact that the Bengal Army was composed largely of the higher castes, viz., the Brahmins and the Rajputs. The policy of recruitment to the army was reorientated. The concept of the 'martial classes' (from particular regions and castes) as the base of recruitment evolved during this period.

Suspicion of high castes therefore dates from the Rising. The valuable lesson so dearly purchased was not going to be lost. It being repeated in the form of the general principle of 'divide and rule' could not have failed to influence the policy and conduct of later officials. It is well to remember in this connection that even the Roman Church, in its desire to propagate its faith, was prepared to accommodate caste in practical programme, though it was opposed to the humanitarian principles of the Church. Pope Gregory XV published a bull sanctioning caste regulations in the Christian Churches of India.[11]

The Nationalist Legacy

The fact that the communal question got the upper hand of caste in deciding the partition of India can be primarily ascribed to the fact that caste is much more diffuse than organized religion.[12] In fact, there is an underlying conflict between caste and religious solidarity in as much as caste splits a religious group. The politics of the Scheduled Caste Federation, only reinforced specialized aspects of the communal question. But when the question of transfer of power arose their fundamental antagonism to the politics of the Muslim League revealed itself.

In fact, casteism got a temporary set-back in the wake of a reinvigorated nationalism that appeared immediately after partition. This nationalism was itself tinged with communalism and resulted in a series of riots throughout the country. In 1957 W.H. Morris-Jones wrote: "Whatever may be the present strength of caste, it is certain that it is already less powerful now than it was even twenty years earlier".[13]

Linguism

Paradoxically, the new nationalism reinforced linguism largely as a legacy of the Indian national movement. The British had never favoured a linguistic organization of the provinces. It was only in 1872 that, after long pressures and persuasion, Assamese was adopted as a court language, in addition to English and Bengali, in the Brahmaputra Valley. In 1874 Assam was constituted as a multilingual province.[14] In 1905 Bengal (then including Bihar and Orissa) was partitioned on religious basis and Assam was merged with Eastern Bengal. The Indian nationalists protested, Partition of Bengal was undone. Assam returned to its old shape; but Bihar and Orissa, having been separated from Bengal, remained one province.[15]

Yet, while framing the Constitution, the Constituent Assembly of India turned down the demand for linguistic reorganization in apprehension of unleashing fissiperous tendencies.[16] Two factors, however, led to the acceptance of the principle of reorganization of states:

(1) The Andhra statehood movement climaxing in the death of Potti Sriramalu, and

(2) The merger of 554 princely states with the new republic.[17]

Even the States Reorganization Commission accepted the language principle half-heartedly. As a result, the process of reorganization continued till 1972. By this time the focus shifted from the major language groups to smaller 'tribal' communities. The reorganization of Northeast India in 1972 went against the language principle, in as much as the newly created hill states were hardly unilingual. All of them, except the Union territory of Arunachal Pradesh, adopted English as their official language.[18] The demands for statehood are still articulate in the tribal belts, particularly in Jharkhand.

Casteism

Selig Harrison postulated that the linguistic demarcation of states' boundaries intensified caste conflict, for "the regional limits of the operative caste units render it inevitable that caste—setting as it does the social boundaries of the competition for economic and political power—will be as divisive as it is unifying."[19]

Universalization of franchise, along with abolition of feudalism, brought to the fore those people whom Risley had considered 'the less advanced races'. Harrison wrote in 1960: "Today the peasant proprietors wield the economic power which made them the most insistent immediate claimants to political and economic power".[20]

Although the caste system acted as an instrument of what Rajni Kothari called the 'intermediate aggregation'[21] by making "available to the leadership structural and ideological bases for political mobilization, providing it with both a segmental organization and an identification system on which support could by crystallized" and forcing the leadership "to make concessions to local opinions"[22] the series of caste riots in the seventies and the spate of conversions first to Buddhism and them to Islam demonstrate the less handsome face of the caste.

For an explanation of this graduation one is apt to look up to the deteriorating agrarian situation in the country. In his J.C. Bose memorial lecture on November 30, 1971, the noted anthropologist, Nirmal Kumar Bose, observed that those tribal people who had been drawn into the vortex of Hinduism but were assigned a low place were perhaps not hurt because of several reasons.

(1) In the villages, the distance between the rich and the poor was not as much as it had become after the introduction of capitalistic ideas even in agriculture.

(2) More honour was showered upon those who spent their wealth in conspicuous expenditure, in gifts to their friends or the poor in the villages than those who accumulated wealth.

(3) Normatively, entry of one caste into the preserves of another's monopoly was forbidden.

(4) There was a slow process by means of which members of hitherto tribal communities could rise higher and higher in the social estimation of the upper castes.[23]

Bose further commented: "But with the increasing pressure of population and, the intrusion of the ideas of competition in economic affairs, under the reorganization caused by capitalism and colonialism, the old norms naturally began to break down". The situation today has turned worse. Ownership of land, share-cropping, agrarian wage are issues critically agitating the 80% of the Indians who still live in the villages. The solution of the problem can be conceived only in terms of overhauling the entire economic system.

1982

NOTES AND REFERENCES

1. Nathan Glazer and Daniel P. Moynihan, *Beyond the Melting Pot*, Harvard University Press, 1970 and the same (ed), *Ethnicity: Theory and Experience*, the same publishers, 1975.
2. H.H. Risley, 'The Race Basis of Indian Political Movements: *Contemporary Review*, May 1890, p. 732.
3. A slightly shocking experience of the present writer in a leading US centre of scholarship was the pronounced distinction made by the US scholars between the Caucasians' and the ethnics.
4. Risley op. cit. p. 747.
5. *Ibid.*, p. 742.
6. *Ibid.*, p. 756.
7. *Ibid.*, pp. 756-57; Selig S. Harrison (*India: the Most Dangerous Decades*, Oxford University Press, 1960) and M.N. Srinivas ('Caste in Modern India' in M.N. Srinivas, *Caste in Modern India and other Essays*, Bombay, Asia, 1962), picked up the thread, after India's Independence.
8. W.W. Hunter, *A. Comparative Dictionary of Non-Aryan Languages of India and High Asia*, (1868) reprint, Delhi, Oriental Publishers, 1975.
9. W.W. Hunter, *The Indian Musalmans*, London, Trubner & Co., 1870.
10. Asoka Mehta and Achayuta Patwardhan, *The Communal Triangle in India*, Allahabad, Kitabistan, 1942.
11. G.S. Ghurye. *Caste and Race in India*, Bombay, Popular Prakashan, fifth edition, 1969, p. 285.
12. For the British role in effecting the partition of India on communal basis see Shibani Kinkar Chaube *Constituent Assembly of India: Springboard of Revolution*, New Delhi, People's Publishing House, 1973.
13. W.H. Morris-Jones, *Parliament in India*, London, 1957, p. 328.
14. Shibani Kinkar Chaube, *Hill Politics in Northeast India*, Calcutta, Orient Longman, 1973.
15. Of course Orissa was separated from Bihar in 1934 primarily on linguistic basis. But in the same year creation of Sind was primarily based on religion.

16. Chaube, *Constituent Assembly of India*, op. cit. pp. 219-22.
17. Shibani Kinkar Chaube, *The Ethnic and Social Bases of Indian Federalism*, Centre for Studies in Social Sciences, Calcutta, Occasional Paper No. 17, pp. 18-20.
18. Chaube, *Hill Politics in Northeast India*, op cit., pp. 121-22.
19. Harrison, op. cit., p. 105.
20. *Ibid.*, p. 134.
21. Rajni Kothari, *Politics in India*, New Delhi. Orient Longman Ltd., 1970, pp. 91-93.
22. Rajni Kothari (ed.), *Caste in Indian Politics*, New Delhi, Orient Longman, 1970, p. 13.
23. Nirmal Kumar Rose, 'An Anthropological View of Indian Civilization, Science and Culture, 37, 2, December 1971.

9

Colonial Context of Regionalism: The Australian and Indian Experience

If we ignore the recent appearance of a number of small states on the world map, as a result of the dissolution of the Western empires and their successor trusteeship regimes, the modern states would generally appear to be large in size and complex in structure. Their societies are pluralistic, their authorities are hierarchical or federal.

A large state comes into being either through annexation or through union. Annexation involves force and hierarchy. Union involves volition and equality. Force is an attribute of authoritarianism, volition of democracy. The distinction between an empire and a federation is determined by the absence or presence of volition, though there could be intermediate regimes like the Canadian Federation of 1867 or the Austro-Hungarian Empire of 1869 (a federation literally means a contracted union).[1]

Pluralism may be expressed either in terms of territorial specificity or that of ethno-cultural specificity. Rigorous control of immigration has not allowed the coincidence of ethno-cultural specificities with territorial divisions in new societies like the USA and Australia, but in the older countries the coincidence is visible.

A major difference between the Indian federation and the United States federation (or, for that matter, the Canadian and the Australian federations) is that, although all of them have historical linkages with the British empire, the Indian federation belongs to the autochthons while the others are made up of immigrants even though they are all results of colonial conquest.[2]

The British rulers of India could not satisfactorily comprehend the socio-cultural complexities of the vast territory they had come to control, far less manage it neatly. In the first place they did not, or possibly could not, define the nature of their control over the territories. In the second place, they did not streamline the limits of their territorial control.

Technically, the British in the shape of East India Company was the *dewan* (revenue collector) of the Mughal ruler of India until 1857, and all Acts of British Parliament about India during that period pertained to the management of the Company and its Indian "possessions'. Within this period the three Presidencies of Bengal, Bombay and Madras were merged under the control of the Governor of Bengal who was redesignated Governor-General by the Regulating Act, 1773. In 1853 the civil and military powers of the governors of Bombay and Madras were transferred to the governor-general. It was only by the Indian Councils Act of 1861 that legislative powers were returned to the governors. In 1870 the power to make regulation in backward tracts (the erstwhile 'non-regulation districts') was restored to the governor-general. It was within this framework that councils were created tor assisting the governors and the governor-general in executive and legislative affairs. Gradually they were made responsive and, after diarchisation, even responsible.

Deliberately or not, the British did not set any precise external limit to their power. By 1858, however, a more or less clear idea of India emerges in British pronouncements. The 1858 proclamation of Queen Victoria brought the East India Company's territorial possessions under her rule and such territories acquired the collective name of British India.The Queen, further, proclaimed to the 'Native Princes of India that all treaties and engagements with them by or under the authority of the Honourable East India Company are by us accepted and will be scrupulously maintained'.

Following this, the Interpretation Act of 1889 defined 'India' as 'British India together with any territories of any native prince or chief under the suzerainty of Her Majesty'. The status of the British Crown over the native princes, thus, legally came to be defined in terms of suzerainty (or, in political jargon, 'paramountcy').

The Indian Ocean and the French and Portuguese enclaves set the southern limit of the Indian empire, but the eastern, the northern and the north-eastern boundaries remained fluid. Annexation of Burma (Myanmar) in the east by 1883 brought

British power almost face to face with the French colonies in South-East Asia but for the hilly buffer zone to the east of the Irawaddy valley. The Durand Line was drawn in the north-west only in 1902 and the McMahon Line in the north-east in 1914. Neither Afghanistan nor China accepted these borders and there remained an unadministered patch of territory to the north-west of British India that came to be designated, after 1935, as a tribal area. A similar tribal area was created in the east when Burma was separated from British India in 1937. And virtually the entire north-east frontier (tribal) tract, now constituting Arunachal Pradesh, was unadministered. Such 'tribal areas' constituted the twilight zone of the empire because they were inside India but outside British India or any native state and yet under the executive authority of the Governor-General.

Even the British Indian territories though were not uniformly administered. Normally, they were divided under two broad types, the Governors' and the Chief Commissioners' provinces. Within the governors' provinces there were 'backward tracts' that, in 1935, were designated 'excluded' or 'partially excluded' areas. The exclusion was from the scope of the reforms. As a result, a wide variety of administrative and control patterns prevailed on the eve of the transfer of power.

British suzerainty over the 566 princely states took the form of different doses of 'political control' exercised by the Governor-General as the Viceroy, either directly or through the governors. For big states political officers were appointed. For small states sometimes neighbouring district officers of British India were assigned responsibility. In discharging his agency functions the governor exercised his discretion. Governors also exercised their discretion with regard to reserved subjects in the provinces as well as in the areas excluded from the reforms either totally or partially.

As in the princely states the territories in British India were not equally developed. The port towns of Calcutta, Bombay and Madras got the most attention in industrial and commercial development. Punjab got attention in development of irrigation. Railways and highways brought about a moderately integrated communication system. Mineral exploitation in middle India, tea plantations in the foothills of north-east India and coffee plantations in south India created enclaves of relative prosperity leading to immigration and urbanization. The economy of the country as a whole, however, was marked by great regional disparities.

The Indian federation was not just an inevitable consequence of the process of devolution of power. It was also a historical necessity—as even the British realized. They had annexed Indian territory at random and at different opportunities.They put such territories in uneven blocs first as presidencies and then as provinces, without attention to their ethno-cultural complexities. When they first sought to impart some rationality to the territorial arrangement they could only think of the religious division. The result was the partition of Bengal in 1905. The anti-partition agitation, dialectically, produced the linguistic (sub-nationalism that became an article of faith with the Indian national movement. But administrative convenience and real politics demanded the reduction of the size of the Bengal Presidency. While the 1905 religious partition was undone in 1912, the new composite province of Bihar and Orissa was split in 1934.

The creation of Sind out of the Bombay Presidency in 1934 was an interesting example of the resolution of the dilemma between religion and politics. The Muslim League demanded its creation on the grounds that it was a Muslim-majority region. The Congress agreed to it on the ground of the distinctiveness of the Sindi language.

The British considered provincial autonomy as a means of managing religious communalism. The Indian National Congress saw it as an instrument of satisfying linguistic aspiration. It had provincialised its own organisation in 1920 on the basis of language. The Cabinet Mission Plan of 1946 acknowledged only three major communities in India, the Hindu, the Muslim and the Sikh, and advocated a grouping plan which reversed the erstwhile British philosophy. The Congress was agreeable to a very high degree of provincial autonomy but not grouping. The irreconcilability of the Cabinet Mission, Muslim League and the Congress positions led to the partition of India on religious communal lines even as there was a strong desire for the political unity of the new nation. The fact that India did not become a unitary state was due to the awareness of the existence of numerous cultural specificities.[3]

From 1905 Indian politics became the victim of the cross-cutting cleavage of religion and language, for undeniably the small Muslim elite of Bengal had largely welcomed the religious division of the Bengal Presidency (as was revealed by the hosting of the Muslim League's inaugural conference in 1906 by the Nawab of Dacca). In the south, where Muslim strength was almost negligible, linguistic sub-nationalism clashed with the administrative boundaries of the provinces as well as the political boundaries of the princely states of Hyderabad Mysore, Travancore and Cochin. In the Bombay Presidency, where international finance capital was taking root, linguistic sub-nationalism was dormant in the British period. Bombay city remained cosmopolitan though Maharashtrian intellectual activities took roots in Poona (Pune).

The partition of India was the victory of the 'religious nationalism' of the Muslim League blessed by the administration. Yet, the irrationality of this victory was demonstrated within a quarter of a century when Pakistan was split by linguistic nationalism.

Although the Congress was committed to the linguistic reorganization of the provinces since 1930, the shock of partition and associated violence made its leaders hesitant. The Constituent Assembly postponed the decision but left scope for it in Article 3 of the Constitution. Half a decade after Independence the demand for the formation of Andhra Pradesh had to be conceded following the violent death of a veteran Congress leader, Potti Sriramalu. Even so the States Reorganization Commission (SRC) was lukewarm about a thorough reorganization on linguistic basis and the work was not completed till 1966.[4]

After 1966, however, linguistic movements were confined to demands for border adjustment as the broad reorganiza-tion had been completed. During this period a kind of anti-linguistic agitation—with stress on ethnic factors—developed, with a common grievance against 'exploitation' by the linguistic majorities in states. Thus, the reorganization of north-east India from 1963 to 1972 was the result of a protest against 'Assamese dominance'. None of the hill people had fought for their own language and most of the hill states, quite small in size, had several languages.[5] They happily adopted English as their official language. Recently, the Bodos of Assam and the Nepalese of the Darjeeling district of West Bengal were fighting for autonomy and citing their languages. But the Bodos are fragmented and scattered on the north bank of the Brahmaputra. On the other hand, the Nepalese of the Darjeeling hills do not unite with the Nepalese in Sikkim on their northern border even though they are an overwhelming majority there too.

Unsuccessful attempts have been made by the tribal groups in the middle Indian hills to develop common languages and scripts. In the most developed of such areas the tribes have ceased to predominate. But autonomy movements, existing essentially on ethnic slogans, occasionally assume regional facades by drafting non-tribal local residents.[6]

It is difficult to theorize on the precise role and impact of religion, language and ethnic affinity particularly if one takes into account the borderline languages. The SRC, for instance, turned down the case ot Punjabi as a separate language and considered it a corrupt form of Hindi. According to Paul Brass Punjabi and Urdu are two languages which are heavily influenced by religious sentiments.[7] The cases of Maithili and Konkani are not affected by religion. But their distinctions flow from the fact that they are on the fringes of two major languages, in each case using distinct scripts.

It can only be said that the various autonomy movements are attempts at correcting the wrongs committed by the territorial arrangements of the British Raj. The operation of democracy, further, is throwing up successive ethno-cultural identities challenging the dictates of political economy. Even the Indian Left, which tried to make use of this process to its benefit, has been swept away by it. The advocacy in the 1940s for conceding the demands of 'Muslim nationalities' was thoroughly misunderstood. Its successful participation in the Samyukta Maharashtra and Mahagujarat Movements was forgotten by the new states. Partition of India strengthened communalism. Bifurcation of the Bombay province strengthened localism.

History and geography together have built the political mosaic of India. States are of different sizes and contain populations of different sizes.Though most of them are unilingual, the hills states in the north-east are multilingual. Structurally, however, there is much greater uniformity now than in the British days.Today there are only states and union territories with Delhi enjoying a somewhat intermediate status as the national capital territory.[8] Within some of the states in north-east India the autonomous districts have district councils enjoying a wide range of powers over local affairs and customary rights under the Sixth Schedule to the Constitution. In the rest of India the Fifth Schedule has provided unspecified powers and administrative machinery for the areas containing substantial tribal populations. Local self-government (LSG) has recently been constitutionalized in the normally administered areas. But the difference between local self-government and full autonomy is that the former has no political identity while the latter has. The jurisdiction of a LSG is determined by mere administrative dictates while that of an autonomy is altered as well as created by political/constitutional decisions. There are, at the same time, ethno-cultural specificities of autonomies while the LSGs may be of a social nature.

There is significant political difference between autonomy and LSG. Pristine autonomy is ethno-cultural because the concept of the first family, first class or first tribe is central to it. The 'we'-'they' dichotomy restricts the admission of the outsider at least on equal terms. Rights of citizens are circumscribed by rights of groups. Thus the states are granted power to restrict public appointments on the basis of residence. Rights to purchase land are denied to outsiders by Jammu and Kashmir and the hill states of north-east India. Even immigration by 'outsiders' is restricted in several states. No LSG can impose such restrictions upon citizens. This in turn implies an authoritarian tendency among autonomies and a democratic tendency in LSG. When the Sixth Schedule to the Indian Constitution granted autonomous district councils to the hills of Assam, election of village councils was foiled in all hill districts except the Mizo. Since the 73rd Amendment several scheduled areas have been resisting elected panchayats. It is also known that many state governments are lukewarm to the 73rd Amendment because it would curtail their power of patronage to the LSGs if not cut into their funds.

The case of the Darjeeling Gorkha Hill Council provides an illustration of such a conflict.The council was formed a few years back as a local body with wide financial and administrative powers.[9] Its chairman, Mr Subhash Ghishing, is demanding central aid to this body to be directed straight to it without being routed through the Government of West Bengal. The Hill Council has so far refused to submit its accounts to state government audit.

On the other hand the Darjeeling Gorkha Hill Council has resisted the holding of local body elections which is mandatory under the 73rd and 74th Amendments to the Constitution. The Darjeeling Gorkha Hill Council was exempted only from the control of the municipal bodies and district panchayat.[10] The Constitution made exceptions for Nagaland, Meghalaya and Mizoram as well as for the hill areas of Manipur where district councils, not under the Sixth Schedule but under an Act of Parliament, exist. It may be noted that under the 1950 Constitution the territories now covered by the states of Meghalaya, Mizoram and most of Nagaland were to have district councils. Because of Phizo's violent resistance, village development boards were set up in Nagaland.Village authorities and village councils were created in the two other areas through mixtures of elective and customary principles. Arunachal Pradesh had its panchayati raj through an election according to 'customary laws'. But the Arunachal Pradesh legislature has so far failed to pass any legislation on panchayat elections. An ordinance issued by the Governor simply says that the panchayats will be elected according to rules to be framed by the government.

While the urban centres of India, as elsewhere, tend to be multi-ethnic and multicultural, Indian villages are monolinguistic though not necessarily monoreligious. And 70 per cent of the Indian people live in villages. This pattern is modified in certain ways in respect of the tribal belts.

The tribal people constitute 7 per cent of the Indian population and they live in certain concentrations. But some of traditional tribal settlements have been infiltrated by non-tribal people who are generally seen as exploiters.

Tribal solidarity movements that have been developing since the 1940s achieved some success in north-east India because of certain geographically and politically favourable factors. In the central Indian hills their political aspiration for statehood has been thwarted by the overwhelming demographic and economic pressure of non-tribal groups. In peninsular India (Andhra Pradesh, Gujarat, Maharashtra and Kerala) they have adopted a peasant character and are fighting, occasionally with the support of political parties, for land. Only for Bihar have the central and the state governments agreed, in principle, on the creation of a Jharkhand Autonomous Council.

A broad cultural mapping of India today would show a Hindu-Hindi heartland of north India (UP, Bihar, Madhya Pradesh, Rajasthan and Haryana), a Hindu-non-Hindi inner periphery and a non-Hindu-non-Hindi outer periphery Jammu and Kashmir, Punjab, most of the hill states of north-east India and parts of Sikkim and Kerala). The tribal people of central and peninsular India have fallen to the impact of this cultural layout. Their number is too small for attainment of territorial autonomy. Even in Jharkhand they are only one-third of the total population. However, as B.K. Roy Burman noted, tribes living at the borderlands of major civilizations have served the important dual role of bridge and buffer, maintaining civilization's continuity on the subcontinent.[11]

On the States Reorganization Commission, Sardar K.M. Panikkar suggested the division of big states like Uttar Pradesh (UP) into smaller ones for administrative convenience. The other two members did not agree. For quite a long time UP supplied the prime ministers of India and served as the bastion of the ruling party at the centre. During the 1970s, Chaudhury Charan Singh, a UP leader, and Jaya Prakash Narayan, a national level leader from Bihar with a socialist background, revived the proposal. It was noted at that time that a partition of UP between an eastern half and a western half would give a relative numerical dominance to certain particular castes. In recent years, after the introduction of reservation for OBCs in the state, an old demand for the creation of an Uttarakhand State in the upper-caste dominated hill districts of UP has become powerful. Similar caste-based demands have been raised on north-east India including West Bengal (Kamatapur / Uttarakhand, Ujani Asom). The Maithili movement has been suspected to have upper caste backing. More than religion, but less than language, caste takes a regional pattern in India though on a smaller scale than both. A large-scale reorganization of UP (probably in three parts—the north, the east and the west) will suit administrative convenience. Extension of the same principle to north-east India will create more minuscule states economically dependent on central assistance.

Reorganizations have thus meant the creation of small states. Their heavy dependence on central assistance has functionally reduced their autonomy. Yet the ever-growing demand for such states indicates two features. In the first place, there is a growth of ethno-cultural particularism—a worldwide trend. Secondly, there is a rising aspiration of the ethnic elite for political power which, in turn, would mean political and administrative positions as well as governmental patronage. On the other hand, removal of their grievances against the 'majorities' brings in a new sense of integration at the national level.

After 1972 no reorganization of states has taken place. But the union territories are attaining full statehood one by one. This vertical movement in status illustrates the role of power in federal relations. Statehood means a full-scale state government with the powers allotted by the Seventh Schedule to the Constitution, a clear-cut autonomous space for the government, more funds, more political and administrative posts for the locals, more trade licenses and so on. The primary beneficiaries of these arrangements are regional literati. However, agriculture being a state subject, farmers have developed a stake in state politics particularly after the ushering in of the Green Revolution. Medium-sized states like Punjab, Haryana, Maharashtra and Karnataka, all products of state reorganization, have made great strides in agriculture. In large states like Uttar Pradesh, on the other hand, the Green Revolution accelerated regional disparity and strengthened the demand for smaller states.

But the crucial question is why the demands almost always seek legitimacy from the plea of regional disparity or internal colonialism. The colonial framework can provide some answer at least as far as India is concerned. The British brought under a common rule a vast territory that had never been under one government. They even rendered this territory a measure of economic integration. On the other hand, they intensified regional disparities by industrialization and spread of irrigation in select areas, ignoring the rest of the country. The total effect was a hierarchisation of the country's economy. It was not until independence that India could even think of removing regional disparity. The result was an endless number of allegations among regions as well as between the centre and the states.

A comparison between Australia and India will reveal more dissimilarities than similarities. Yet dissimilarities may be as instructive as similarities. The emergence of both federations out of the framework of British dominion probably was the major reason for Sir B.N. Rau examining, among others, the Australian governmental structure and suggesting a finance commission in line with the Commonwealth Grants Commission of Australia. This is as far as any similarity goes. Among the major dissimilarities is the headship of the two governments, one monarchical, another republican. Secondly, the Australian federation was born in the centripetal way, the Indian federation in the centrifugal way.

The differences are not symptomatic but caused by specific political circumstances. The Australian federation was the result of administrative union of the six British colonies and their territories on that continent, a process that had been completed in India by 1833. The federation also registered virtually total transfer of power from the Crown to the Australian Government (except the power over appeals). This was completed in India only by 1947 when the Governor-General was granted unlimited power of assent on behalf of the British Crown in Parliament.

Until the end of the nineteenth century Australia was a continent and not a country. Its six colonies had grown up as colonial outposts supplying raw materials to Britain and receiving her excess population. The formation of the Commonwealth literally turned the sights of the colonies onto themselves. But the geography of Australia is such that the Commonwealth members could only look sideways and not inward. For 80 per cent of Australia's territory is arid or semi-arid. They could serve the colony economically (through mining and grazing) but not by hosting human settlement.

The weakening of Australia's links with England, particularly after World War II, has strengthened her national and regional orientation. Her major trade partners today are the United States of America, Japan, the United Kingdom, New Zealand, Korea and Germany, in that order. She is clearly carving out her immediate world at the southern half of the Indian Ocean-Pacific Ocean region.

Thanks to regulated immigration, Australia does not have an ethnic problem. Yet one feels that territory, which is the primary parameter of modern nationhood, offers a certain challenge to the nation-building programme of Australia. This feeling is based on the hypothesis that physical contact/proximity is a basic condition of community. For a state which is an extended community this contract must be continuous and multifaceted. Australia is a highly urban country with people tending to settle mainly in the urban centres at the coasts.

This discontinuity affected Australian government structures in the past. While six colonies united in a federation in 1901 and called themselves states, the Northern Territory was kept under exclusive control of South Australia till 1911. That year the Australian Capital Territory was created by the transfer of Canberra from New South Wales to the federal jurisdiction. The Northern Territory got limited self-government in 1978, the Australian Capital Territory a similar deal in 1988.

Australia's progress towards self-government is equally steady for the whole as well as for the parts. It will probably lead to the declaration of the country as a republic in the near future. The symbol of the British crown has so far served as a unifying force for the country even if vaguely. The removal of that symbol may necessitate the strengthening of other bonds including those of place. Australia's population geography does not contribute to such strengthening.

1999

NOTES AND REFERENCES

1. Douglas Varney puts federation in the framework of popular sovereignty and sees federalism as an expression of pluralist democracy: 'In setting up a republic the Americans made a complete break with the notion of the monarch as sovereign. And in organising government on the basis of the separation of powers and limited government, they also did away with the idea of parliamentary sovereignty ... if none of the institutions of government could be sovereign, where was sovereignty to lie?'

For Varney, who argues that the Americans, in 1787, consciously established a federal political system, 'popular sovereignty was an essential feature of federalism'. At the same time he concedes that 'the Americans were not proposing populism.' Their idea of popular sovereignty was republican and anti-feudal (Douglas Varney, 'Are all Federations Federal?' In Balveer Arora and Douglas Varney (eds.), *Multiple Identities in a Single State* (New Delhi, 1995), pp. 9-50 at pp. 30-1.

2. I have provided a summary of the process of British annexation of the Indian subcontinent in my *Colonialism, Freedom Struggle and Nationalism in India* (Delhi, 1996).
3. See Shibani Kinkar Chaube, 'Ethnicity and the Dynamics of Federalism in India' in Amal Mukhopadhyaya (ed.), *Political Miscellany.* (Calcutta, 1986), pp. 125-42, at pp. 125-7.
4. This contention has been put forward in my *Constituent Assembly of India: Springboard of Revolution* (New Delhi, 1973).
5. Shibani Kinkar Chaube, *Hill Politics in Northeast India* (Calcutta, 1973).
6. See K.S. Singh (ed.), *Tribal Movement in India*, Delhi, Vol. 2.
7. Paul R. Brass, *Language, Religion and Politics in India* (Delhi, 1975), pp. 404-405.
8. Article 239 AA of the Constitution of India inserted by the 69th Amendment in 1991. Delhi has been promised statehood by the new BJP government.
9. Article 243ZC(2) inserted by the 74th Amendment in 1992.
10. Article 243M(3) inserted by the 73rd Amendment in 1992.
11. B.K. Roy Burman, *Tribes in Perspective* (Delhi, 1994), pp. 81-2, 86-9.

10

The Cultural Frame and the Dynamics of Federalism in India*

The Historical Perspective

Popular textbooks on the Indian constitution usually trace the history of federalism in India to the devolution of provincial autonomy in the British period, particularly since the Government of India Act, 1919. A simplistic approach to this history may result in confusing federalism with decentralization of administration. Decentralization is a matter of administrative policy flowing from the top. The British in India experimented with it, as well as its opposite, namely, centralization, ever since the merger of the three presidencies of Bengal, Bombay and Madras, under the Governor-General of Bengal, through the Regulating Act of 1773.

Decentralization was the inevitable consequence of the fast growth of the empire. So, although the civil and military powers of the Governors of Bombay and Madras were transferred to the Governor-General in 1833, through the Indian Councils Act of 1861, the legislative powers were returned to the Governors. Meanwhile, in 1853, the government of Bengal was placed under the direct charge of a Lieutenant-Governor (subsequently replaced by a Governor). Yet, in 1870, the power to make regulations for the administration of the 'backward tracts' was restored to the Governor-General by the Government of India Act. On the other hand, the Montford Commission of 1917 found even the centralization of military powers in 1833 'shadowy'. The Bombay and Madras military commands were abolished only in 1893[1].

---

* This is a revised version of a paper presented at the Indo-Soviet symposium on the Problems of the Federal Polity in India and the USSR at Moscow in May 1979.

The administrative initiative of Curzon led to a 'marked concentration of authority in the hands of the central Government'.[2] Immediately after him, however, a decentralization commission was set up. Before the report of the commission was submitted in 1909, the Moriley-Minto reforms, confirmed the decentralizing trend as well as the British government's desire to increasingly associate loyal Indians with the administration, expressed in the Queen's proclamation of 1858.

It was only with Montford reforms that the Indian people were granted an element of 'responsible' government. This led to a kind of bifurcation (however notional) between the respective domains of the rulers and the ruled. Hence the beginning of 'federalism'. Federalism is an offshoot of democracy, a union with power, not a loyal subjection.[3] In this sense, federalism under the British Raj was an internal administrative arrangement circumscribed by the overall demand for loyalty to the Crown. The reforms of 1919 and 1935 did not spring directly from the power of the people; they were grants of the British government, although forced by the pressure of the nationalist movement. Therefore, although a federal 'form' emerged in India even before 1947, the political essence of federalism was missing.

It can be said that the British experiment with 'federalism' set the pattern for the federal growth of independent India. The devolution of autonomy initiated in 1919 culminated in a constitutional division of power in 1950. Yet in independent India, as in the British period, the central control over the provincial affairs remained tight. The Governor remains the agent of the centre with unlimited power to intervene in the affairs of the states. The redeeming feature is the replacement of the British Governor-General with unlimited discretionary power by an elected Indian President who is guided by the advice of a responsible Council of Ministers. As the Council of Ministers is ultimately controlled by an elected House of the People and as the Council of States is supposed to represent the interests of the states, the federal principle is apparently protected, not by any constitutional machinery, but by the operation of democracy.

In the past the constitutional provision and democratic principles have in fact frequently collided in the matter of the supersession of the elected state governments. Such supersessions were resorted to by means of the declaration of constitutional breakdown whenever the central government, on the basis of a report from the Governor, or otherwise, was satisfied that lawful government had become impossible in a particular state. The practice has been followed until the recent supersession of the Congress-run state governments in northern India by the Janata-led central government. But there were certain differences between this last supersession and its preceding ones. There was no report by the Governor recommending the supersession in the last case while in the preceding ones the Governor's report was always available for the purpose. Such reports of Governors in the past have often been controversial, and occasionally censured by public opinion, when the party/coalition superseded managed to win the subsequent election, as in the case of West Bengal's United Front Government (1967 and 1970). The supersession of the Congress-run state governments of north India following the Sixth Lok Sabha elections (1977) was based on the plea of the loss of public confidence by the Congress party; and the central government was vindicated in its stand by the electorate even before the Congress-dominated Council of States had an opportunity to disapprove of it. The democratic principle took precedence over the constitutional form.

The point can hardly be missed even in a legalistic approach to federalism which locates the volitional character of a federation either in the form of a treaty at its origin (as in the USA) or in that of a constitutional right to secession that can terminate it (as in the USSR). The Indian federation did not emerge out of a treaty among its constituents. On the other hand, whatever uncertainty about the rights of the Indian states (after 1950) might have existed at the beginning, it was removed in 1963 with the 16th amendment to the Constitution.[4]

There is one unreality about the federal system of India. In the Indian Union no state can boast of its 'indestructible' character which is the cornerstone of US federalism. In the USSR the Karelo-Finnish Republic was abolished in 1958 on the formal request of the Soviet Republic. In India the formation and alteration of boundaries of the states is within the sole competence of the Union government.

But in one respect the treaty element is present both in India and in the USSR. If the formation of the United States federation was due to a treaty among the representatives of the people of the 13 former colonies, the size of the USA grew in the next two centuries through the annexation of the native people's territories. The size of the USSR grew through the success of the socialist revolution in the neighbourhood and eventual voluntary unions. In India too, the merger of the princely states was forced by popular democratic movements of the states' peoples. The French colonies were transferred in deference to popular demands. Although the Indian army had to be moved into the Portuguese colonies, the people welcomed them. The last country to join the federation was Sikkim, where, in 1974, the ruler was overthrown and the specific proposal for merger was passed by the local legislature elected by universal adult franchise. Secessionist forces have indeed been active in some parts of India. Even though 'secessionism' is prohibited by law and the coercive power of the state, it is important to note that even the disguised parties of secession have never been able to win a single election in any part of the country. The treaty element in Indian federalism can be located only in the consent of the peoples comprising it.

This theoretical clarification is necessary in order to avoid the formalist bias of the constitutional lawyers who focus their attention merely on the division of power between the Union and the units, the written constitution and the federal judiciary. The questions that need some additional probe in the light of the nearly two hundred years' of federal history of the United States of America is: how much of this 'autonomy' is real and how much of it is relevant to the social reality? When the Anglo-Saxon constitutional lawyers frown upon the federal system of the USSR, for instance, on the ground of the unreality of the right to secession of the Soviet Republics, the question of the reality of state autonomy in the USA, against the increasing assault of the defence and commerce powers of the centre, becomes pertinent. Even Beard's[5] dichotomy between the 'substantial personalty interests on the one hand and the small farming and debtor interests on the other' as the respective proponents and opponents of the US federation fails to hold good in the era of monopoly capitalism.

As the US federal system cannot be comprehended today in terms of either legal categories or economic categories, its relevance to the social reality becomes problematic. The 'functionalist' approach, fashionable among the Western scholars, therefore, seeks to re-interpret the precepts of federalism in terms of the concept of a 'plural society'. 'Instead of a single centre of sovereign power there should be multiple centres of power' because, as 'one centre of power is set against another, power itself will be tamed, civilised, controlled, and limited to decent human purposes'.[6] However, the pluralist theory tends to reduce the states as well as the federal centre to the level of any other public organization and to dilute the sanctity of the power vested in the state by means of the constitution.

The only tangible criterion of federal autonomy today, therefore, can be found in the cultural world. The United States will, of course, not fit in this scheme, as it does not recognize any cultural minority (except, probably, the American Indians living in the federal reserves and yet to acquire political rights). But many other federations will surely fit—Switzerland, Canada, the USSR and India. Popular textbook writers have marvelled at the similarity of certain features of the Indian federation with those of the Commonwealth countries including the racist South Africa. Even the structural similarities of the Indian federal system with that of the USSR have, on the other hand, missed their attention.

The Imperial Legacy

The British can be said to have set the pattern for India's federal growth in another way by leaving a set of administrative boundaries which were mostly incongruent with the cultural boundaries of the Indian people. As their 'military and political exigencies led to a great extension of the empire', the political map of British India was drawn 'with small regard to the natural affinities or the wishes of the people.'[7]

The partition of Bengal (1905) and its subsequent reconstitution (1912), through separation of Bihar and Orissa, showed the basic contradiction between imperial policy and the cultural patterns in the country. The province of Eastern Bengal and Assam, created in 1905, would have been a predominantly Muslim-majority area and would have, it was hoped, cut the Bengali bhadralok Hindu unrest to size. It was also a bait to the Muslim elite in British India until the beginning of the *khilafat* controversy. The annulment of the partition of Bengal was announced when the controversy had already begun. It probably made Indian Muslims more unhappy; but this unhappiness was not articulated in a violent form. The annulment gave Bengal the shape of a linguistically homogeneous province.

For the freedom movement in India this had great consequences.[8] There emerged a counterpoise between religion and language. Against the Muslim League's continuous assertion of religious nationalism, the Congress asserted the territorial integrity of nationalist India. They recognized the linguistic communities as sub-national identities. The Congress constitution was amended in 1920 by Gandhi, recognizing the linguistic provinces as its units, and the Provincial Congress committees were largely reorganised on linguistic lines. On the other hand, the British continued to give priority to the considerations of 'convenience or economy'[9] when it bundled together Bihar and Orissa, although some concessions were granted to religious as well as linguistic aspirations in the subsequent constitution of the provinces of Orissa and Sind,[10] which came into existence in 1937. Yet Orissa contained a portion of Andhra (Telugu-speaking) territory, just as Madras did another portion. This fact left some critical problems for the nationalist leaders of India. The nationalist definition of India exactly corresponded to what Lytton's 1877 proclamation described India to be and the Interpretation Act of 1899 confirmed.

The idea of Pakistan was accommodated within the Cabinet Mission's 'grouping' plan rather innocuously. It could save the unity of India under the then conceived dominion status. But if it is assumed that the Indian leaders were visualizing a sovereign, independent India, their opposition to grouping may be justified. They did not want a repetition of the Irish tragedy in this country to an extent far in excess of the impact of the communal riots that occurred around the time of the transfer of power. Yet, even the partition of India was a half-hearted admission of religious nationalism, it created a Hindu-majority state (India) and a Muslim-majority state split in two parts (Pakistan). It did not end the 'communal problem' in either of the successor states even after a partial transfer of population. On the other hand, the religious unity of Pakistan was shattered when the language movement in East Pakistan developed into the liberation war of

Bangladesh. What the partition ensured was the end of the 'political' problem with religious minorities. The constitution of new India scrupulously ensured that only the backward areas and communities were entitled to special status.[11]

End of Religious Nationalism

Of course this radical step was taken ignoring the claim of one religious community which, though not very large, was geographically concentrated and important enough to have acquired the status of a political minority in the British days; the Sikhs had identified themselves with the nationalist mainstream after the emergence of the idea of partition. At the end of the proceedings of the Constituent Assembly of India, however, their frustration could hardly be suppressed. Sardar Hukum Singh (later, a Speaker of the Indian Lok Sabha) protested: 'Does it stand to reason that because the Muslims have secured Pakistan, therefore, the Sikhs have ceased to be a minority?'[12]

Although the constitution of a Punjabi *suba* in 1966 has been viewed by some as a grant of Sikh 'homeland' only in a different 'garb',[13] it was preceded by the transfer of the leadership of the *suba* movement from the religion-oriented, sometimes secessionist, Master Tara Singh, to the more moderate, language-oriented, Sant Fateh Singh. The apprehension of the Punjabi Hindus about the Tara Singh movement can be gauged from the fact that since 1921 the number of declared Hindi-speakers was steadily increasing in each census, so much so that, in 1961, the number of Punjabi-speakers in the Indian part of the Punjab fell from 64.13 per cent (in 1911) to 41.9 per cent and the strength of the Hindi-speakers rose from 13.94 per cent (in 1911) to 55.64 per cent in 1961.[14] On the other hand, the formation of the Punjabi *suba* on professed linguistic ground did not invoke any major controversy and, in 1971, the strength of the Punjabi-speakers again rose to 65.61 per cent. The corresponding figure for the strength of the Sikhs in the Punjab is 60.22 per cent.

The end of 'religious communalism' did not lead to any negative repercussions in the form of a majority chauvinism. Punjab is not the only state in India with a non-Hindi majority. Jammu and Kashmir is a Muslim-majority state (65.85 per cent) and the Laccadive, Minicoy and Amindivi group of islands is a

Muslim-majority Union territory (94.37 per cent). Political history (and, in the second case, geographical distance too) separated them from Pakistan. There are three religious concentrations in Jammu and Kashmir. The Jammu division is Hindu-majority, the Ladakh division Buddhist-majority and the Kashmir division Muslim-majority. Suggestions for splitting the state according to the religious concentrations were turned down in the past not only by the government of India, but also by Sheikh Muhammad Abdullah, the unquestioned leader of the people of the state. The Lakshadweep (Laccadive group of) islands is yet politically inarticulate, and is administered directly by the Centre.

A group of Christian-majority states have emerged in northeast India as a result of the fast spread of Christianity and political re-organisation. Nagaland (66.76 Christians in 1971) became a state in 1963. Meghalaya, born in 1972, had 46.98 per cent of its population as Christian in 1971. But the spread of Christianity is so fast in that area that it can reasonably hope to be the religion of the majority. In the Union territory of Mizoram the Christian strength rose to 86.09 per cent in 1971. Christian strength is fast growing in the hill areas of the neighbouring states of Manipur and Tripura too. But the strength of the hill population constitutes a minority in each of these states so that the Christians comprise respectively 26.03 per cent and 1.01 per cent of the total population of Manipur and Tripura. The only new hill state with a Christian minority is the Union territory of Arunachal Pradesh (26.35 per cent).

The existence of several states and Union territories with non-Hindu majority is a proof of the equal status of all religions in India. But it was not until the 42nd amendment that India was formally declared to be a secular state. Although the overwhelming majority of Indians is Hindu, Muslims and Christians are spread over the whole of the country. In a way the fact of some of the border states of India being non-Hindu is a guarantee of secularism. For any attempt to convert India into a Hindu state will certainly affect the territorial integrity of the country.

Neither Jammu and Kashmir nor any state in northeast India was created as a religious state. Jammu and Kashmir is in fact a revolt against religious politics. This Muslim-majority former princely state was integrated with the Indian nationalist aspirations through an anti-feudal struggle against the Hindu prince. During the merger negotiations the prince toyed with the idea of a union with Pakistan, while the National Conference, led by Sheikh Abdullah, threw its lot with India. The union was qualified by the retention of a vast amount of autonomy by the state[15] and, although strains have occasionally appeared over the question of autonomy, the accession to India has never been put to doubt. Even in the Assembly elections of 1977, when the National Conference was set against both the Congress and the Janata Party, no secessionist demand was entertained.

In spite of the Christian concentration in Nagaland, Meghalaya and Mizoram, and the fact that their political leadership is almost entirely Christian, religion did not enter the demand for their creation. Only the secessionist movements in Nagaland and Mizoram sought to use religion by propagating the idea of 'Christian states', but the Christian churches not only dissociated themselves from the movements, they also positively opposed the sessionists when the latter became involved with communist China.[16]

Problems of Reorganisation

The three Presidencies of Bengal, Bombay and Madras developed into the British empire of 'India', and the empire was organised and administered, as we have seen, according to 'convenience and economy', marked by the strategy of *divide et impera.* At the time of the British departure, 'India' consisted of the following categories of territory:

1. British India, under the direct rule of the Governor-General, was divided into (a) Governor's Provinces and (b) Chief Commissioner's Provinces.

   Within the Governors' Provinces 'backward tracts' were categorised as 'excluded' and 'partially excluded areas', the local legislatures having no control over the excluded areas and partial control over the partially excluded areas. Most of such backward tracts were inhabited by tribal or semi-tribal populations.

2. 566 princely states in which the Governor-General of India, as the Viceroy of the British Crown, exercised different degrees of agency powers; their sizes differing greatly, but

their total territory constituting about one third of the territory of India.

3. Two tracts of 'tribal areas', defined as 'the areas along the frontiers of India or in Baluchistan which are not part of British India or of Burma or of any Indian state or of any foreign state'[17] and placed, according to the government of India Act, 1935, under the executive control of the Governor-General of India.

The partition of India was the final outcome of *divide et impera.* Though it solved no problem for India, the Indian leadership of course had reasons to be grateful to their former masters who chose not to aggravate the problems of the merger of 554 native states with India. Complex arrangements had to be evolved in order to accommodate the princely states within the democratic framework of independent India with the minimum use of coercive power. Yet the enforcement of one national constitution in the disparate units was a great achievement of the Indian leadership. After the mergers, the country was put under four categories of state administration: Part A (former Governor's Province), Part B (some big princely and groups of princely states). Part C (some princely states and their groups as well as most Chief Commissioner's Provinces) and Part D (the Andaman and Nicobar Islands). Specialised administration of most of the former backward tracts was provided through two separate Schedules (the Fifth and the Sixth). The areas under the Fifth Schedule were called Scheduled Areas, and the areas under the Sixth Schedule were called the Tribal Areas (differing from the 'tribal areas' of the British period).[18]

The merger of the princely states with India (as also with Pakistan) gave the question of linguistic reorganisation some urgency. The initial territorial arrangement of the constitution was largely *ad hoc* and some rational realignment of territories was obviously necessary. To quote the Madras government memorandum to the Simon Commission: 'The separation between British Indian territory and that of the various native states follows neither nationality, language nor geography. If we admit the linguistic provinces theory, we raise inevitably the question of the separate existence of the Indian States as they are at present'.[19] It fell to the States Reorganisation Commission to suggest territorial realignment not only in regard to the linguistic principle, but also with a view to the administrative integration of the former princely states.

There were practical hurdles to the linguistic reorganisation of India as were revealed in the early period of the working of the Constituent Assembly of India. Jawaharlal Nehru told the All-India Congress Committee in April 1948 that there were more serious problems requiring the government's attention than the linguistic re-organisation of the provinces. Yet in June 1948 the Constituent Assembly appointed a Linguistic Provinces Commission (popularly known as the Dar Commission) to examine the possibility and the implications of the constitution of the linguistic provinces of Andhra, Karnataka, Kerala and Maharashtra. (Significantly, Punjab was not yet on the agenda.) The Commission submitted its report on 10 December 1948, recommending the postponement of such reorgnisation on the ground that it would have 'a sub-national bias and militate against the working of India into one nation'. They recommended 'administrative convenience' as the principle of reorganisation.[20] The constitution of course left scope for such reorganisation.[21]

Reorganisation—A Continuous Story

It required some agitation by the Andhras and the fast unto death of a saintly politician, Potti Sriramalu, for the government of India to finally concede the creation of a separate Andhra state, out of the territories of the then Madras state, on 1 October 1953. This unleashed all sorts of demands for reorganisation of states along two lines:

(1) creation of new states out of the old, occasionally involving territories of two or more contiguous states.

(2) Adjustment of the existing borders of the states.

The common criteria proposed for such reorganisation, in most cases was language. In a few cases religion (as in the demand for a Moplastan on the western coast in Malabar, Kerala) and caste (as in the demand for a Jat-dominated union of western Uttar Pradesh and the Haryana region) seem to have influenced the demands.

The government's apprehensions came true. The country threatened to be split into a large number of small states, economically and administratively non-viable. Parochial jealousies and rivalries threatened to break out in local riots which the country could hardly afford within a few years of independence and the communal holocaust. The principle of language itself became open to doubt, as regional dialects such as Maithili (covered by Hindi) asserted autonomy. On top of all, the established administrative boundaries had developed some economic and political integrity of their own which would undoubtedly collapse in case of a radical reorganisation. Within three months of the formation of the Andhra state, therefore, the States Reorganisation Commission was set up.

The States Reorganisation Commission[22] was aware of the constraints. The recommendations for linguistic reorganisation were only partly based on the Eighth Schedule (enlisting the major languages of India).[33] The commission did a great deal of integrative work in respect of the former princely states (Part B and Part C States under the constitution) by recommending their mergers with contiguous former British Indian territories. Though the principle of such mergers was basically the linguistic affinity, the consideration of some practical problems such as administrative convenience, geographical proximity, communication facilities, etc., compelled its occasional modification. Thus, they recommended the separate continuation of Hyderabad for five years, the 'eventual' merger of Manipur and Tripura with Assam and the continuation of the direct administration of the North-East Frontier Tracts by the Central government, for reasons of security. The only controversial major recommendation was the creation of a Vidarbha state out of the Maratha caste-dominated territories of Bombay and Madhya Pradesh. Ultimately the size of Bombay was enlarged through transfer of territories from Madhya Pradesh by the States Reorganisation Act, 1956.

It was clearly impossible for one commission to map out the ethnolinguistic jigsaw of India. A number of border problems were yet to be solved. The border question between Bihar and West Bengal, together with the unsolved problems of Bombay and Punjab gave birth to a rather short-run experiment in bilingualism. The proposal for the merger of Bihar and West Bengal, mooted by the chief ministers of the two states and blessed by the national leaders, was aborted through popular pressure. Although the States Reorganisation Commission found that 'the minority Gujarati community in Bombay were content to remain in the composite state of Bombay',[24] the addition of further Marathi-speaking areas to the state made them apprehensive. In 1960, therefore, Bombay was split into the states of Gujarat and Maharashtra. The formula of bilingualism in Punjab also failed in 1966 when that was split into Punjab, Haryana and Himachal Pradesh.[25]

Border readjustments and creation of new states have, therefore, been a continuous story. Contrary to the desires of the States Reorganisation Commission, in 1963 Nagaland was made a state. In 1969 Meghalaya became an 'autonomous state' within Assam. In 1972 there was a large-scale reorganisation of northeast India.[26]

The Special Problems

Reorganisation of northeast India was not only contrary to the vision of the States Reorganisation Commission but also a departure from the erstwhile policy of forming linguistic states on the basis of the Eighth Schedule alone. In a way, it was a negative reaction to the language approach. One of the stimuli for the movement for the creation of 'hill states' in northeast India emerged from the opposition to the adoption of Assamese as the official language in the composite state of Assam in 1960. On the other hand, none of the hill states that was created out of the territories of Assam did have any standard language of their own. They have retained English as the official language. These states can probably be regarded as 'tribal states' in the sense that the bulk of their populations belong to the 'scheduled tribes' (a constitutional category), and the customary rights of such tribes are constitutionally protected. Perhaps some ethnic implications may be derived from their ascriptive origin from the great Tibeto-Mongoloid stock of the Himalayas or even religious implications from their profession of Christianity. But these are hardly articulated by the political leadership of those states. At the level of articulation the creation of the hill states was based on grievances against their 'exploitation' by the 'plains-men', particularly the Assamese.

For the Indian national leaders of all hues northeast India had been a 'special problem' (among many) left by the British Raj. Its intensity was partly due to the concentration of the scheduled tribes in relatively inaccessible and underdeveloped areas near India's international borders. Similar areas with less acute problems are strewn over the interior highland areas of the country. Around the hilly trijunction of Bihar, Orissa and West Bengal a multi-tribal Jharkhand movement has long been alive. The tribals belong to the Munda and Oraon stocks speaking different languages. Hence they cannot claim statehood on linguistic grounds. Naturally such problems are mainly viewed as emerging from the poverty and exploitation of the tribals by their advanced neighbours and sought to be tackled by the developmental and protective strategy of the Fifth Schedule and the Directive Principles of the Indian constitution.[27]

The more complex and more exclusive types of 'special problems' are treated as Union territories at present numbering nine: (1) Delhi is the national capital; and (2) Chandigarh is the common capital of Punjab and Haryana; (3) Dadra and Nagar Haveli as well as (4) Goa, Daman and Diu were liberated from the Portuguese empire and are yet to be integrated with their neighbourhood; so is (5) Pondicherry, transferred from the French, although Chandernagar which was also under French rule has been merged with West Bengal: (6) Mizoram is a small hilly tribal territory strategically forked by Bangladesh and Burma; and (7) Arunachal Pradesh is a larger but hilly and extremely backward tribal territory on the border with China; and finally (8) The Lakshadweep and (9) the Andaman group of islands are small, isolated, extremely backward tribal territories, although parts of the Andaman groups have been colonized. Even at the time of the framing of the constitution the state of Jammu and Kashmir was regarded as a special problem and a bar was placed on the automatic application of Union laws to that state.[28] The state of Nagaland got certain other kinds of protection from Union laws in a subsequent amendment.[29] Certain special constitutional provisions were made in view of the political situation in the new and small state of Sikkim.[30] These special provisions are different from the ones which are intended for special areas in the states of Maharashtra, Gujarat,"[31] Assam,[32] Manipur[33] and Andhra Pradesh.[34] This second category of special provisions relates to the specific necessities of backward regions with somewhat limiting effects on the powers of the concerned state legislatures.

At the opposite end of this tendency towards segmentation is the scheme for inter-state collaborations through central intervention.[35] Further, in 1956, a Zonal Councils Act was passed creating five multi-state Zones for coordinating economic affairs. The number rose to six in 1972.[36] Such Zonal Councils are mainly consensual apparatus not affecting the local autonomy of the states. Only the North Eastern Council has a statutory establishment with developmental funds from the Planning Commission of India.

The Emerging Pattern

The pattern of the evolution of the state structure of India may now be summed up. The partition of British India was the point of departure. The size of the country since then had increased through the accession of territories under the pressure of democratic movements. One strong point of India is the growth of political democracy. Partly it has attracted the democratic elements in the neighbourhood and partly it works for the consensus which maintains the territorial integrity of the state. Of course the coercive power of the state is the ultimate sanction behind this integrity through legal means. But the use of such coercive power in India has been rare.

The aversion to secession in India is no exception to the federal norm. More significant is the aversion to religious nationalism, springing from her historical experience, which disapproves of even the formation of states on the basis of religion, even though some states numerically dominated by the national religious minorities have actually come into being. As an alternative to religion, language has been recognized as a sufficient ground for nationality-formation with three qualifications: (1) the process of formation of states has gone beyond the limit of language in northeast India, (2) in the case of Hindi one language spreads over several states, and (3) the language boundary occasionally differs from the political boundary on administrative grounds.

Three notionally concentric circles may present the cultural topography of India in this way. The heartland consists of the Hindu-majority and Hindi-speaking states of north India.

Haryana, Rajasthan, Uttar Pradesh, Madhya Pradesh, Bihar, Chandigarh and Delhi contain 93.67 per cent of Hindi-speaking population of India which constitute 39.67 per cent of the Indians. The inner periphery of the heartland consists of Hindu majority but non-Hindi speaking states. The outer periphery contains the non-Hindu majority and non-Hindi-speaking states of Jammu and Kashmir (Muslim, Kashmiri), Punjab (Sikh, Punjabi), and the northeastern hill states of Nagaland, Meghalaya and Mizoram (Christian, tribal languages/dialects).

The most impressive aspect of the linguistic composition of India is the strength of Hindi which is the national language of the country. Because of the official policy and by virtue of its commercial use it has become the most important second language of the non-Hindi speakers. English is of course the elite language. The bulk of the Indian elite, however, has come to have a fair acquaintance with Hindi making it the most effective link language. At the same time, it is the non-Hindi elite which mainly resents the status of Hindi as the 'national language'.[37]

In the religio-linguistic complex of India Hindi has two major disadvantages: (1) All major languages of India, other than Hindi, extend beyond the religious boundary, (2) By virtue of its antagonism with Urdu, Hindi has acquired a communal character. The dialectal difference between Hindi and Urdu is negligible. But Hindi is written in Devnagari script (like Sanskrit, considered identical with the language of the Hindu scriptures), Urdu in Persian (a legacy of Muslim rule in India). Gandhi visualised Hindustani (including Hindi and Urdu) as the national language. The growth of communal politics pushed the two components apart. The partition dealt the final blow to the concept of Hindustani.[38] As Hindi was increasingly Sanskritised, the religious minorities came to regard it as the language of the Hindus, though many Hindus in northern India continued to use Urdu.

Brass observes that 'language in north India has generally played a secondary role to religion as a source of social and economic differentiation'. He is impressed by the speed at which Hindi has assimilated the wide spectrum of regional dialects of north India. Only Punjabi has been able to assert its autonomy, not because of any linguistic distinctiveness, but because 'it became an important secondary symbol in the struggle of the Sikhs to preserve their separate religious identity and to acquire a new territorial unit in which they would be dominant'. In South India, on the other hand, he finds language as the stronger basis of identity formation.[39] He could find it in eastern India too. In fact, the frequency and intensity of language riots in Assam have been fairly comparable to, if not greater than, those in south India.

Factor of Unity

One of the factors of political stability in a plural society is claimed to be the existence of cross-cutting cleavages that neutralize themselves.[40] Federalism is a praxiological extension of this theory. The basic characteristic of a federation is the regional clustering of diversities. Yet there must be some overwhelming considerations of common interest to keep the diverse components together. The geographical implication of this theory is that, when the boundary lines of the regionally identified diversities overlap to a certain extent, the ideal conditions for federalism are achieved.[41] The question is whether such an overlap of diversities is in itself a sufficient condition for the formation of federation. The disintegration of the Austro-Hungarian, as well as the Ottoman empire, led to the birth of several successor nation states with overlapping cultural boundaries. No federation was born. This leads one to the conclusion that the birth of a new state, unitary or federal, is ultimately governed by overwhelming political-economic forces, rather than cultural considerations.

For India, not only the birth, but also the continued stability of the federation is hardly explained by the cross-cutting cleavage theory. Dikshit finds the persistence of the Indian federation against 'seemingly impossible conditions'. There is no regional specialisation of production which necessitates complementarity as in the industrialized federations of the USA and Canada. Caste boundaries in India coincide with the linguistic boundaries giving the latter an exclusiveness. His explanation of the stability of India is cultural: (1) 'the fundamental unity of India preserved in the cultural realm', (2) the charismatic leadership of Mahatma Gandhi and Jawaharlal Nehru and (3) the new *tirthas* (places of pilgrimage) of industry where workers from different parts of the country mingle.[42] The problem lies in that, to consider such mingling as a major factor of unity, one must assume the level of industrialisation to be so high as to cover the majority of India's working population. India is clearly not that industrialised.

India's cultural layout, in fact, favours more division/fission than cohesion. Religion builds a strong case for constituting India into a Hindu state to the exclusion of the states in the outer periphery. Language confines the focus to the Hindi heartland. Yet these cultural factors work against the political division of the country by disfavouring the growth of any counterpole. The religious minorities in the outer periphery are so small, so divided in language and ethnic affinities, so situated that there is hardly any option for them to secede. Only the Muslim-majority Kashmir valley has the option of joining Pakistan. But the leadership of the long democratic movement in Kashmir is shy to throw its lot with the unpredictable course of politics in that country. Anti-Hindi agitations have indeed occasionally rocked the country, but they could not crystallize around any other native language even on a regional basis. Only, sections of the English-knowing elite have joined temporary platforms of protest which lacked mass support. The anti-Hindi agitations never acquired democratic depth.

Besides this law of inertia, which sustains the Indian political structure, worked out through the transfer of power, the sub-regional conflicts contribute in no small measure to the federal unity of India. One view that emanated from the States Reorganisation Commission, for instance, was the division of the big state of Uttar Pradesh for sheer administrative convenience. No heed was paid to it even though some noticeable cultural differences between the eastern and the western parts of the state exist, and there is a demand for the formation of an Uttarakhand state with the northern hill areas of the state. In the big non-Hindi states of Andhra Pradesh, Gujarat and Maharashtra, on the other hand, there are regions, under the 'special responsibility' of their Governors, which are administratively distinguished. In Andhra Pradesh the differences between the parts formerly belonging to Madras and Hyderabad threatened the integrity of the state. In West Bengal the question of the status of the Nepali language lurks behind the demand for autonomy of the hill areas of Darjeeling. Even after the 1972 reorganization of northeast India, the integrity of Assam is threatened by the regional pulls of languages and communities. The effect of all these is the fragmentation of the peripheral states which strengthens the bargaining position of the heartland.

The political unity of any country is ultimately dependent on the socio-economic factors rather than the ethno-cultural affinities. The plural and multi-structured Indian union is sustained by the dominant interest of capital that, because of the very fact of under-development, needs to operate throughout the national market. The capital of the industry in West Bengal (one of the most industrialized states of India), for instance, is in the bulk non-Bengali. In this respect geography comes to the aid of the federation. Most of the heavy industry of the country (metallurgical and chemical) are situated in the non-Hindi belt, while agriculture, husbandry and related middle-range and small-scale industry are the mainstay of the Indo-Gangetic Hindi region working for their complementarity.[43] The pulls of the peasants and tribals, who account for 80 per cent of the Indian population, may disfavour centralism. The language and the counter-language agitations may further split the states. But there is no immediate possibility of a real disintegrative tendency to develop in its structure.[44]

Reorganisation of Northeast India—A Case Study

A summary of the political evolution of the multi-ethnic and multi-structured northeast Indian region, based on the writer's personal fieldwork,[45] may corroborate some of the formulations made above. In 1950 the area comprised the composite state of Assam and the Union territories of Manipur and Tripura. The bulk of their territories was hilly and inhabited by scheduled tribes with different dialects and ethnic backgrounds but practising subsistence agriculture. The benefit of missionary education, however, had given rise to an educated elite which generally stood for integration with India but with autonomy over local affairs. The hill districts of Assam were constituted as Tribal areas.

The Part A Tribal areas got autonomous district-councils, resembling the autonomous regional soviets, with the power of local authorities and of regulating tribal customary rights. The Part B Tribal areas (the frontier tracts and the 'Naga tribal area' of the British days) were placed under the direct administration of the Centre. By 1972 some of these hill areas grew into states and Union territories, but the autonomous districts system survived in Assam as well as the new hill states. In Manipur, new district councils were created in the hills.

Superficial analyses of the northeast India situation put premium on 'tribalism' (by definition, microcosmic), role of Christianity (vis-a-vis the Hindu-majority plains), historical separation of the hills from the plains (through restrictions put on travels) and the language controversy in Assam. The arguments can be countered. First, the leaders of the hill districts are, except as a legal category, hardly 'tribal'. They are as much educated, sophisticated and affluent as most other Indian politicians are. The Christian church has always discouraged secessionism. Although there is a great deal of truth in the argument of historical separation, that will hold only partly good after thirty years of independence. The argument about the language controversy is also valid only partly. While the negative attitude towards Assamese as a state language strengthened the autonomy movement in the hills, there was hardly anything positive about it. The hill states have no indigenous language with the status of a state/official language. In any case, these hypotheses fail to answer the supreme question: why have they not chosen to leave India?

The solution of the problem rests in the answer to a positive question: What have they achieved through the statehood? They have achieved Councils of Ministers of their own, responsible to elected legislatures. This is true not only of the new states (including Manipur and Tripura) but also of the Union territories of Arunachal Pradesh and Mizoram. The state bureaucracies are rapidly swelling with the induction of local bureaucrats not only creating employment opportunities for the local elite but also imparting it a voice in the local administrative policy. More important, it entitles them to a share of national revenue without the capacity for reciprocal contribution. Their political leadership is intensely aware of the impossibility of insular existence.

Part of this awareness springs from the apprehensions about the transborder situation: the uncertain political conditions in Burma and Bangladesh (formerly East Pakistan) and communism in China. (Acceptance of China's help by the Naga and the Mizo underground has been disapproved by the church). The visionary in the north-east Indian hills dreams of a prosperity along capitalist lines. With practically no industrial development and a low productivity of agriculture, the hills can provide for the affluence of their elite only out of central subvention (which flows at an annual average of about Rs. 30 crore). Whatever business there is, it is either directly or indirectly controlled by plainsmen. The economy of the hills is tied with that of the rest of the country by that peculiar component of twentieth century capitalism: underdevelopment. The secular cultural policy of the Union government has, on the other hand, been reassuring to the hill men.

1984

NOTES AND REFERENCES

1. 'A curious echo of this state of things lingers in the language of section 45(2) of the Government of India Act, 1915, which still contemplates the possibility of a provincial Government 'making peace and war' (*Report on Constitutional Reforms in India*, cmd 9109, Government of Great Britain, 1918, paragraph 37, p. 26).
2. *Ibid*, paragraph 10, p. 3.
3. Numerous examples of what a federation is not can be cited from history. The Austro-Hungarian empire, for instance, was a sham federation. In spite of the Scottish 'autonomy', Great Britain is not a federation.
4. Some of the circumstances leading to the 16th amendment were the separatist movement of the Dravida Munnetra Kazagham, the Chinese claims on some of the border territories of India, and the impending grant of statehood to Nagaland which was troubled by underground secessionism.
5. Charles A. Beard, *An Economic Interpretation of the Constitution of the United States*, New York, Macmillan, 1961, p. 325.
6. Robert A. Dahl, *Pluralist Democracy in the United States: Conflict and Consent*, Calcutta, Scientific Book Agency, 1969, p. 24. See also pp. 42-52.
7. *Report of the Commission on Constitutional Reform*, paragraph 39, 27-28.
8. For the story of the growth of the demand for linguistic reorganisation of provinces out of the agitation against Bengal partition, see K. V. Narayana Rao, *The Emergence of Andhra Pradesh*, Bombay, 1973, pp. 13-14 & 29.

9. *Report of the Commission on Constitutional Reform,* paragraph 41, p. 29.
10. Narayana Rao (op. cit, pp. 119-27) argues that the creation of Sind and Orissa was actually meant to weaken the nationalist movement.
11. See Shibani Kinkar Chaube, *Constituent Assembly of India: Springboard of Revolution,* New Delhi, People's Publishing House, 1973; particularly, chapter 12.
12. *Constituent Assembly Debates,* Delhi, Manager of Publications, Government of India, Vol. 10, p. 235.
13. Paul R. Brass, *Language, Religion and Politics in India,* Delhi, Vikas Publishing House, 1975, p. 17.
14. The percentages have been worked out by Brass, op. cit., pp. 293-95, with reference to the period subsequent to the partition of India but prior to the creation of the Punjabi *suba.*
15. Article 370 of the Constitution of India.
16. See Shibani Kinkar Chaube, *Hill politics in Northeast India,* Calcutta, Orient Longman Ltd., 1973, pp. 156 & 226.
17. Section 311 (1) of the Government of India Act 1935.
18. See Chaube, op. cit, pp. 215-19.
19. *The Hindu,* February 21, 1929, quoted by Narayana Rao, op. cit., p. 130.
20. See Narayana Rao, op. cit., pp. 204-09.
21. See Chaube, op. cit, pp. 219-22.
22. *Report of the States Reorganisation Commission,* Delhi, Manager. Government of India Press, 1955.
23. Assamese, Bengali, Gujarati, Hindi, Kannada, Kashmiri, Malayalam, Marathi, Oriya, Punjabi, Sanskrit, Tamil, Telugu, Urdu. In 1967 Sindhi was added to the list, though there is no Sindhi-speaking state. Sanskrit is a classical language and Urdu may be regarded as a dialectal variation of Hindi/Hindustani. English enjoys the status of the official language of the Union, along with Hindi.
24. Report of the SRC, p. 113.
25. See Brass, op. cit, pp. 339-45.
26. The North Eastern Area Reorganization Act, 1971, promoted Meghalaya (an autonomous state), Manipur and Tripura (two Union territories) to statehood and created the two Union territories of Arunachal Pradesh (formerly centrally-administered North-East Frontier Tracts) and Mizoram (formerly Mizo district) out of Assam.
27. Article 46 directs the state to 'promote with special care the educational and economic interests of the weaker sections of people, and, in particular, of the Scheduled Castes and the Scheduled Tribes'. The Fifth

Schedule provides for the administration of Scheduled Tribes and Scheduled Areas (inhabited, mostly by Scheduled Tribes).

28. Article 370 of the Constitution of India.
29. Article 371A, by means of the 13th amendment to the Constitution.
30. Article 371F, by means of the 36th amendment to the Constitution.
31. Article 371, by means of the 7th amendment to the Constitution.
32. Article 371B, by means of the 22nd amendment to the Constitution.
33. Article 371C, by means of the 27th amendment to the Constitution.
34. Article 371D, by means of (he 32nd amendment to the Constitution.
35. Article 263 of the Constitution.
36. By the North Eastern Council Act. The Zones are the northern, the central, the western, the southern, the eastern and the north eastern.
37. See Jyotirindra Das Gupta, *Language Conflict and National Development: Group Politics and National Language Policy in India*, Bombay, Oxford University Press, 1977, particularly chapter V.
38. *Ibid.*, pp. 110-11. Also see Granville Austin, *The Indian Constitution: Cornerstone of a Nation*, Oxford University Press, 1966, pp. 273-78.
39. Brass, op. cit., pp. 404-05.
40. Alexis de Tocqueville *(The American Democracy)* was the first proponent of this theory. Also see Seymour Martin Lipset, *Political Man: the Social Basis of Politics*, Garden City, N.Y., Anchor Books, 1963, p. 77.
41. Ramesh Dutt Dikshit, *The Political Geography of Federation: An Inquiry into Origin and Stability*, Delhi, The Macmillan Company of India, 1975, p. 234.
42. *Ibid.*, pp. 125-28.
43. The following situation obtained in the industrial geography of the country in 1963: 'Amongst the five major industrial regions the Hooghly belt is prominent in the country with 0.59 million factory workers. It is being followed by the Bombay-Poona and Ahmedabad-Baroda Regions as the second and third major industrial regions of India. There appears to be a keen competition between the Hooghly and Bombay-Poona regions for the first position as the latter is on the way to catch up the former if its present rate of growth persists. The Bombay-Poona Region has increased its industrial labour force from 0.475 million in 1950 to 0.564 million in 1960.... On the contrary the Hooghly industrial belt has declined in its factory employment from 0.594 million to 0.591 million during the same period. Among all the major industrial regions Chotanagpur plateau has recorded the maximum growth (2.6 per cent). The annual rate of growth works out to be 2.6 per cent as against 1.8 per cent of the Bombay-Poona and Ahmedabad-Baroda regions. Madurai-Coimbatore-Bangalore region

in the Peninsular India has a very slow annual rate of growth, only 1.6 per cent per annum during 1950-60).' (B. N. Sinha, *Industrial Geography of India*, Calcutta, World Press, 1972, pp. 19-21). Four of these five major industrial regions were in the non-Hindi states. Chotanagpur (in Bihar) is in a tribal area where a strong Jharkhand state movement is alive.

In 1973-74, basic metal and alloy industries were concentrated in West Bengal, Maharashtra and the tribal hill areas of Bihar and Madhya Pradesh, cotton and jute textiles in Maharashtra, Gujarat, West Bengal and Tamil Nadu, while chemicals and chemical products (except petroleum and coal products) were mostly in Maharashtra. Uttar Pradesh was second to Maharashtra as the manufacturer of food products. Here other industries were far below that level (*Annual Survey of Industries* 1973-74, Government of India, New Delhi, pp. 38-45).

44. The present-day problem of Punjab deserves a separate discussion.
45. See Chaube, *Hill Politics in North-East India*, Bombay, 1973.

11

The National and Ethnic Problems in India and Canada*

Race and Nation

An oft-quoted letter of Hector St. John de Crevecoeur (1735-1813), a French farmer who first settled in French Canada and then in Orange Country, New York, in 1782, has been a source of a few theoretical formulations in US politics:

> Here individuals of all nations are melted into a new race of men, whose labours and posterity will one day cause great change in the world.[1]

Besides projecting the 'great American vision', which later branched off into 'manifest destiny', it became the source of the 'melting pot' theory.[2] It also reflected the changing conceptualization of 'nation' and 'race' at the end of the eighteenth century. The nation is viewed as a constituent of race. According to some historians this letter is also the first formulation of the emerging American nationalism. The irony of the anecdote is that Crevecoer finally returned to France.[3]

By the end of the nineteenth century, roughly corresponding to the Dreyfus trial in France, 'race' became a somewhat dirty word in social categorization and its application tended to be restricted to the anthropological—particularly, physical

*The research on which this paper is based was funded with the assistance of the Government of Canada through the Canadian Studies Programme of the Shastri Indo-Canadian Institute (SICI). Neither the Government, of Canada nor SICI necessarily endorses the views herein expressed.

Though I am particularly thankful to Professors C. E. S. Franks, J.K. Lele and P. M. Leslie for warm interaction on the lovely campus of the Queen's University, Kingston, On, during the Fall of 1994, I cannot hold them responsible for any of the views expressed in this article.

anthropological— literature, while in the US social sciences the word 'ethnic group' tended to be favoured.[4] The precise distinction of 'nation' from either 'race' or 'ethnic group' was, however, never streamlined with differential-stresses on origin/ascription and culture/achievement.

But there is a contextual difference. For nearly two centuries Europe and Asia have cradled the concept of a 'nation' with regard to political rights of identified groups. The USA never recognised group rights. Consequently, in Europe the minority groups have often retained the status of 'nationalities' and, occasionally, earned the right to self-determination. The USA, however, tended to call their minorities 'ethnic groups' and disapproved of minority consciousness.

In 1890, H.H. Risley, while sceptically examining the possible impact of enfranchisement of the agrarian classes in India, called them the Dravidian people and entitled his article as 'The Race Basis of Indian Political Movements'.[5] In 1937 the *Encyclopaedia of Social Sciences* defined 'ethnic communities' as 'groups bound together by common ties of race, nationality or culture, living together within an alien civilization but remaining culturally distinct.[6] Thus, the phrase 'ethnic group' was conceived in the USA as the other name of 'minority group'.

Defining the Ethnos

The phrase 'ethnic group', of course, has a longer pedigree than the word 'nation'. The former is derived from the Greek word 'ethnos', meaning a group of people identifiable by origin and culture, used by Homer. Aristotle used it in a pejorative meaning by applying the term to non-Greeks—'the Barbarians'—and by prescribing that only such people could be enslaved. Interestingly, the US social scientists first picked up the Aristotelian conception of ethnic group and then tended to move towards the Homeric conception. The change of mood is reflected in Glazer and Moynihan's well-known book on 'Ethnicity': They ask rather dramatically :

> Do we not now tend increasingly to apply the term 'ethnic group' to any group of distinct cultural tradition and origin, even if it is the majority ethnic group within a nation, the *staatvolk?*[7]

The ethnic group is thus seen as a constituent group of a nation, majority or minority. The concept is bereft of any association with rights. On the other hand, there is, in the US social sciences, a general disapproval of ethnocentrism which, as early as 1907, was described as a 'folkway'[8] not quite compatible with civilization. The disapproval is writ large in D. Reisman's otherwise anti-marxist manifesto of 1953. Propounding a strong defence of McCarthyism vis à vis the 'liberal fancies' of the urban intellectuals in the US political life Reisman noted

> a tendency for the older 'class struggles' rooted in clear hierarchical antagonisms, to be replaced by a new sort of warfare : the groups who, by reason of rural or small-town location, ethnicity, or other parochialism, feel threatened by the better educated upper-middle class people (though often less wealthy and politically powerful) who follow or create the modern movements in science, art, literature and opinion generally.[9]

The other dilemma is with regard to the bond of ethnic group. A nation of immigrants cannot very much stress the blood relation or kinship and the overwhelming opinion in the USA was in favour of cultural affinity being the criterion of an ethnic group. Yet Parsons spoke of an ethnic group as 'an aggregate of kinship units the members of which either trace their origin in terms of descent from a common ancestor or in terms of descent from ancestors who all belonged to the categorized ethnic group.'[10] Immanuel Wallerstein abstracted this dilemma and held that 'Membership of an ethnic community is a matter of social definition, an interplay of the self-definition of members and the definition of other groups.[11]

Fredrik Barth echoed Wallerstein's view while he looked for the social significance of ethnic consciousness and stressed the belief in a 'common origin' :

> The critical feature then becomes . .. the characteristics of self-ascription and ascription by others. A categorical ascription is an ethnic ascription when it classifies a person in terms of his most general identity, presumptively determined by his origin and background.[12]

'The critical focus of investigation from this point of view', writes Barth, 'becomes the ethnic boundary that defines the group, not the cultural stuff that it encloses.[13]

Nations and Self-determination

In the British political tradition the term 'nation' acquired salience only in the twentieth century—the formation of the National Governments, for instance. In the continental Europe, on the other hand, the word had a more frequent use—possibly because of the Latin connection. But it certainly acquired a radically different meaning during the French Revolution which declared that sovereignty belonged to the French Nation. It at once upheld the power of the people above the power of the dynastic rulers.[14] Secondly, it defined sovereignty in terms of a territorial population rather than any kinship or cultural groups. The cultural contours of nationhood developed in continental Europe later—in reaction to Napoleonic conquests.

It is easy to take Delisle Burns' classic formulation—'Out of Renaissance Sovereignty combined with Revolutionary Rights comes Nationalism'—simplistically. For Renaissance Sovereignty created modern states around dynastic rules. In Germany alone 300 states were created. Neither was the concept of 'rights of the people' clearly outlined by the French Revolution. But, together, they had the following effect:

> The local independence of the sovereign state was at last connected with the rights of the inhabitants to choose their own form of government; and the result has been the conception that every group of sufficient permanence and with enough of a distinct tradition to have a 'national' character should have an opportunity for developing its own forms of law and government.[15]

From a purely political angle, therefore, nationhood is rooted in the right to self-determination of a people identifying themselves as such. It is on the question of identification of a people entitled to local independence that the problem arises. The criterion of common ancestry is the easiest but possible only in a simple/primitive society. Organized religion sought to give medieval Europe a continental unity and West Asia an oppressive Khilafat. The only feasible criterion in the modern states is language.

Even language has its limitations. Ellie Kedourie tells us, for instance, that 'the French were originally Teutons who forsook

German speech for a neo-Latin idiom,[16] In 1789 less than 50 per cent people of France spoke French. For nearly two centuries after that the world saw several wars aimed at bringing about a rational correspondence of linguistic boundaries with·political boundaries (the latest being in 1971). It has tried multi-cultural federalism as in Canada and India. A 'perfect' solution is still far off.

This does not mean that self-determination/autonomy movements of necessity have to be culture bound. Throughout the nineteenth century European states were splitting and uniting into national autonomies while the United States was seeking to build a national unity out of political autonomies. The results were varied. Whereas France, Italy and Germany grew into nation states, Belgium grew into a multi-cultural unitary nation and Switzerland into a multicultural federal nation. The United States evolved into a political nation of autonomous states. The point to note is that the demand for autonomy is territory-specific and a minority group may claim the status of a nationality only if it controls a definite territory. If a portion of the same group lives elsewhere in a dispersed manner, it has to be regarded as an ethnic minority. Whether it will get group rights or will have to be satisfied with individual rights will depend upon the historical conditions and existing circumstances.

Stated differently, in a nation state, minorities can be settled in two different ways : (1) they may be concentrated in a locality/ region, and (2) they may be dispersed. The solution of the minority problem of the first type lies in political federation, the extent of regional autonomy depending upon negotiation/ bargain/struggle. If a union with autonomy is impossible to achieve separation become inevitable. The solution to the second problem lies in a social federation in the sense of acknowledgement of the rights of citizens as not only individuals but also members of identifiable groups.

The Impact of Colonialism

The moment political power was transferred from one sovereign to many people number became important for the realization of power. Persons seek affiliation along the lines of kinship, culture or class creating identifiable majorities and minorities. This leads to the issue of minority rights. It is superfluous to stress that in complex societies majorities and minorities are constructed along different lines frequently cross-cutting each other. As the size of a territorial community varies the complexity of cleavages also varies. This critical problem of reconciliation of sectional interests with general interest becomes further complicated by colonialism. For a colonial state is an arbitrary entity and rarely, if at all, corresponds to ethno-cultural criteria.

Neither does colonialism have a uniform impact. For there are different kinds of colonialism in different kinds of countries. Thus the Spanish-Portuguese colonialism in Latin America resulted in partial annihilation, partial isolation and partial mixing of the indigenous people, while the Franco-British colonialism in North America and Australia resulted mostly in annihilation or isolation of the local people. European colonization of Africa resulted in enslavement of the indigenous population while in Asia the effect was less demographic than economic. Decolonization after World War II ended direct economic exploitation of Asia and Africa but created new problems of nation-building.

The American and Australian continents were not decolonized. By 1781 the New England colonies were free. In the first half of the 19th century metropolitan power of Latin America moved from Europe to the USA. However, the white colonies of Britain slowly moved toward independence through the framework of dominion status. Canada falls in this last category—but with a difference.

Of all colonial powers the British have two distinctions: (1) They appropriated territories of continental dimensions by annihilating and cornering the indigens (2) They conquered colonies of other European Powers-in America, Asia and Africa. In their new homes, unlike the other European colonists, they not only refused to mix with the local people, they adopted a scrupulously regulated immigration policy. Canada is a victim of both these features of colonialism.

Because of historical and geographical reasons the population of Asia and Africa could not be decimated. Instead, an oppressive political system enabled ruthless plunder and then, sustained economic exploitation. As a result, the ostensible similarities between the Canadian and the Indian experiences cannot hide the fact that the Canadian and the Indian experiences are fundamentally different. And yet there is a great deal of similarity between the *problems* that Canada and India have faced.

Canada and India : Historical Experience

The British reached New Foundland in the mid-fifteenth century. The French came to Canada, in 1608, when the British were building a factory at Surat, India. The Anglo-French conflict in the mid-eighteenth century drove the French out of the North American continent (as well as from most of the Indian sub-continent). When, in 1774, the British united Lower Canada (Quebec) and Upper Canada (Ontario), the British population was one-eighth the size of the French population. The War of Independence in the New England colonies caused huge immigration of the royalist British population to Canada, and the late nineteenth century outmigration of French Canadians to the USA radically altered the demographic picture of Canada.

The Union Act of 1840 united the two Canadas and gave the new country a parliament where the British and the French parts were equally represented. Fresh British immigration to Canada strengthened the demand for greater British representation to the Canadian parliament. Finally, another split, followed by a federation of the two Canadas, was felt necessary. In the Charlottetown conference in September 1864, however, not only Quebec and Ontario took part but also the maritime provinces except New Foundland sent their delegations. The New Foundland delegates attended the Quebec conference in October 1864. The 72 resolutions passed there were approved by the Canadian parliament but opposed by the maritime provinces. The British North America Act, 1867, united Quebec, Ontario, Nova Scotia and New Brunswick. The provinces of Alberta, British Columbia, Manitoba, New Foundland, Prince Edward Island, Saskathewan, the Yukon Territory and the North-West Territories joined later. Of these states Quebec has French-speaking population constituting 82.1% of the total population and New Brunswick 33.6% (1991 census). In the other states the proportion of the Francophones vary from 0.5% (New Foundland) to 5% (Ontario).

Basking in the 'glory' of imperialism the British were satisfied that the federal formula had solved the problem of Anglo-French relations in Canada. Reginald Coupland, who had studied the Durham Report as a young scholar and visited India in the company of the Cripps Mission, suggested the adoption of the Canadian model in British India.[18] Indeed the Canadian and the Indian constitutional evolutions have a great deal of similarity in the reverse. In India the federal experiment was begun in 1935 on the Canadian model essentially to settle the communal divide between the Hindus and the Muslims. That formula was sought to be institutionalized on the sub-continental scale through the Cripps Mission and the Cabinet Mission but failed. Hence partition.

The Canadian Mosaic

The Canadian political system seemed to have worked tolerably well for a century, that is, till the nineteen sixties when the Quebecois nationalism articulated itself.[19] By that time non-British, non-French immigrants had swelled to about a third of the country's population while the Francophones were reduced to a third of the total population as the immigrants joined the ranks of the Anglophones. By 1991 the Francophone population of Canada has been reduced to about 22% of Canada's population. Interestingly the Francophone population in Quebec had a proportional growth in percentile number[20] from 78% in 1921 to 82.6% in 1991 indicating either immigration of Francophone Canadians or outmigration of Anglophones or secular population growth among the Catholic Francophones or all these factors combined.

Until World War I Quebec carried the burden of Francophone Canada's leadership. That burden restrained her own secessionist aspirations. The two major national political parties of Canada—the Conservative and the Liberal - dominated Quebec's politics too but through a peculiar federal arrangement whereby the provincial party organizations controlled nomination to the provincial legislature and the central party organizations controlled the nominations to the Central legislature. As these two parties controlled the Canadian politics. Quebec's representation to the Canadian parliament was more federalist than its representation to the provincial legislature until the formation of the *Partie Quebecois* in the 1970s with an openly secessionist programme.

But the moral leadership of the Francophone Canadian society belonged to the Catholic Church which had a Pan-Canadian following. For it Quebec was only the symbol of protest of Francophone Canada. The wave of modernization since the end of World War I generated popular indifference toward the Catholic church. The end of World War I may have inspired the dream of national self-determination among the Quebeckwans at the same time rendering them a sense of frustration that the principle of self-determination did not apply to the colonies of the Allied powers. The *Quebecois* concern for the Francophone Canadians outside Quebec's boundaries, consequently, started weakening. A contradiction arose between the demand for minority right of the Francophone Canadians and that for Quebec's separation.

British officials and historians never failed to remind us that the Hindus and the Muslims were on two sides of a great divide and, therefore, India was not a nation. A section of the 'nationalist' historians like R.C. Majumdar dispute such a view but assert that the Indian nation has been a Hindu nation and that Muslims were the detractors. The common argument is that the Hindus were the majority whereas the Muslims had been the ruling race. While the Hindus welcomed British rule at first they became disillusioned and turned nationalist. The Muslims at first hated British rule, avoided English education, fell behind the Hindus and, on realization of their folly, turned collaborators of the empire and invented the 'two nations' theory the inevitable result of which was partition.

Even if this motivated and inaccurate version of modern Indian history is accepted, however, it cannot compare favourably with the story of Canada's national divide. For, in British India, the loss of political power was a memory for the Hindus and the Muslims under the empire, as far as their mutual relations were concerned. For the French settlers in Canada the experience was live. For they had lost power to the British. Although when New France was conquered by the British the Anglophones were about 1/8th the size of the Francophones, yet the over-all demographic balance between the two groups in the 19th century somehow averted the crisis. When this balance was increasingly tilted in favour of the Anglophones after World War I the Francophone Canadians became anxious about their identity. Hence their sharp opposition to the concept of a multi-cultural Canada in which they would be reduced virtually from a nationality to an ethnic group.

And there lies the empirical significance of the theoretical distinction between a 'nation'/'nationality' and an ethnic group. What the Francophone Canadians, particularly, the Qubeckwans, are demanding is the political right of a nationality and not the cultural rights of an ethnic group. The dominion status of Canada, however liberally operated, adds fuel to their smouldering fire. The Canadian government is still headed by the British Crown, the Canadian cabinet is still a committee of the British Privy Council, the Canadian Senate is still made up of Life Peers created by the British Crown. 'History stands between the Anglophone and the Francophone Canadians', said one of my learned resource persons.

Logically the Francophone political aspiration may probably be fulfilled-at least partly-if Canada declared herself a republic. But that will create a crisis of legitimacy for Anglophone Canada now aggravated by the pull of NAFTA*. Will Canada want to live rather than join the USA?

The political division between the Francophone and the Anglophone Canada is projected in the cultural domain in the form of a two-nation theory based on language as well as religion. Since about the beginning of the twentieth century, on the other hand, continuous immigration has changed the cultural map of Canada and the two-nation theory shrank in its territorial focus to Quebec. It is doubtful if the bilingualism evolved by Pierre Trudeau for the whole of Canada will surrive Quebec's secession in which case Quebec may actually weaken the position of the Francophone Canadians in the other provinces in the same way that the partition of British India weakened the position of the Muslim in India and Hindus in Pakistan.

Liberal democracies today are essentially majoritarian and unitarian and opposed to group rights in the form of reservation,

*The North African Free Trade Agreement.

separate electorate, quota and communal codes. Strict secularism can take care of only a part of the composite societies. The dividing line between the sacred and the secular is thin and there are many socio-cultural spheres outside religion where minority sensitivities are as intense as in the case of religion.

In real life situation the problem can be more complicated. A religious division and a linguistic division may or may not coincide. Secondly, in any country a section of a minority may be localized lending themselves to federalization and another section fairly spread out. Federalization or separation of the localized section has an inevitable backlash over the dispersed section of the minorities' rights.

Paul Brass has shown in the case of India that, except for Urdu and Gurumukhi Punjabi, there is no co-extensiveness of religion and language.[21] Even these two languages have become embroiled in political controversy only after partition and independence. There is a much greater correspondence between religion and language in Canada as the Catholics constitute the whole of the Francophone Canadian population but are by no means confined to them.

Secondly, when India was partitioned, the greatest victims were the minorities in both the parts. Their existence was 'delegitimized'. The Francophone Canadians outside Quebec realized the dangerous implications of Quebec's independence for them and strongly urged the Quebeckwans to vote against Quebec's independence.

Religion and Nationalism

Objectively, the consciousness of a nationality is heightened by, if not altogether built around, the notion of a territorial attachment. This creates an interesting dilemma on the national question in Canada. The French Canadian consciousness of the late 18th century shrank into the *Quebecois* nationalism in the course of the next two hundred years because of this association. Subjectively, *Quebecois* nationalism has been associated by Eric Hobsbawm with disorientation of the Catholic church that governed' a conservative, Catholic, clerical, child-producing society not only among the farmers but among townspeople. It seems that in the course of 1960s church attendance in the province dropped from well over 80% to 25%, while the Quebec birth rate has become one of the lowest in Canada. Quebec nationalism has been argued to be a surrogate for the lost Catholicism for a disoriented new generation'.[22]

Springing from his equal dislike for nationalism and religion Hobsbawm's observation has an important bearing on the Quebec problem. It also reflects a certain crisis in the Canadian Catholic church which seeks to serve the entire Catholic Francophone Canadians. There is no doubt that separation of Quebec will undermine the Catholic church's pan-Canada influence. There is, however, a certain neglect of the long-term socio-economic factors in Hobsbawm's observation on *Quebecois* nationalism. For Canadian nationalism came under economic pressure in the 19th century when hundreds of thousands of French Canadians had to migrate to the USA. By 1921 the urban population of Quebec surpassed the rural population.[23]

In the depression years voices were raised in Quebec for separation. Conservative politics of the *Union Nationale* party of Quebec survived from 1945 to 1960 probably because of the tight web of patronage politics of Maurice Duplessis. But the first several years of the 1960s saw radical change in Quebec politics. The election of the provincial liberals under Jean Lesage in 1960 opened the way for political reforms and social changes. The state replaced the authority of the Catholic church in the areas of social services and education. It also undertook much broader economic functions. Quebec nationalism gradually replaced French Canadian nationalism.[24] The *Quebecois* became a nationality while the Francophones outside Quebec became ethnic groups.

The Francophone-Anglophone relationship was further complicated by the Metis and Inuits who are the mixed or pure off-springs of the original inhabitants of Canada. Their position is better than that of the American Indians. They have acquired advantage by playing the Anglophone-Francophone differences by virtue of their enfranchisement by 1969. The Metis live predominantly in Maintoba while the Inuits are concentrated in the North-West Territory, northern Quebec and Labrador. The Meech Lake Accord of 1982 was frustrated by the veto of one Metis Legislator of Manitoba where the constitution requires unanimity for all legislative decisions.

And here lies the third dimension of the Canadian nationhood. Historically, the Metis, an advanced section of the Canadian population born out of European-aboriginal marriage/relations have had more pleasant relations with the Frenchmen. But, when a Metis member thwarted the Meech Lake Accord he was understandably accused of acting at the bidding of the Anglophones. However, the Metis population seeks its roots not in either of the European peoples but in the indigenous population. In fact the report of the Metis and Non-status Indian Constitutional Review Commission held that

> Canadians suffer from the lack of national identity because they have not been taught to value an identity rooted in this land.... What is forgotten in the national unity debate is the extent to which Canada has been shaped by the aboriginal heritage.[25]

The Indian story almost totally replicates that of Canada but in the reverse. In the early British period the leaders of the two major communities respected their cultural distinctions but assembled on the liberal platform of the Indian National Congress to wage an elitist constitutional struggle for self-government. After World War I Gandhi brought the Indian masses into politics and led the Khilafat-NCO Satyagraha on an apparently Muslim religious cause. This alienated the liberal, constitutionalist Congressman, M.A. Jinnah. The religious leaders of the Indian Muslims joined the Khilafat agitation and, later, the Congress. M.A. Jinnah, later, became the leader of the Muslim League, propounded the 'two nations' theory, claimed the status of the sole spokesman of the Indian Muslims and obtained Pakistan. In this crucial communal divide the Scheduled Castes of India played a marginal role with alternating alliance with the Congress and the Muslim League. However, the Scheduled Castes never as a whole abandoned the nationalist cause for they were as much native as the Congressmen were and they worked within the Hindu fold.

It is interesting to note that Hobsbawm's thesis on *Quebecois* nationalism is applicable to India too-in the reverse. In India religion has frequently acted as the surrogate of nationalism. Khilafat saw the open admission of religion in India's struggle for freedom. Within a decade Gandhi was turned into a God. He was assassinated by a religious fanatic within a year of earning independence for India. For a decade now in India a religious cult is being sedulously built as the surrogate of nationalism (one hears a reverberation of the same slogan in the rise of the so-called fundamentalism in the Third World as a whole).

1995

NOTES AND REFERENCES

1. Hector St. John de Crevecouer, *Letters from a Farmer, quoted in Glazer and Moynihan see fn. 2.*
2. For the 'melting pot' concept see Nathan Glazer and Daniel P. Moynihan, *Beyond the Melting Pot: The Negroes, Puerto Ricans. Jews, Italians and Irish of New York City*. Cambridge, Mass, and London, the Harvard University Press & M.I.T. Press, 2nd ed., 1970.
3. An illustration of the confusion between 'the nation' and 'the race' is J.W. Burgess's 1891 definition of nation as 'a population of ethnic unity inhabiting a territory of a geographic unity' (Quoted by J.G. Garner, *Political Science and Government*, Calcutta, World Press, 1952, p. 110.
4. For a short history of the concepts of 'ethnic groups' and 'ethnicity' see Dr. S.K. Chaube. 'Ethnicity and Nationality a theoretical prelude'. *Asian Studies*, 14, I. January 1986.
5. *Contemporary Review*, May 1890.
6. *Encyclopaedia of Social Sciences*, Vol. V, 'Ethnic Communities' 1937.
7. 'Introduction' in Nathan Glazer and Daniel P. Moynihan (eds) *Ethnicity : Theory and Practice*, Cambridge, Mass. The Harvard University Press, 1975, p. 4.
8. W.G. Sumner, *Folkways*, Boston, 1907 as quoted in Glazer and Moynihan, op. cit., pp. 18-19.
9. D. Reisman, 'Some observations on Intellectual Freedom', *American Scholar*, Vol. 23, No. I, Winter 1953-54.
10. Talcott Parsons, *The Social System*, Glencoe, The Basic Books, 1951, p. 172.
11. Immanuel Wallerstein, 'Ethnicity and National Integration. *Cahiers' Etudes Africans* 1960, quoted by Donald R. Horrowitz, 'Ethnic Identity', in Glazer and Moynihan (eds). *Ethnicity*, p. 113.
12. Barth. 'Introduction' in Fredrik Barth (ed), *Ethnic Groups and Boundaries: the Social Organisation of Cultural Difference*, Oslo, Johnsen & Nielsen, 1969, p. 13.
13. *Ibid.*, p. 15.

14. For the origin and growth of the concepts of 'nation'and 'nationalism' see. Ellie Kedousia, *Nationalism,* Hutchinson of London 1960, pp. 13-15, and Eric Hobsbawm, *Nations and Nationalism since 1780: Programme, myth, reality,* Cambridge University Press, Second edition, 1992, pp. 14-17.
15. Delisle, Burns, *Political Ideals,* Calcutta, World Press, 1960, p. 135.
16. Kedourie, op. cit., p. 65.
17. Hobsbawm, op. cit., p. 60.
18. Reginald Coupland, *The Constitutional Problem in India,* Oxford University Press, 1944. For a comparative overview of the Canadian experience see Shibani Kinkar Chaube, *Constituent Assembly of India: Springboard of Revolution,* New Delhi, People's Publishing House, 1973, pp. 300-02.
19. 'The first several years of the 1960s are justly considered a turning point in the history of Quebec'. Mary Beth Montcalm and Alain-G. Gagnon 'Quebec in the Continental Economy' in Alan-G. Gagnmon and James P. Biescerton (eds), *Canadian Politics: an introduction to the discipline,* Broadview Press, Petersborough, On, 1990, p. 320.
20. C.E.S. Franks, 'Canada and India : Vertical and Horizontal Dimensions of Language, Culture and the Polity' (mimeo, 1992).
21. Paul R. Brass, *Language, Religion, and Politics in India,* Vikash Publishing House, 1975.
22. E. Hobsbawm, op. cit., p. 172.
23. Mary Beth Montcalm and Alan-G. Gagnon, op. cit., p. 328.
24. *Ibid.,* pp. 320-21.
25. *Native People and the Constitution of Canada : the Report of the Metis and Non-Status Indian Constitutional Review Commission; Commissioner H.W. Davids,* Ottawa, Mutual Press, 1981, pp. 43-44.

12

Caste, Politics and the Indian Federation

The term 'caste' is derived from the Latin word 'castas', meaning *chaste*. It is supposed to have been used by the Spaniards in the sense of race and applied to India by the Portuguese first in the middle of the fifteenth century. The English adopted it in the same sense a century later.[1] In India today it denotes two apparently contradictory concepts - *varna* (stratification) and *jati* (ethnic group). I call them contradictory as *varna* splits a people vertically and *jati* horizontally. The rules of caste, atleast where and when they are observed, reveal the following features:

(i) a notional or actual division of labour prescribing for each group a certain or a certain type of occupation;

(ii) exclusiveness in matters of marriage and contact; and

(iii) a status ranking frequently mixed up, positively, with what some sociologists call 'esteem'[2] and, nagatively, what some anthropologists call 'purity-pollution syndrome'.[3]

If this status ranking will be called 'hierarchy' is a moot question. Although Louis Dumont defines 'hierarchy' functionally as the principle by which 'the elements of a whole are ranked in relation to a whole',[4] the term literally means a 'chain of authority'. The three twice-born castes of Brahmin, Kshatriya and Vaishya, mentioned in the early *Vedic* texts, are professionally specialized but are very much regarded as species of the same genre. It is only in the later *Vedic* texts that the Sudra enters as the servant. It is doubtful, however, that the Sudra could be identified with the slave even if we ascribe the Sudra's status to racial conquest. For one thing, the classical Greeks or Romans employed slaves individually from those groups of people whom they called barbarians. In no case did they identify a whole people as slaves.

For another, Karl Marx, whose theoretical paradigm of class contradiction was used to discover slavery in the ancient Indian society, himself regarded caste as a guild-like phenomenon springing from hereditary division of labour.

> The conversion of fractional work into the life-calling of one man corresponds to the tendency shown by earlier societies to make trade hereditary; either to petrify them into castes, or whenever definite historical conditions beget in the individual a tendency to vary in a manner incompatible with the nature of castes, to ossify them into guilds. Castes and guilds arise from the action of the same natural law, that regulate the differentiation of plants and animals into species and varieties, except that, when a certain degree of development has been reached, the heredity of castes and the exclusiveness of guilds are ordained as a law of society.[5]

Max Weber, who is credited with all the 'answers' to Marx, finds in the caste system combined with the religious ideology in India a reflection of the spirit of Indian religion which is 'irrational', 'world escapist' and 'anti-progressive', being based on the theory of *karma*. According to Weber the *karma* doctrine transferred the world into a strictly rational, ethnically determined cosmos. The devout Hindu was accursed to remain in a structure which made sense only in the intellectual context; its consequences burdened his conduct. One could move to a higher or lower life only through rebirth. Weber even finds in the commandment of Christianity - 'let everyone abide in the same calling' - the reflection of the Hindu promise of rebirth more than of any 'organistic social ethics'.[6]

While M.N. Srinivas shares this Weberian perception,[7] Nirmal Kumar Bose finds an inconsistency in the theory that *karma* and transmigration of soul are used as a justification of fatalism. Precisely these two concepts were used by the Buddha for the justification of endeavour. Bose noted that, according to *Yogavasistha Ramayana, purusakar* (endeavour) can undo the heritage of *daiva*. 'Now, if two meanings of an opposite nature are thus given to the same word *karma,* and if both high and low castes remain more satisfied with one and reject the other, then there must be some other reason why such a choice is made'.[8]

Bose, a rockbottom Gandhian, could never reconcile himself to this celebration of fatalism. His 'Hindu Method of Tribal

Absorption' provides us with a model which is indistinguishable from that of Marx:

> From what has been observed among the Juangs and from a reading of the law books, it is to be noted that Hindu society when absorbing a new tribe or while creating a new jati by differentiation of occupation, always guaranteed or tried to guarantee monopoly in a particular occupation to each caste within a given region. The last point is very important; for the same jati may be found practising slightly different trades if it finds the prescribed hereditary occupation no longer economically satisfactory. But the careful way in which correspondence was established between jati and occupation is proof of what the economic and social legislators of ancient India had in mind. They tried to build up a social organization on the basis of hereditary monopolistic guilds. That lay at the base of the caste system; and it is because capitalism has, in modern times, completely upset the old productive organization, that we are witnessing the fast decay of the entire social system of ancient India. Today we are also witnessing the rise of the middle classes on the one hand and of the proletariat on the other; and each of these two classes draws recruits from all the ancient castes without discrimination.[9]

Bose's 'functionalist' justification of the caste was as follows:

> It gave security in spite of obvious inequalities; and this security was guaranteed both by law and custom. Sudras knew very well that they could not rise to a higher status in their present life; but as long as differences were not sky-high, and justice was meted out to all according to recognized dues, caste also endured.
>
> It is our belief that it was precisely this element of deliberateness born out of a recognition of the advantages of complementary hereditary guilds, but modified by a feeling of racial superiority, which created the caste system in India, and whose absence in other parts of the world prevented its growth even when most of the other conditions for its formation were present in one form or another.[10]

Thus, while the origin of the caste system may be traced to a whole range of phenomena from racial conquest to voluntary adoption of caste practices, as envisaged in M.N. Srinivas's model of 'Sanskritization',[11] its nature is structural. It is pointless to tie it up with religion or religious philosophy through the doctrine of *karma*. Caste is a *dharma* (attribute) of one's social position. *Karma* is, of course, a belief and may be regarded as a religious faith. But it does not necessarily justify or oppose caste.

Nor does caste entail production relation. The economic basis of caste is division of labour. Socially it is a form of stratification with attendant privileges or disadvantages. But it is a special kind of stratification. It is a closed system; it does not permit vertical individual mobility,[12] though there may have been collective mobility of *jatis*.[13] Besides, at individual level, there is no down-casting, there is only outcasting.[14]

The political attributes of the caste are, however, almost the opposite of its social and economic attributes. Politically, caste forges new cohesions and challenges the old cohesion based on stratification.

It was H.H. Risley, for the first time, who, towards the end of the last century, opposed the extension of voting right on the basis of property qualification in India as ownership of property - particularly landed property - was not confined to what he called 'the Aryan races'. Extension of franchise to the 'agrarian classes', Risley prognosticated, would lead to the formation of caste associations and competitive politics.[15]

M.N. Srinivas merely picked up the cue from Risley when he noted that universalization of franchise after Independence politicized the castes and turned them into competitive groups.[16] Early British rule was territorial and ethnic groups had no administrative recognition (even the 1905 Bengal partition was effected in the name of administrative convenience). There was, however, political recognition of ethnic groups as in the declaration of certain groups as "martial races' and certain others as 'criminal tribes'. In 1883, along with the introduction of election - at the local government level - the system of separate electorates was created. It was extended to legislative elections - when they were introduced by the Indian Councils Act of 1909. As the system of separate electorate went on being elaborated - their number reaching 18 under the Government of India Act, 1935 - the concept of 'depressed classes' was introduced by the Government of India

Act, 1919. The Government of India Act, 1935, called them the Scheduled Castes.

The Constitution of republican India rejected the concept of political minorities and abolished the system of separate electorate. All kinds of discrimination on the basis of race, religion, sex, caste or place of birth were prohibited. But the concept of social equality in the Indian Constitution is dynamic. It would not leave the various classes of people, where they are and then provide them with equality of status and opportunity. It was an acknowledgement of the prevalence of social inequality and the need for its removal that led the Constitution to accord a special status to the Scheduled Castes and Scheduled Tribes - as a temporary measure.

This the Constituent Assembly did by providing for reservation of seats in the legislatures for Scheduled Castes and Scheduled Tribes. (For representation of the Anglo-Indian community provision was made for nomination).

Though successive extensions of the legislative reservation for Scheduled Castes and Scheduled Tribes only raised a few eyebrows, reservation in public employment has proved to be more contentious. Atleast a part of this contention springs from defective drafting. It will be recalled that partition of India effected considerable discontinuity in the work of the Constituent Assembly.[17] In April 1947 the Minority Rights Sub-Committee of the Advisory Committee recommended reservation in services for the minorities. The Advisory Committee forwarded this recommendation to the Constituent Assembly with the stipulation that such claims of the minorities shall be taken into consideration consistently with the consideration of etficiency of administration.[18] Following the decision to abolish all kinds of political minorities reservation in services was connected with backwardness and took the form of two provisions of the Constitution:

Art. 16(4): Nothing in this article shall prevent the State from making any provision for the reservation of appointments or posts in favour of any backward class of citizens which, in the opinion of the State, is not adequately represented in the services under the state.

Art. 335: *Claims of the members of the Scheduled Castes and Scheduled Tribes to services and posts:* The claims of the members of the Scheduled Castes and Scheduled Tribes shall be taken into consideration, consistently with the maintenance of efficiency of administration in the making of appointments to services and posts in connection with the affairs of the Union or of a state.

The difference in terminology may mean either of two things:

1. The Constitution confines 'any backward class of citizens' to Scheduled Castes and Scheduled Tribes permitting the inclusion of any other backward group among them.
2. Whereas the special provision for appointment of the members of the Scheduled Castes and the Scheduled Tribes is subject to consistency with efficiency of administration, for any *other* backward class such a permission is unlimited.

The second interpretation is clearly untenable by any rule of interpretation for an unlimited exemption makes a law infructuous.

Nor did the first amendment adding Clause 4 to Article 15 clarify the situation. The clause runs as follows:

> Nothing in this article or in clause (2) of article 29 shall prevent the State from making any special provision for the advancement of any socially and educationally backward classes of citizens or for the Scheduled Castes and the Scheduled Tribes.

In the first place, it restricts the concept of 'backward classes' to socially and educationally, which does not necessarily mean caste and which certainly cannot be interpreted to exclude communities. In the second place, Article 15 can by no means be associated with employment, for there is a separate Article (Article 16) relating to that. Historically, also, Clause (4) of Article 15 was included through the first amendment to obviate the difficulty posed by the judgements in *Champakan Dorairajan v. State of Madras* and *Venkataramana v. State of Madras* which said that the Indian Constitution allowed special benefits only in respect of employment and excluded other benefits like reservation in educational institutions. In the context of the Mandal agitation, the Supreme Court has passed an advisory opinion excluding 'the creamy layer' of the other backward classes from the benefit of job reservation. It has not passed a judgement on whether Clause 4 of Article 15 permits job reservation at all.

One of the first students of Indian politics, W.H. Morris-Jones hoped in 1952 that democratic progress would sweep away casteism.[19] This did not happen. On the other hand, Selig Harrison reports organized casteism practised by the Congress party in the first Assembly elections in Andhra Pradesh for fighting the Communist Party of India. In this election (1955) the Indian National Congress put up candidates in the delta region, heartland of Communist challenge, 'matching' them caste by caste.[20] Successive election studies since then have revealed consideration of caste and community by almost all political parties in the matter of nomination though open advocacy of caste voting is muted due to electoral laws and also the need for putting up a 'secular' face.

Selig Harrison's own thesis was that communism in Andhra region had grown among the land-owning Kammas since World War II. But by no means did he insist that caste was the sole factor in Communist strategy in 1955. In fact he spoke of 'a timely confluence of events'.[21] He recorded the presence of a large proportion of agricultural labour in the delta. Thirty-seven per cent of the total agricultural population in the delta is landless labour, a concentration second only to Malabar district on the West Indian coast.'[22] Harrison was, however, surprised(!) to find Communist support in the 'general seats' - 'ranging from a low of 11.5 to a high of 31.9 with the median falling just above 20 per cent in the 1946 election in which, due to the franchise property restriction, the landless labourers had no vote.[23] But, then, Harrison admitted that several Andhra communist leaders, of high prestige, belonging to the Kamma caste and that Kamma Congressmen were factionalized. Ajit Singh's predicament since 1991 would show that caste is an important factor in Indian politics, but not the only factor and not necessarily the main factor in all elections.

At the Amritsar Congress in April 1958, on the other hand, the Communist Party of India decided to launch a campaign against casteism, communalism and untouchability. It may be recalled that both communalism and casteism were liberally used at this time to remove the Communist government in Kerala in 1959. At the Vijaywada Congress of the CPI, Ajoy Ghosh observed that, 'Caste sentiments, instead of loosening, has grown prodigiously. In elections the tendency is more and more based on caste. Members of the Congress party themselves set the example which get followed by others. Panchayats and other local bodies get divided into factions based on caste'[24] E.M.S. Namboodiripad wrote in June 1962: 'Whereas caste as a social bar has weakened specially after independence, it is precisely in this period that caste has emerged as an important factor in current politics, deciding, in many cases, the fate of the elections and choice of ministers.'[25]

Thus, caste, from a system of status ranking associated with privileges has been transformed into competitive horizontal groups due to a number of reasons. The most important of them has been industrial capitalism with its attendant occupational mobility and urbanization. The second factor has been Independence and democracy which has granted basic legal equality to its citizens. The third factor has been the universalization of franchise (compared to a mere 14 per cent) immediately before Independence.

It is in the domain of economy that caste has now become most volatile. In the entire rural area of the country land relations have become embroiled in caste conflict, its most violent manifestation being apparent in Bihar. There was a qualitative shift with the beginning of the Mandal agitation when the Other Backward Classes staked their claim to jobs, hitherto regarded as an urban preserve. Besides the increasing pressure on land, spread of education was the main catalyst.

Another important dimension of caste is geographical. Whereas *varna* is a pan-Indian notion, *jati* is localized owing to two factors: (1) endogamy and (2) relative immobility of an agrarian society. Agrarian societies are immobile because agriculturists need to remain attached to land during the major part of the year. Furthermore, endogamy is favoured by linguistic affinity. As a result, *jatis* are restricted to particular linguistic regions, sometimes constituting sub-regions within them, like the Jats in north India and Rajbanshis in north Bengal and lower Assam. In both these cases, interestingly, there are political memories which strengthen the demand for 'Jatland' and 'Kamatapur' state respectively. In other cases local concentration has created Srinivas's 'dominant castes' and the political scientists', 'pressure groups', 'caste lobbies' and 'vote banks'.

As the authority of the central government dwindles slowly but steadily, the alternating alliances of the castes (as well as communities and tribes) increasingly become significant forces of regional as well as national politics.

For these very reasons there cannot be an all-India casteist party.

1997

NOTES AND REFERENCES

1. Louis Dumont, *Homo Hierarchicus* (London: Paladin, 1972), pp. 57-58.
2. Talcott Parsons, *The Social System* (Glencoe: The Free Press, 1951), p. 132.
3. Dumont, op. cit., pp. 80-103.
4. *Ibid.*, p. 104.
5. Karl Marx, *Capital* (Moscow: Progress Publishers, 1954), Vol. 1, p. 321.
6. See Max Weber, *The Religion of India (The Sociology of Hinduism and Buddhism)*, translated and edited by Hans Gerth and Don Mertindale, (Glencoe: The Free Press, 1958), pp. 121-23.
7. M.N. Srinivas, *Caste in India and Other Essays* (Bombay: Asia Publishing House, 1962), pp. 151-52. He wrote: 'The progress and retrogression of a soul goes on until it attains salvation.... Birth in a particular caste becomes an index of a soul's progress towards salvation'.
8. Nirmal Kumar Bose, 'An Anthropological View of Indian Civilization' (J.C. Bose Memorial Lecture at Science College, Calcutta, November 30, 1971), *Sciences and Culture,* 37, 2, December 1971.
9. Nirmal Kumar Bose, 'The Hindu Method of Tribal Absorption', in Nirmal Kumar Bose, *Cultural Anthropology and Other Essays* (Calcutta: Indian Associated Publishing Company Ltd, 1953), pp. 156-70, at p. 163.
10. Nirmal Kumar Bose, 'Caste in India', *Ibid*, pp. 171-91, at p. 177.
11. M.N. Srinivas, *Social Change in Modern India,* New Delhi, Orient Longman, 1960.
12. Parsons, op. cit, p. 172.
13. Bose, 'The Hindu Method of Tribal Absorption', op. cit., p. 161.

14. Fredrik Barth, 'Introduction' in Fredrik-Barth (ed.), *Ethnic Groups and Boundaries: The Social Organisation of Culture Difference* (London: George Allen & Unwin, 1969), p. 28.
15. H.H. Risley, 'The Race Basis of Indian Political Movements', *Contemporary Review,* May 1890.
16. M.N. Srinivas, 'Caste in Modern India', *Journal of Asian Studies,* August 1957.
17. See Shibani Kinkar Chaube, *Constituent Assembly of India: Springboard of Revolution* (New Delhi: People's Publishing House, 1973).
18. The Advisory Committee of the Constituent Assembly formulated the following recommendation:

    Nothing herein contained shall prevent the state from making provision for reservation in favour of classes not adequately represented in public services (See B. Shiva Rao, *The Framing of India's Constitution: Select Documents* (New Delhi: Indian Institute of Public Administration, 1966, Vol. V, p. 194).

    The recommendation of the Minority Rights Sub-Committee, forwarded by Vallabhbhai Patel, after adoption by the Advisory Committee, ran as follows: *Recruitment in Services*

    9. *Due share to all minorities guaranteed:* In the all-India and Provincial Services the claims of all the minorities shall be kept in view in making appointments to these services consistently with the consideration of efficiency of administration, (*ibid.*, Vol. II, p. 418).
19. W.H. Morris-Jones, *Parliament in India* (London: Longman, Green 1957), p. 329.
20. Selig Harrison, *India: The Most Dangerous Decades* (Princeton: New Jersey, Princeton University Press, 1960), p. 239.
21. *Ibid.*, p. 217.
22. *Ibid.*, p. 215.
23. *Ibid.*, p. 220.
24. Ajoy Ghosh, 'New Situation and Our Tasks', 'in Ajoy Ghosh, *Speeches and Articles* (Moscow, Publishing House for Oriental Literature, 1962), pp. 176-249, at p. 227.
25. E.M.S. Namboodiripad, 'Caste as a Political Factor and the Work of National Integration,' *New Age* (monthly), June 1962.

13

The Domain of Secularism: Religion, State and Society in India

The foremost requirement in a discussion on secularism in India is demystification of the term and its precise definition. It is necessary to note that India is the only major democracy in the world to inscribe on her Constitution the logo, 'secular'.

The Bharatiya Janata Party accuses the government and the Left parties of practising pseudo-secularism and advances a doctrine of 'positive secularism' which would require the Muslims of India to surrender their claim to what they call the Babari Masjid and accept a common civil code. It also requires the Kashmiris to abandon the special status of their state under the Constitution of India.

To Bhikhu Parekh it appears striking "that no Indian social or political theorist has seriously attempted to grapple with the question of secularism". His own critique, however, fails to provide any positive guidance toward this objective. He admits that in a multi-religious society the state cannot afford to be identified with a particular religion. He also admits that the state is primarily concerned with the material interests of its citizens rather than with the salvation of their souls. But he passes the stricture that the complex problem of relation between the state and religion "cannot be solved by importing an alien, and much misunderstood, model from the West."[1]

Parekh's insistence on an 'Indian' political theory, besides being social scientifically unsound, brings him close to the BJP's prescription of 'positive secularism'. He writes:

> No government since independence has explained why India should be a secular state. Most have argued that secularism is necessary to ensure religious tolerance and harmony. But the argument is false. A secular state is not necessarily

> tolerant, for example, the Soviet Union during the communist rule or France after the French Revolution. And conversely a religious state is not necessarily intolerant or discriminatory against minority religions, for example, traditional Hindu kingdoms in India and Muslim kingdoms in the Middle East. It could also be argued that, by denying religion public identity and expression, a secular state might *provoke* religious conflicts (emphasis in original).

In the first place, the examples furnished are not quite accurate. Though revolutionary France and communist Russia may both be regarded as *anti-religious* in a general way, Soviet Russia did not abolish religion as France did in 1793. The Catholic church in France was restored to its glory through the Concordat in 1802. Communist Russia, on the other hand, separated the church from the state and the schools from the church. Although in some of the Muslim republics people have the freedom to practise other religions, in the best known Muslim kingship of today, Saudi Arabia, it is not done. On the other hand, although in the medieval Hindu kingships Islam was tolerated, this could not be said about Buddhism or Jainism. There could be solid sociological reason for that besides the military one.

Muslims could not be 'redeemed' to the *sanatana* Hindu society while the Buddhists could be absorbed. In fact, Buddha himself was petrified into a Hindu *avatar.*

But the larger fallacy of this argument, like most other similar arguments, lies in the confusion of categories. Secularism is identified with religious tolerance and, therefore, counterposed with communalism. Divine right kingship is identified with theocracy and religion is identified with *dharma.* It is to be noted that divine right kingship is not necessarily an offshoot of Catholic Christianity. It is also pre-Christian and extra-Christian. Hindu, Theravadi Buddhist and Muslim kingships can hardly be considered theocracies. In fact, besides the Gelukpa Lamacracy of Tibet and Khomeini's Iran, it is difficult to find a pure theocracy in the recent period. Even in these countries heretical religions are not forbidden.

All political orders live on congenial social alliances and convenient myths. The legitimacy of the Saudi kingship is solely derived from its supposed defendership of the holy shrines of

Islam and its unofficial claim to *Khilafat*. Buddhism's challenge to the caste system undermined the authority of the 'Hindu' kings who themselves claimed high caste status. The point that is important to note is that a king did not need communalism to crush opposition. His 'peace-keeping', 'law-enforcing' police and army were enough for the purpose. Communalism goes along with democracy, its electoral and pressure politics.

An examination of the entire gamut of theoretical issues involved in the question revolves around a few key words. The two words which have a Western origin and a Western context are 'religion' and 'secular'. One word that has a Western origin but an Indian context is 'communalism'. And the one word that has an Indian origin and an Indian context but is very much misunderstood by the anglophils is '*dharma*'.

According to the *Concise Oxford Dictionary* (COD) 'religion' is rooted in the Latin word 'religio' and is perhaps connected with re(*ligare*=bind). The word has five meanings: (1) Monastic condition, being monk or nun, (rare) a monastic order; (2) (rare) Practice of rites; (3) One of the prevalent systems of faith and worship; (4) Human recognition of superhuman controlling power and especially of a personal God entitled to obedience, effect of such recognition on conduct and mental attitude; (5) Action that one is bound to do.

The word 'secular' has its equivalent in 'temporal', time-bound, and, therefore, this worldly. The word is the antithesis of 'sacred' which is other worldly. The secular courts emerged in medieval Europe under the auspices of the states. Serious criminal cases were transfered by the parish courts controlled by the clergy to the secular courts for trial. Thus, even in the period of papal hegemony, the domain of the state was regarded to be this worldly.

Though COD gives the general meaning of "communal" as "of a commune", for India the meaning is "of the antagonis-tic religious and racial communities in a district". Since the British period, however, the core of communalism in India has been treated to be the antagonism of the religious communities.[2] But, as the meanings of 'religion' have both an individual and a collective implication all communal activities need not be religious and all religious activities need not be communal. Mohammad

Ali Jinnah, who emerged as the communal leader per excellence, was not famous for his religious conviction. He opposed the Khilafat agitation which had a profound religious significance and brought several ulemas to the nationalist fold.

Except Saudi Arabia there is no major state today which officially prohibits public practice of heretical faiths. Such prohibition is characteristic of tribal societies in which totems and cults are integral to the system of social control. 'Saudi Arabia's speciality may be partly explained by its problem of legitimacy in the context of the history and geographical importance of the land to the Islamic world. In the other authoritarian systems the ruler takes upon himself the role of arbiter among feuding communities. It is only when an autocrat is not sure of his ground that he chooses to promote feuds among contending religious sects and communities. That applies also to the colonial rulers. Mehta and Patwardhan put this phenomenon succinctly in the phrase "the communal triangle in India".[3]

When Lord Krishna said *swadharme nidhanam shreya, paradharmo bhayabhah,* there was no Hindu, Muslim or Christian around. He was speaking of the duty of one's caste status. When the Buddha spoke *of dharma* he meant what the Greek idealist philosophers like Socrates, Plato and Aristotle later called 'virtue'. There is no synonym of 'religion', in the Western sense of collective faith, in the Sanskrit words *yagna* (performance), *achara* (rite), *prarthana* (prayer), *puja* (worship) and *bhakti* (devotion). P.V. Kane translated *dharma* as 'religious and civil law'.[4]

In other words, whereas the domain of secularism in social scientific theory is legal-political, that of communalism is socio-political, that of *dharma* is social and that of religion personal. Yet pretenders right from the days of the papacy have claimed authority upon the faithful frequently with the aid of "defenders of the faith" simultaneously giving birth to the divine right theory of kingship. Worse people have claimed the leadership of communities by using its association with religion.

Our hypothesis that authoritarian rulers or colonial masters need to resort to communalism *only* when they are unsure of their ground explains why Aurangzeb had a Hindu general and Shivaji a Muslim. It also explains why the South African white regime ruthlessly oppressed all black people until the Second

World War but later adopted a policy of "divide and rule" using inter-tribal feuds (that now stand in the way of black emancipation). It goes a long way in explaining 'the communal triangle in India' since the suppression of the 1857 revolt.[5]

This hypothesis, further, goes against a prevailing misconception that communalism is a product of feudalism.

When we say this we have in mind not the emaciated feudalism of India under the British *raj*. We mean the feudalism that developed in the wake of the collapse of the Mughal empire. When a Muslim feudal lord would fight a Hindu feudal lord or vice versa for property or any other thing, he would hardly resort to 'mass mobilization' on communal basis. He would depend upon his paid *paik* or mercenaries. When a Muslim or Hindu feudal lord would punish his defaulter subjects, he would do exactly the same. It is true that many Muslim *zemindars* backed the Muslim League,[6] it is equally true that Hindu *rajas* and *zemindars* financed the Indian National Congress at the early stage. When the freedom struggle took an increasingly democratic popular character, the Hindu *zemindars* fell out with the Congress. The *zemindars* feared not freedom from the British rule, they feared democracy which would challenge their exploitation of the peasants, Hindu or Muslim.

This does not mean that the religious faith of a ruler or a feudal lord has nothing to do with the administration of the people. More often than not governmental assistance to priests, temples and mosques is extended for the purpose of imparting legitimacy to the rulers or raise their social status. Tribal chiefs of pre-British India paid the Brahmins lavishly and obtained the caste status of Kshatriya supported by appropriate myths of origin. More Saudi money is said to be spent on building of mosques all over the world and free distribution of the Holy Quran than on ameliorating the economic conditions of the followers of Islam. Otherwise, the rulers would prefer to keep their religious convictions to themselves and would hesitate to split their regimes over questions of faith.

Had Aurangzeb's administration been not set in mortal combat with Dara Sekoh, and, had he not taken a major military initiative in south India, he might have ended as another Nasiruddin presiding over a larger empire. Had the English East India Company been not threatened with closure by the Charter Act of 1813, it would not have allowed the Christian church within its territory in India. And had the British Parliament been not constantly pressurized by the British rivals of the Company, including the emerging industrial bourgeoisie, the British Parliament would not concede the demand of the protestant church to allow its establishment in British India. It is interesting to note that the Church of England, the official church of the British state, was the least favoured establishment in the matter of distribution of licenses.

The fact that the British government sponsored some of the social reform measures like the *sati* abolition is not due to its keenness to interfere with Hindu religion but the support such measures received from Hindu intellectual leaders like Rammohan Roy and Iswar Chandra Vidyasagar. The facts that Rammohan Roy opposed the establishment of the Sanskrit College at Calcutta inspite of being a reputed Sanskrit scholar himself and Iswar Chandra Vidyasagar, a great Sanskrit scholar and a Brahmin, supported the teaching of English—a *mlechchha* language—in the Sanskrit College demonstrate the amount of autonomy that the Hindu society enjoyed from religion. In fact Vidyasagar drew support for widow remarriage from one of the ancient scriptures—the *Parasura Samhita*. And this fact demonstrates that the Hindu society is polycentric too.

These two facts—autonomy of Hindu society from religion and its polycentrism—enabled the state, both colonial and post-colonial, to pass social legislations for the Hindus. The Islamic and Christian social laws flow from their religious systems. The fact that they differ between themselves is due to the fact that their own norms differ, particularly about the status of women.

The important point to note is that while, in India, laws of succession and marriage of the Christians were replications of the advanced British laws on the subjects, the Hindu social reformers over a century and a half sought an approximation to that model. No such movement occurred among the Muslims in India. Though Muslim women traditionally had the right to succession to property, their conjugal rights compare unfavourably with those of the Christian and modern Hindu women.

The relation between the state, the society and religion is, as a result, quite complex. Islam binds both the society and the state. Though Christ laid down a distinction between state and religion by his famous dichotomization of "Caesar and God", his attempt at laying down the social norms of his followers brought the Roman empire's wrath upon him. The adoption of Christianity by the empire brought in a historic conflict between the state and the church for hegemony over the civil society.

The Hindu has never been a religion, least of all a religious order. The name had its origin in the geographical ascription by India's north western neighbours who actually called the residents of Hind 'Hindi'. 'Hindu' came into use through the British census practice since the late nineteenth century. Even then social movements like the Brahmo Samaj, the Arya Samaj and the Sanatanis shunned the designation 'Hindu'. The 'Hindu Mela' in Calcutta was hardly a religious affair; it was in fact one of the earliest nationalistic undertakings by the Bengalee middle class.

It is important to note that in the colonial 'reforms' initiated in the late nineteen century and continued till July 1947, when the Indian Independence Act was passed by the British Parliament, the word 'Hindu' finds no statutory recognition though it is acknowledged in the common law practice of the courts in the form of 'Hindu law'. Correspondingly, there was the 'Muslim law'. Never was a 'Hindu' constituency set up under the scheme of separate electorate that went on being elaborated till 1935, though 'the Hindu-Muslim divide' was writ large on the colonial politics since the late nineteenth century. The infamous 'Bengal partition' of Curzon was done, officially, not on the ground of Hindu-Muslim division but of administrative rationalization. When the Cabinet Mission gave its 'plan' in 1946, it spoke of three communities 'the General', 'the Muslim, and 'the Sikh'. In July 1947 the British Parliament passed a law creating just two 'independent dominions' because 'it was expedient'. It did not create either a 'Muslim dominion' or a 'Hindu dominion'.

Inspite of the bitterness of partition not a single proposal was mooted in the Constituent Assembly of India, which included Syama Prasad Mookerjee, the Hindu Mahasabha leader who later founded the Bharatiya Jana Sangh, as a very active member, to declare India a 'Hindu Rashtra'. In fact it was considered unnecessary to even declare India 'a secular state' as demanded by a Congress member, K.T. Shah. Ambedkar's brief answer was that a Constitution does not enshrine a social philosophy.[7] The Constituent Assembly, on the other hand, laid down an elaborate system of rights ensuring equality and even providing for cultural safeguard of the minorities.

The British, therefore, did not hand over India to the Hindus. There is no historical justification for declaring India a 'Hindu Rashtra' particularly because the India of today was defined by the British. The declaration of Pakistan as an 'Islamic Republic' through the aberration of a military dictatorship is just no ground for declaring India a Hindu state. None of the Western democracies calls itself a 'Christian state' inspite of the fact that all of them have a Christian majority. The argument of 'sentiment' of the majority has no ground in rational politics that is the basic assumption of any stable democracy for the simple reason that sentiments can be manipulated.

Any attempt to define India as a Hindu state is, moreover; bound to be self-defeating. If the Hindus do not have one religion they do not lend themselves to determination on religious ground. Even the Rashtriya Swayam Sevak Sangh think tank admits it:

> It is not a way of worship. It *is* not ruled by one book, one prophet. One who does not believe in God is a Hindu and one who believes in God is also a Hindu. So Hinduism is not at all a religious concept. The Britishers deliberately...made Hinduism parallel to Christianity and Islam. They did it in their census operation and many other things.[8]

V*arnashrama* and *chaturashrama* are the two most important *dharmas* of the *sanatani* (traditional) Hindu. First, there is no Hindu outside the varna system. Second, every Hindu is bound to go through the four stages of life, *brahmacharyya* (studentship), *garhastha* (family), *banaprastha* (retirement), and *sannyasa* (total withdrawal). By the same token, the life-long mendicant (sannyasi/sant) has no place in the Hindu society. One has to forego his caste and perform his own *sraddha* (post-death rites) before entering into *sannyasa* The Ajeevakas, the Jainas and the Shramanas of ancient India did not perform these duties and were, therefore, excluded. They lived mostly on charily of the trading castes which were themselves looked down upon. (The impression that the traders were *vaishyas* and, therefore, belonged to the upper *varnas* is wrong because *vaishya* literally means 'settler'—the land-owning cultivator. All agrarian societies in the world have looked down upon trade as a profession.)

It was Shankaracharyya who first organized an anti-Buddhist monastic order. But he could not bring all monks into the Vedic mainstream as his *mathas* were under brahminical leadership. By the eighteenth century the sannyasis were found to be engaged in long-distance trade. They became mercenaries in several places. In the seventeen seventies they even revolted.[9] They had captured the decadent Buddhist shrines. When the Sikh *gurudwaras* faced a crisis following their conflict with the Mughal power, the *mahants* took over their control. Contrary to the popular image of being total renouncers, many *sannyasis* are rich as one can easily find at the Kumbha melas.

Varnashrama lays down the the structure of Hindu society while *chaturashrama* periodizes the individuals' life span. There are other specific *dharmas* according to one's station and situation. One important determinant of the Hindus' *dharmas,* however, has been the purity-pollution syndrome which a *sannyasi* (renouncer) may ignore but a *gruhi* (householder/layman) may not. Over the last one thousand years the *sanatani* (traditional) Hindus have rejected everything 'polluted' by contact with the *mlechchhas* (Muslims and Christians) swelling the number of converts. Hence the failure of the *suddhi* movement of the Arya Samaj. Even though, at the folk level, there has been a great deal of approximation between the two major communities of India—through the *bhakti* and the *sufi* movements—at the ritualized institutional level mobility of personnel and objects of veneration is far from achieved.

The BJP-RSS-VHP project of *Hindutwa* (symbolized, at the moment, by the temple-building call) is aimed at what, in over a thousand years, *sannyasis* (from Shankara to Shraddhananda) have failed to achieve, namely, a monolithic, if not monotheic, religious sect built by the *sants, sannyasis* and cemented by the financial strength of the trading classes and overarching the caste-structure which, notwithstanding the laying of 'foundation stone' by a

'Harijan', has not been really challenged. The imponderables are the still overwhelmingly agrarian social structure and, notwithstanding the respect of the masses for the renouncer—next only for the martyr, the exclusion of the *sants* from the social hierarchy. Moreover, the Indian peasants, like all other peasants, are awe-struck by wealth but contemptuous of the traders who, in their (physiocratic) view, possess wealth without earning it. Finally, notwithstanding the lone pilgrim out of a million, peasants are still overwhelmingly attached to their local gods and village priests and lack any pan-Indian religious consciousness. Leaving aside the mercenaries, the 'Hindutwa' wave sways only the urban and suburban Hindus. But, then, there are new trends since the partition of India.

In the first place, there has been a certain kind of lumpenization. Taking the life or the property of a 'bidharmi' or a 'kafer' has become not only legitimized but also invested with a patriotic halo. Secondly, exchange of population between India and Pakistan led to the exchange of property including places of dwelling. Out of necessity such properties are usually 'purified' through some kind of religious performance. Nothing, not even a masjid, is irredeemable to the new Hindu. Thirdly, electoral politics has politicized religion. Fourthly, a new breed of jet-set gurus have grown as the centres of political manipulation and economic cartelization. Their off-the-cuff, 'modern,' interpretations of religion correspond very little to the purity-pollution dichotomy. All these have contributed greatly to a communalization of the Hindu society.

In independent India 'Hindu' has become a statutory category. It found its place in the Constitution of India. Article 25(2)(b) of the Constitution provided that notwithstanding every person's right to freedom of religion, nothing shall affect the operation of any existing law or prevent the state from making any law providing for social welfare and reform or the throwing open of Hindu religious institutions of a public character to all classes and sections of Hindus. For the same purpose the phrase 'Hindu religion' includes 'Sikh, Jaina and Buddhist' religions. (In fact Islam and Christianity do not find mention in the Constitution).

This, incidentally, has been viewed by some Hindus as negative discrimination. They consider Muslims to be privileged against social reform like prohibition of polygyny. In practice this Article contains nothing prohibiting social reform for the non-Hindus. It only enables the state to open Hindu religious institutions of public character to all sections of the Hindus. The context of this Article is the great temple entry movements during the British days. For the Muslims and the Christians the question does not arise as they do not practise untouchability. This Article in fact corresponds to Article 17 that abolishes untouchability. The criticism of a section of the Sikhs against being regarded as Hindus for that purpose is groundless too.

Criticisms against the legislations like the Muslim Women's Protection (Amendment) Act spring from the interpretation of Article 26 which gives "every religious denomination or any section thereof the right (a) to establish and maintain institutions for religious and charitable purposes, (b) to manage its own affairs in matters of religion, (c) to own and acquire movable and immovable property, and (d) to administer such property in accordant with laws. "By an extension of the right (b) a section of the Muslim leadership has opposed the enactment of a uniform civil code as they claim that Muslim civil law is derived from the *shariat*, that is religious code.

This is no doubt a contentious issue. In the colonial days Muslim law, like the Hindu law, was treated as a common law. The very fact that republican India has passed the Hindu Code shows that it does not recognize marital rights as religious affairs. Neither did the highest law court in the country recognize it when, in the Ahmed vs. Shah Bano case,[10] it offered compensation to a divorced Muslim lady on the basis of Muslim Women (Protection of Rights on Divorce) Act, 1966. The political reaction to the judgement was so violent that the central government had to amend the Act. It ignored the Supreme Court's recommendation calling for a uniform civil code. The prevailing view in the government was that Muslim opinion in the bulk must accept the idea before such an endeavour is made.

The Constitution of India, even before the 42nd Amendment, had, in fact, laid down the distinction between the religious and the secular domains. Under Article 25(2) (a) the state had, and still has, the power to make any law "regulating or restricting any economic, financial, political or rather secular activity which may be associated with religious practice". The incorporation of the term 'secularism' in the Preamble to the Indian Constitution is merely ornamental. Under the Directive Principles of State Policy which, however, the state cannot be forced to implement, the state "shall endeavour to secure for its citizens a uniform civil code throughout the territory".[11] If a certain government or a certain political party is unable to live up to this directive the fault does not lie with the Constitution. On the other hand, the concerned community/communities need to be educated with bonafide intentions.

A characteristic of the Indian Constitution is the distinction it made between religion on the one hand and culture on the other by treating them under separate headings. Further, cultural rights are distinguished from educational rights by treating them under separate Articles. Religious rights *per se* are granted to 'all persons'. Freedom to manage religious affairs (Article 26) is given to "every religious denomination or any section thereof". Cultural rights *per se* [Article 29(1)] are given to "any section of the citizens residing in the territory of India or any part thereof having a distinct language, script or culture of its own". Under clause (2) of the same Article, individually, "no citizen shall be denied admission into any educational institution maintained by the state or receiving aid out of state funds on grounds only of race, religion, caste, language or any of them". As this clause offers protection against injustice, it is negatively worded and individual oriented in nature.

Though the phrase in Article 29(1) is "any section of citizens", for all practical purposes, the provision concerns the minority groups who really need it. Hence the marginal note: "Protection of interests of minorities". Yet the minorities here are not merely religious minorities but also linguistic and cultural minorities. This also applies to Article 30 in which the minorities are allowed to set up their educational institutions and the state is forbidden to discriminate against them. Article 30, incidentally, is the only place in the *text* of the Constitution in which the term 'minorities" occur. The majority automatically has this right; it is the minorities which need constitutional guarantee about them.

To sum up, the Constitution of India makes a clear distinction between the religious and the secular domains as well as between the domains of religion and culture. Logically, therefore, culture is in the secular domain of the state. The facts that the state has passed the Hindu Code, The Muslim Women (Protection of Rights on Divorce) Act and an amendment of the Act further show that the state has jurisdiction over the social customs of all communities which are regarded as secular.

Yet in India, unlike in the USA, there is not a total ban on legislation "respecting an establishment of religion".[12] The Indian state, therefore, cannot be called secular as such. But the question whether, in the complexity of India's social and historical compulsions, such a state ideology is feasible or even desirable may probably be answered only in the negative.[13]

1990

NOTES AND REFERENCES

1. Bhikhu Parekh. *The Poverty of Indian Political Theory,* Hull Papers in Indian Politics, ed. by Noel O'Sullivan, N.D.
2. In 1944 Reginald Coupland wrote that the core of the 'Indian Problem' was the Hindu-Muslim rivalry, see *The Constitutional Problem in India,* Oxford University Press, 1944, part III, p. 16.
3. Asoka Mehta and Achyuta Patwardhan, *The Communal Triangle in India,* Allahabad, Kitabistan, 1942.
4. Pandurang Vaman Kane, *History of Dharmasastra (Ancient and Medieval Religious and Civil Law),* Puna, Bhandarkar Oriental Research Institute. Vol. I, Revised and Enlarged, part I (p. 3) noted that "Dharma is one of the Sanskrit words that defy all definitions. That word has passed through several vicissitudes". Kane, however, synthesized the following definition of *dharma;* "the privileges, duties and obligations of a man, his standard of conduct as a member of one of the castes, as a person in a particular stage of life". His own book, according to Kane, was devoted to *acara* and *vyavahara* (law and administration of justice), ibid., p. 4.
5. The rationalization of the administrative 'Hindu-Muslim divide' was laid down in W. W. Hunter, *The Indian Musalmans,* London, 1870.
6. See Jawaharlal Nehru, *An Autobiography,* Oxford University Press, 1989, p. 606.
7. *Constituent Assembly Debates,* Vol. VII, p. 336. There is a background to this discussion. On April 3,1947, the subcommittee on Fundamental Rights reported to the chairman of the Advisory Committee on Minorities, Fundamental Rights, etc, recommending a draft set of rights

which included the following statement (Clause 19): "The state shall not recognize any religion as State religion" (See B. Shiva Rao, *The Framing of India's Constitution: Select Documents,* New Delhi, Indian Institute of Public Administration, 1967, Vol. II, pp. 137-43, p. 140). According to B. N. Rau's note the provision had been borrowed from the first amendment of the US Constitution and Article 137, paragraph I of the Weimar Republican Constitution (ibid., p. 149). During discussion in the meeting of the same subcommittee on the basis of certain objections from its members, K.M. Munshi and K.M. Panikkar appear to have raised objection to the clause and it was dropped. According to a rather cryptic statement in the minutes of the report dated April 14, 1947, "Mr Munshi and Sardar Panikkar promised to bring a redraft so as to provide for those cases where religion is already accepted as a state religion" (*Ibid.*, p. 165). This draft is not available, but the clause was dropped on April 15, 1947 (*Ibid.*, p. 169). Given the stature of the two members in the Constituent Assembly, such an ill-drafted and incomplete minute is just incomprehensible. Munshi and Panikkar obviously had in maid the princely states.

8. Nanaji Deshmukh interviewed by Vinod Sharma in *The Hindustan Times,* March 10, 1991.
9. B. P. Misra, *Sannyasi Rebellion—The Sociology and Economics of a Conflict in Sub-Himalayan Bengal,* Occasional Paper I, Centre for Himalayan Studios, University of North Bengal, 1985.
10. A.I.R. 1985, S.C. 945.
11. Article 44, *The Constitution of India.*
12. *The Constitution of the USA,* the First Amendment.
13. V.P. Luthra, in *The Concept of Secular State and India,* Bombay, Oxford University Press, 1964, holds India to be a 'jurisdictionalist state'.

14

Communalism and Secularism in India

Then there is the question of Article 25 which gives the state the power to legislate for the social welfare and reform of Hindu religious institutions, whilst making no such provision for any other religion. Which Hindu can accept this public humiliation of his religion in the Constitution itself, which marks out Hindu religious institutions as being so perverted as to need state intervention for their reform? If the BJP says that Article 25 should be amended, how is it communal? Again, so far as Article 30 is concerned, the BJP quite rightly says that either let every community administer its own educational institutions without state intervention or remove the special exemption given to minority communities alone.[1]

The Meaning of Secularism

The above statement about sums up the confusion, if not orchestrated disinformation, about Indian secularism. At the theoretical level it is sought to present basically three arguments aimed at obfuscation: (1) that secularism is opposite of religiosity, and like communism, bad and against the spirit of India's culture, (2) that secularism is equal treatment of religions and neither repression nor patronization of a particular religion, and (3) that secularism is the opposite of communalism and co-terminal with tolerance.

The confusion had set in right at the time of Constitution-making in India when at least two amendments to the Draft Constitution seeking to declare India a secular republic (one moved by Maulana Hasrat Mohani, a Muslim Leaguer, and another by K.T. Shah, a Hindu Congressman) were turned down and excathedra statements were made by the leaders that Indian society *is* secular.

The assertion has had its resonance in academic and journalistic writings[2] and even judicial decisions at the highest level[3] frequently along with the refrain that 'our secularism is different'. As it is easier to stress a difference than to spell out its fundamental characteristics, the 'Indian version' of secularism has indeed become quite impossible to define. In the *Bommai* case some of the judges endorsed the definition offered by Mrs. Indira Gandhi — *Sarva dharma samabhava*. Two judges kept silent. One of them (Ahmadi, C.J.) held that the state should not fund any religious body/project. One of them judges who kept silent on the question of secularism subsequently held that *Hindutwa* is not quite antithetical to secularism. Of course the Bharatiya Janata Party rejected the judgement in the Bommai case altogether.[4]

To go back to the arguments of what may be called 'India's special theory of secularism'. The first argument is patently wrong. The United States of America is a secular state 'by the Western view'. It is, at the same time, a highly religious society. Indeed the birth of the United States was connected with the exodus of religious zealots from England.

The second argument is a statement of laudable intentions that are just not amenable to translation into a public policy, at least as far as public confidence is concerned. In the democratic framework of competitive politics the prescription is a sure way toward antagonizing all the religious communities.

The third argument has a somewhat mischievous underpinning. Tolerance is an offensively undignified concept implying one section of the society living at the mercy of another. The opposite of communalism is not tolerance, it is assimilation or identification. But the theoretically important fallacy is that it is only in a communally charged society that the element of secularism is absent. Nobody can blame the United Kingdom of religious intolerance but nobody can call her a secular state. The argument should be that secularism mitigates communal conflict because an aggrieved community is assured that a secular state will after all protect it. Secularism must be seen as a condition of communal amity, not as a consequence of communal tension.

A theoretical point stressed by this author in an earlier writing is that communalism is a socio-political concept while secularism is a legal-political concept.[5] Therefore there is neither a positive nor a negative correlation between the two though there may be overlappings. Therefore India's special theory of secularism has severe loopholes in terms of sociology, politics and law. All these are social sciences and the fundamental basis of a social science is conceptual, if not definitional, clarity. Such clarity has to be universal, otherwise an assertion of faith will lead us to the sphere of black magic.

Etymologically, 'secular' is 'this worldly'— mundane, profane. It is the opposite of sacred — other worldly. No average human being is secular, no society is secular. There is in the life of an individual or a society a concern for the other worldly. A few individuals may be total atheists. But the bulk of a society is concerned with both the secular and the sacred domains of life. Secularism can be the attribute of only a state— if it so chooses — not of a society.

Secularism is a religious *laissez faire* preventing the state from either positively or negatively interfering with the sacred activities of individuals or societies and their concerned institutions. The model is that of the First Amendment to the Constitution of the United States of America.

Indeed secularism is a negative right of the individual organized in society. Even the Soviet Union, which established total state-control over the material life of its citizens, followed this form of cultural *laissez faire* by separating the church from the state and the schools from the church. Positively speaking, therefore, secularism involves a rolling up of the state from the sacred domain of the individual/society.

The Meaning of Communalism

If secularism is a legal-political doctrine prescribing a policy of cultural *laissez faire,* communalism is a socio-political ideology which, according to Bipan Chandra, has three basic elements or stages, one following the other: (1) the belief that people who follow the same religion have common secular interests, *(2)* in a multi-religious society like India the secular interests of the followers of one religion are dissimilar with the interests of the followers of another religion, and (3) a perception that the secular interests of different 'communities' are antagonistic to each other.[6]

Like all other ideologies, however, communalism needs to be

propagated. But there is a fine point to note — communalism is different from other 'isms" because, by definition, communalism must be shared by a community. Otherwise it just remains a false consciousness of one or some individuals—a prejudice.

The second point about communalism is that the community itself is a human construct unlike the class. This is not to say that the identification of a class is unproblematic. In fact, there are several definitions of a class. Whatever definition is adopted, however, every class may be identified by some standard external to it (like wealth, power, education). A 'community' is defined by the faith of its members which may not even be expressed in ritualistic practices. At the same time, ritualistic practices are not the accurate guide to one's faith.

The most important point about communalism, however, is that it is perfectly possible for a person to be communal without being religious. Conversely it is perfectly possible for a devoutly religious man to be non-communal. Mohammad Ali Jinnah and Abul Kalam Azad are the perfect examples of the two types respectively as would be illustrated by their opposite attitudes to the Khilafat question.

But the fundamental difference between secularism and communalism is that they operate at different levels. Secularism concerns an institution, communalism concerns the collective mind. Hence the two may co-exist as well as conflict. It will, for instance, be a travesty of truth to claim that the Indian National Congress before Independence did not contain communalism. But the INC never took a resolution on a religious issue except for the highly politicized question of the Khilafat. Patronization of all religions 'impartially' by the governments of the country may demonstrate a non-communal attitude. It is certainly not secular.

Theoretical Formulations

From the above argument certain theoretical formulations follow:

For an individual

1. It is possible to distinguish between the secular and the sacred domains of life.
2. It is possible to be religious without being communal — Azad, Gandhi.

3. It is possible to be communal without being religious — Jinnah.
4. It is possible to be both communal and religious.
5. It is not possible to be secular without being an atheist.

For a group/society (macro and micro)

1. It is not possible to be totally secular.
2. It is possible to distinguish between the secular and the sacred domains of life.
3. The stress on religiosity is a cultural attribute depending on historical circumstances.
4. Inter-group societal relations are determined by historical conditions that may or may not involve religion.
5. Sustained inter-group/societal relations involve, in the main, secular interests.
6. Modernity involves materialist/secular rationality.
7. Formulae for inter-group/societal cooperation and conflict resolution, therefore, must be looked for in the secular sphere of life.
8. Modernity has forged cohesion of smaller groups but have also created wider rifts among bigger groups.
9. The state is a product of modernity and is capable of distinguishing the secular from the sacred better than the simpler social formations.
10. A secular state is more capable of handling inter-group/ societal differences, defined by religions than a theocratic or sectarian state.

Dictates of secularism—

1. The state shall not have an official religion.
2. The state shall not favour or discriminate against any particular religion — far less be identified with a religious sect.
3. Office-holders of a state are free to profess and practise religion in private — individually and collectively — without using the benefits of office.
4. The secular concerns of the state include the maintenance of law and order and protection of freedom of individuals and groups.

Secularism in India

As far as the negative rights of the individuals are concerned the Indian Constitution forbids state interference and discrimination. Article 25 of the Constitution grants explicit freedom of conscience and free profession, practice and propagation of religion. Clause 1 of the Article says: 'Subject to public order, morality and wealth and to the other provisions of this Part [i.e., Part III] all persons are equally entitled to freedom of conscience and the right freely to profess, practise and propagate religion.'

In the same way Article 26 grants to every religious denomination or any section thereof the right (a) to establish and maintain institutions for religious and charitable purposes; (b) to manage its own affairs in matters of religion; (c) to own and acquire movable and immovable property; and (d) to administer such property in accordance with law.

Article 27 forbids the state to impose any tax the proceeds of which are specifically appropriated in payment of expenses for the promotion or maintenance of any particular religion or religious institution. A related question is, can the state impose a tax selectively on members of any religious community *not* with a view to aiding any religion or religious denomination? The answer is: discriminatory taxing of members of any religious community is forbidden by Article 14 that forbids the State to deny to any person equality before the law or equal protection of the laws within the territory of India and Article 15 which prohibits discrimination of any citizen on grounds only of religion, race, caste, sex, place of birth or any of them.

There is, however, nothing in the Constitution which forbids the state to spend money from its consolidated fund for the benefit of religion. Neither is there any ban on positive discrimination in favour of a particular religion. In fact, there is a constitutional mandate on the governments of Kerala and Tamil Nadu to pay fixed sums of money, annually, to the *Devaswom* fund of the respective states and such payments are charged on the Consolidated Fund of India (Article 290A).

The reason for such a provision is to be traced to the story of the merger of the princely state of Travancore which was incorporated with the presiding deity of the state, Padma Nabha, and the massive wealth of the temples which the government of the state had grabbed through the *Devaswom* trust[7]. In fact, K.M. Munshi confessed in the Constitutional Assembly of India that adoption of secularism could create hurdles for the integration of the princely states[8].

There was, therefore a clear reason for rejecting the proposal for declaring India as a secular state. Consequently, governments since 1948 have been spending money on repair/ reconstruction of temples, mosques, churches and monasteries, financing the wakfs and similar other religious purposes provoking unnecessary controversies. Seen thus, the 42nd Amendment is nothing but a joke.

Yet the framers of the Indian Constitution made a clear distinction between the sacred and the secular paths in clause 2 (a) of Article 25 permitting the state to legislate 'regulating or restricting any economic, financial, political or other secular activity which may be associated with religious practice.'

Incidentally, even if the *Devaswom* Fund is interpreted as a secular activity, this clause certainly does not permit contribution to it by the state. On the ether hand, it may be argued that, like the special status of Jammu and Kashmir, contribution to *Devaswom* fund is an obligation flowing from the agreement of accession of a princely state and should be treated specially. Even then, the assertion of the secular character of the constitution will depend on the complete cessation of grants towards any religious purpose by the state.

Clause 2 (b) of Article 25 has been subjected to serious misunderstanding. This clause allows the state to make laws 'providing for social welfare and reforms or the throwing open of Hindu religious institutions of a public character to all classes and sections of Hindus.' An "explanation" offered on this clause says that 'the reference to Hindus shall be construed as including a reference to persons professing the Sikh, Jaina or Buddhist religion and the reference to Hindu religious institutions shall be construed accordingly.

The 'Hindu' protest to this clause is against the alleged discrimination against Hindus on the question of social reform and exemption of the religious minorities from its scope. The protest zeroes in on the question of Muslim personal law. Some foolhardy statements of Muslim League members of the Constituent Assembly to the effect that they would not allow the tampering of Muslim personal law has led to the misunderstanding that the clause allows only Hindu social reform.

The language of the sub-clause warrants no such conclusion as the clause does *not* speak of Hindu social reform. There is nothing in the Constitution that prohibits social reform of the minorities. The word 'Hindu' qualifies only 'temples of public character'. It does not relate to private temples.

Anyone familiar with the Indian freedom movement knows the crucial significance of the 'temple entry' movement led by Gandhi. Everyone also knows that this problem does not affect the Muslims and Christians. The problem belongs to all religions containing 'untouchables' in its ranks. This clause, in fact, should be read along with Article 15 (Prohibition of discrimination on grounds of religion, race, caste, sex or place of birth or any of them/ particularly with regard to access to public places/utilities) and Article 17 (Abolition of Untouchability).

Another misunderstanding concerns Article 30 which grants to 'all minorities, whether based on religion or language' the right to establish and administer educational institutions of their choice. This is seen as a manifestation of 'minority pampering' forgetting that linguistic minorities are as much benefited by this right as the religious minorities are. But the more important point is that in a democracy, that is governed by number, it is a minority which needs protection and not the majority.

1997

NOTES AND REFERENCES

1. M.N. Buch, 'Who is Secular', *The Hindustan Times*, May 17, 1996.
2. T.N. Madan, 'Secularism in its Place', *The Journal of Asian Studies*, 46, 4, November 1987 is the classic case of confusion of a political problem with a sociological view.
3. *S.R. Bommai and Others v. The Union of India and Others, Judgements Today*, 2, No. 8, 21 March 1994. See also S.K. Chaube, 'The Supreme Court, Federalism and Secularism in India', *Trends in Social Science Research*, Vol. 1, No. 1, June 1994.

4. A.G. Noorani, 'Hindutva Debate', 2 parts, *The Statesman,* 26-27 December 1995.
5. S.K. Chaube, 'The Domain of Secularism: Religion, State and Society in India', *Social Science Probings,* Vols. 7-8.
6. Bipan Chandra, *et. al., India's Struggle for Independence,* Penguin, 1989, pp. 398-99.
7. V.P. Menon, *The Story of the Integration of the Indian States,* Orient Longman, 1961, pp. 269-71. 8.
8. Munshi was backed by Vallabhbhai Patel. See *Constituent Assembly Debates,* Vol. V, pp. 385-91.

15
Minority Problem in India

All peoples or races of the Indian Union are component parts of the Indian nation and shall be equal...

There shall be no state religion. The state shall observe neutrality in respect of all religions.[1]

To all minorities in India we give the assurance that they will receive fair and just treatment and there will be no discrimination in any form against them. Their religion, their culture and their language are safe and they will enjoy all the rights and privileges of citizenship, and will be expected in their turn to render loyalty to the country in which they live and to its constitution.[2]

The most grievous feature of this post-independence development is that the Minorities have held up their vote as a bait and political leaders of the majority community *belonging to different parties have* indiscriminately swallowed that bait in their Election Manifestos and alliances, irrespective of the ideologies which ushered in the Independence of India and which form the bedrock of the existing Constitution. In this background, it is the duty of an impartial academician to point out to a nationalist Indian (every Indian citizen cannot be assumed to have narrow political ambitions) that to accept such anti-nationalist demand of the Minorities (which, though sponsored by the Muslims, are being reiterated by the other minorities, such as the Christians, the Sikhs, the Buddhists, in so far as such demands would serve their respective communal or sectional interests) would be to tear India into pieces, with a second Pakistan for Muslim-majority areas or a Christendom for the Christians, or an Islamic Republic for the Muslims, or a Khalistan, so far as the Sikhs are concerned, or a Buddhist Republic so far as the Buddhists are concerned, and so on.[3]

An Overview

The first of the above quotations is from a memorandum submitted to the Minority Rights sub-committee of the Advisory Committee on Fundamental Rights, Minorities and Tribal and Excluded and Partially Excluded Areas of the Constituent Assembly of India, dated April 7, 1947, by member, Executive Council of the Governor-General of British India and the Constituent Assembly of India. President the All-India Hindu Mahasabha then and, subsequently, the founder President of the Bharatiya Jana Sangh, earlier incarnation of the ruling party at the centre now, Dr Syama Prasad Mookerjee. The second quotation is from a speech at the mid-night of August 14-15, 1947, by Chairman, Constituent Assembly of India, and later the first President of the Indian Republic, Dr Rajendra Prasad. The horrendous scenario that the third quotation projects is from a recent edition of *the Bible* of every graduate student of the Indian Constitution, *Introduction to the Constitution of India* by *Acharya* Dr. Durga Das Basu.

Together, they say it all about the attitude of the Indian elite toward the minority problem in India. Perhaps the timings of their delivery are important. The first statement was made before the Partition decision was taken and the task of the Constituent Assembly was still seen to be to constitute India into a liberal, pluralistic, democracy. The second statement was made immediately after Partition. The commitment to a liberal, pluralistic, democracy was still there. But a cloud of suspicion appeared on the head of the minorities, a particular minority - the Muslims - for that. The third tells the story of degeneration of Indian politics to such a vicious level as to poison the mind of an eminent authority on the Constitution to the extent of his offering a political comment. Not only the Indian Muslims, who are, against the evidence of history, all held to be responsible for the partition and loyal in their hearts to Pakistan, but also the Indian Christians and the Sikhs, who were firm allies of the Indian National Congress during the freedom struggle, along with the numerically insignificant Buddhists, turn into potential 'traitors' to India.

Listing of the causes of the degeneration is a Herculean task. The Partition, the scores of Hindu-Muslim riots since then, three major wars with Pakistan, the perennial Kashmir dispute and the vote-bank politics of the major as well as minor political parties have been partly responsible for the plight of the Muslims. The Sikhs, the spine of India's defence, have been the victims of the adventurous 'Khalistan' movement. The only point that 'nationalist' India can hold out against the Indian Christian is the fact that in some of the hill states of north-east India where political violence - sometimes on secessionist slogan - occurred there is a Christian preponderance even though the Hindu-majority states of Assam, Manipur and Tripura are as susceptible to violence as Nagaland, Meghalaya and Mizoram. The only point against the Buddhists perhaps would be that they are fighting the Hindus in Sri Lanka.

There is now ample historical evidence to show that, whereas 'Pakistan' was a Muslim League idea, Partition was the idea of the Indian National Congress with the backing of the All-India Hindu Mahasabha.[4] The only reason why the Indian Muslims can, probably, be blamed on the Partition is the assumption that most of them - though certainly not all - voted for the Muslim League in the provincial elections of early 1946. The All-India Shia Muslim Association opposed the Cabinet Mission Plan as the Congress did. So did the All-India Christian Association and the Shiromani Akali Dal. The Buddhists in India were too insignificant to take a political position. Several Muslims and Christians, on the other hand, have died in wars with Pakistan and in quelling violence in the border states, though the Sikhs surpass them all in the sacrifice of life for the integrity of India. Why, then, is this cruel suspicion of the minorities? To understand this suspicion a look at the constitutional status and the plight of the minorities is necessary.

Minority Status

'Minority' is a contextual term with reference to number. Without a context the word has no meaning. In parliamentary politics or in general elections the context is provided by the political parties. Such majority-minority dichotomy is ephemeral there. A Constitution, being a permanent document, does not use the word in isolation. Articles 29 and 30 of the Indian Constitution use the word in definite contexts. Part III of the Constitution grants two kinds of fundamental rights. Most of the rights, including the freedom of religion, are given to individuals. Some rights are given to groups (Articles 26, 27, 29 & 30). Though Explanation I of Article 25 mentions the right of the Sikhs to wear *kripan*, it actually means that *every* Sikh is *entitled to* wear *kripan*. It is an individual right. Article 29 speaks of 'sections of citizens ... having a distinct language, script or culture' and Article 30 speaks of 'all minorities whether based on religion or language.' This categorization springs from the census that relies on declaration by the subjects counted. A political minority, on the other hand, is one that is accorded a political status because of their number.

The Roman imperial practice of *divide et impera* is perhaps the first instance of treatment of minorities within the empire. Their 'minorities' were, however, subject peoples. The majority-minority paradigm does not strictly obtain between the masters and the subjects. The British residents in colonial India and South Africa would hardly be regarded as political minorities. The paradigm works between two or more co-lateral groups of people. The 'problem' does not even arise substantially in an absolutist/ authoritarian regime where the people live on the favour of the ruler who may or may not practise discrimination among his/her subjects. The minority problem arises only where people have a share in the governmental power. In other words, it is a problem of representative government not only in respect of legislative and policy-making powers but also in respect of administration.

There is only one case where the Indian Constitution recognized a political minority - that of the Anglo-Indians. The President of India has been authorized to nominate up to two Anglo-Indians to the House of the People if that community is not adequately represented in the House (Article 331). The Governor of a state is similarly authorized to nominate one Anglo-Indian to the State's Legislative Assembly if in his opinion the community is not adequately represented (Article 333). Of course this practice of nomination is temporary. This special provision was made on the consideration of the small number of Anglo-Indian in the country and also an understanding reached by the leaders of the Constituent Assembly of India with the All-India Anglo-Indian Association. The Anglo-Indians were granted reservation of posts in certain services (railways, customs and posts and telegraph) temporarily.

The reservation of seats in the Union and the State legislatures as well as in the public services for the Scheduled Castes and the Scheduled Tribes population of the country was not based on the grant of a minority status to them but on the consideration of their extremely weak and backward status in the Indian society. The legislative reservations are temporary but the reservation in the public services is not. The claims of the members of the Scheduled Castes and Scheduled Tribes shall be taken into consideration consistently with the maintenance of efficiency of administration (Article 335).

The Constitution of the United States of America - the model of liberalism - put a premium on the individual citizenship and did not recognize any group - religious or otherwise - for the grant of rights. By abolishing state control over religion by the First Amendment to her Constitution the USA outlawed religious discrimination. By establishing the hegemony of the English language in public affairs she steam- rollered all linguistic differences. By forbidding deprivation of voting right on the basis of race, colour or previous condition of servitude by the Fifteenth Amendment (1870) she abolished political discrimination against the black people. The references to groups, if implicit, were negative in the sense that the state was prohibited from discriminating against denying a citizen equal protection of the laws (Fourteenth Amendment, 1868). However, the principle of affirmative action has by now been well established in the US constitutional practices. And, though the US Constitution does not recognize any racial, linguistic or religious minorities, such minorities are free to practise their faiths and use their own languages at the family and community levels.

The Indian Constitution prohibits discrimination among citizens on the basis of race, religion, language or place of birth. But it also positively recognizes the cultural and educational rights of the minorities - based either on language or religion. As far as the political rights of the minorities are concerned, the only group enjoying them - the Anglo-Indians - depend solely on the policy of the Union or the State government. The temporal uncertainty about reservation of posts in public services for any 'backward' class of people - including the Scheduled Castes and Scheduled Tribes also pushes it to the domain of policy. Technically they are permissive and not mandatory. Their implementation greatly depends on the ideology and commitment of the Government and the interpretation of the courts of law.

The positive cultural and educational rights granted to religious and cultural minorities in India were provided on the model of the minority treaties that were ordained in several European states created after World War I. During the period between the two World Wars a number of European states were born on the ruins of the Austro-Hungarian Empire. These states had to sign minority treaties before their constitution. Three countries - Poland, Czechoslovakia and Yugoslavia - expressly recognized such rights in their constitutions[5]. They were hardly respected. Most of the new states even resorted to ethnic cleansing.[6] One of the major reasons of World War II was the minority problem.

Race, Religion and Language

Next to gender race is perhaps the oldest method of identification and differentiation. Ancient India had its *mlechchhas,* ancient Greece had its 'barbarians.' One of the causes of the fall of the Roman Empire is said to have been the invasions of the Mongolian 'hordes.' Modern Europe distinguished people by the colour of their skins. Language and religion have been the other criteria of differentiation.

The Reformation and the related bloodbath in Europe taught the people that religion is best kept to the private domain of life. This led to the freeing of the state from the clutch of the church. In England the church was brought under the authority of the state. The First Amendment to the Constitution of the United States of America brought about a complete separation of the church and the state and set up the principle of secularism. This term - 'secularism' - has been given distorted meanings in India ranging from *'Hindutwa'* to *'sarva dharma samabhaba'* ignoring its simple dictionary meaning of attachment to the secular - mundane, profane - fields of society as against the sacred one. Secularism by no means implies atheism. The United States is one of the most devout countries of the world.[7]

The last religious-sectarian war fought in Europe was in Switzerland, and in the year 1847, due to the *Sonderband* secessionist move of seven Catholic cantons led by the Jesuits. The revolt was crushed and the Jesuits expelled after which Switzerland settled down to peaceful inter-sectarian relations to such an extent that, in 1955, the expulsion was rescinded and the Jesuits readmitted. Yet religious identification survived in Europe as a legacy of the Crusade (against the Muslims) besides the traditional dislike for the Jews. The latest manifestation of the Christian-Muslim conflict is the concept of 'clash of civilizations' and the phenomenon of *al Quaida*[8]. Britain tried to make good the past humiliation of the Jews (at the cost of Muslim Arabs) by settling some of them in Palestine. Hitler's slaughter of the Jews only aggravated the Palestine problem.

But since at least the eighteenth century language has been the major rallying point of political divisions as it held the key to power, wealth and education.

The Minority Problem in India in Historical Setting

For a country of India's size, number of population and antiquity the 'race' question can only belong to the domain of myth. The question of religion is almost equally complex. The *sanatana* (traditional) dharma followers got the Arabic name 'Hindu' during the British period. Buddhism and Jainism were indigenous sects that grew as a revolt against the traditional *varna* system in India. Most of the Muslims and Christians in India are converts from indigenous faiths while Sikhism belongs to the synthesizing *bhakti* tradition.

A peculiarity of the Indian religious demography is that no one speaks the language of one's scripture. The only language mistakenly identified with religion is Urdu, a compound of Arabic, Persian and Hindustani *khari boli,* and spoken equally by the Hindus and Muslims in urban north India. (By an equally profound misunderstanding Urdu has been adopted by Pakistan as her national language though it is spoken by the refugees from India alone.) Consequently, there is a great incoherence between religious and linguistic divisions. If organized religion may be said to be the 'national' divider of the Indians, language divides it regionally. (This, incidentally, is the reason for linguistic reorganization of States). At the village level, however, one notices great religious uniformity. On some inexplicable reasons the British thought it prudent to see the Indians through the prism of religion. Though in the Councils of the Governor-General and the Governors, created by the Indian Councils Act of 1861, Indian members were nominated on the communal line, the fact that the British acquired sovereignty on India from a Muslim ruler initially prejudiced them toward the Muslims. Hindus and Sikhs were favoured for government services, civil and military. In 1870 came out *The Indian Musalmans* by W.W. Hunter demanding a re-look at the Government's policy toward the Muslims.

Contrary to popular belief that separate electorate was introduced in India by the Indian Councils Act of 1909 separate electorate was actually introduced in India in 1883, with the introduction of a partly representative local bodies system under the Ripon Reforms. (This, again, is mysterious because in India villages are usually dominated by single communities.) The Indian Councils Act, 1909, introduced representational system at the provincial and the central levels and a separate electorate for the Muslims was introduced there. This separate electorate system was elaborated by the time of the 1935 Reforms into 18 electorates. Since 1925 the Government was reserving a certain portion of services for the religious minorities. Under the Government of India Act, 1935, 25% of the posts were reserved for the communal minorities[9].

Yet the British Cabinet Mission in 1946 recognized only three main communities in their constitutional scheme: Muslim, Sikh and General. Incidentally, it is necessary to note that none of the electoral laws and rules in the British period recognized the Hindu as a community. For that matter, the Indian Independence Act, 1947, did not establish any denominational Dominion.

There is a subtle conflict between minorityism and localism in India both in structural and in behavioural terms. As held above, religion divides the country more than language while language divides the regions more than religion. This does not mean an irrelevance of religion to the composition of a region. There were in the British period and there are still now regions with numerical majority of the 'national minority' population. Pakistan was created with areas having Muslim majority. But, when Pakistan was created more Muslims were left in India than were in Pakistan. The position is unaltered till now. On the other hand, Curzon's misadventure with Bengal Partition in 1905 proved the strength of language over religion at the regional level. Secondly, minority safeguards become important at a larger level of political unity than at a smaller level where the concept of autonomy becomes relevant.

The point has been quite aptly made by Ayesha Jalal though she overstresses it in the case of Mohammad Ali Jinnah who, she claims, was against provincial autonomy and in favour of a united centralized polity with a share of power for the Muslims.[10] She ignores the fact that it was at the Muslim League's 1924 session, presided over by Jinnah, that the demand for a federal structure of India was first raised. The fect is that both the Indian National Congress and the Muslim League were unsure of their strategies. In 1916 at Lucknow the Congress and the League agreed on separate electorate for the Muslims. In 1928 the Nehru Committee conceded federalism but reneged on a separate electorate and Jinnah's Muslim League walked out of the All-Party Conference. The Cabinet Mission messed up the two issues by upholding the principle of provincial autonomy but forcing them to join 'groups' and still sanctioning the communal veto in the proposed Constituent Assembly[11].

Right from the beginning the Indian National Congress denied a separate nationhood to the Indian Muslims. The 'two nations' theory was first expounded by V.D. Savarkar in 1928 and then by Mohammad Ali Jinnah in 1939. In 1920 the Congress Constitution organized its provincial units on linguistic basis. Yet the Nehru Report conceded provincehood to Sindh, a Muslim-majority area, on the ground that Sindhi is a distinct language. According to Paul Brass a similar compromise was made after Independence on the grant of a *Punjabi suba*.[12] Some of the hills states created in 1972 in northeast India happen to be Christian-majority. But they were created as tribal /ethnic states. Two of the three states created in 1990 - Jharkhand and Chhattisgarh - are similar, though there is no Christian majority in either. The creation of Uttarakhand, on the other hand, was solely on geographic and economic considerations.

The religio-linguistic lay out of post-partition India may be described as a Hindi-Hindu 'heartland' surrounded by an 'inner periphery' of non-Hindi, Hindu states and by an 'outer periphery' of non-Hindi, non-Hindu states.[13] The Government of India is firm on the inalienability of Jammu and Kashmir in spite of the overall Muslim majority in the State. It has also resisted the demand for trifurcation of that state along religious-communal lines as demanded by the *Hindutwa* zealots.

The Minorities under the Constitution

After the decision on the partition of India the Constituent Assembly felt free to abolish separate electorate enjoined by the Cabinet Mission plan. In fact, it abolished the concept of political minorities except for the Anglo-Indians as a special case, and that too temporarily. It abolished reservation of posts for the minorities too. Reservation of seats in the legislatures for the Scheduled Castes and the Scheduled Tribes were immediately provided for not as minorities but as underprivileged groups (Articles 330 and 332). Also immediately provided was the recognition of their claims to services and posts of the Government (Article 334). States were allowed to identify other backward classes of citizens not adequately represented in the services for reservation of posts for them (Article 15/4). None of them had a minority status.

A tricky question arises here. The Constitution recognizes religious and linguistic minorities. It has allowed linguistic reorganization of states. It has also allowed tribal states to be constituted. Are the Scheduled Tribes of India on way to be recognized as a minority? One suspects that this apprehension motivates the *Hindutwa* zealots to be violently sensitive to the question of conversion causing the murder of Graham Staines and the Dangs carnage in 1998. The fear is unfounded. Of the total tribal population of India that itself is 8% of India's total population only about a quarter is Christian. In fact, among all the religious communities in India the Christians have the lowest population growth and their share in India's total population is decreasing. The three Christian-majority states of northeast India that alarm the zealots constitute less than 0.5% of India's total population.[14]

The *Hindutwa* zealots make a major mistake in counting Buddhists, Jainas and Sikhs as Hindus. The Constitution of India considers them as equivalent to Hindus, as will be presently seen, only for a specific purpose. They are religious minorities for all other purposes. Even the Census counts them separately from the Hindus.

Secularism and the Indian Constitution

But the greatest confusion relates to the concept of secularism. In a simplistic way even some intellectuals, including members of the highest courts, define it in terms of *sarva dharma samabhava* whereas its literal meaning is to be attached to secular, that is, the mundane/profane affairs. The principle is embodied in the First Amendment to the Constitution of the United States of America: 'Congress shall make no law respecting an establishment of religion, or prohibiting the free exercise thereof. This is not the 'Protestant spirit'. Protestantism freed the state from the clutches of religion. In England the Reformation actually put the Church of England under the authority of the state. The First Amendment not only freed the church from the state but also prohibited the state's patronage as well as hostility to religion. If Congress could not make a law on religious establishments it could not punish or grant favour to any of them.

The Indian Constitution, originally, did not use the word 'secular' in the Preamble. The Forty-fourth Amendment brought the term in. The criticism that the Constitution did not define the word secularism is naive because no Constitution defines the terms it uses. Not even the Constitution of the USA defined secularism. But the Indian Constitution made a distinction between the secular and the sacred affairs of the society in the very Article that sanctioned the right to freedom of religion (Article 25) when it authorized the state to control the 'secular' activities associated with religious practice (Article 25/2/a). Of course Article 25 grants all persons the freedom of conscience and the right freely to profess, practise and propagate religion subject to public order, morality and health and other provisions in Part III of the Constitution. Article 26, further, grants to every religious denomination or any section thereof, subject to public order, morality and health, the right to establish and maintain institutions for religious and charitable purposes, to manage its own affairs in matters of religion, to own and acquire movable and immovable property and to administer such property in accordance with law and, certainly, within the overarching limitations of Article 25(2)(a).

Article 27 forbids the state to collect taxes from any person specifically toward payment of expenses for the promotion or maintenance of any particular religion. This is not the prohibition of *Jaziya* that was actually a tax collected from the non-Muslim pilgrims for the general revenue. This is a prohibition of general collection of taxes toward the benefit of particular religions. The prohibition, however, is deceptive. The Indian state, both at the Union and the unit levels, collect general revenue for general purposes. Nothing prevents it from allocating portions of the government money to religious institutions and religious affairs. Support to the maintenance of religious institutions, pilgrimages and even religious festivals and functions to the extent of financing free lunch *(prasadam, a la* Jayalalitha 2002) violate norms of secularism. More important, it dissatisfies every religious community.

The extent of confusion about secularism even at the highest level of the judiciary is revealed in the benchmark judgement on the *S.R. Bommai* case that generally upheld the inviolability of secularism. From a nine-judge bench six separate judgements were issued, Chief Justice, A.M. Ahmadi's judgement being a 'dissenting' one. Apparently, the only major difference of Ahmadi's judgement with the others consisted in the following observation of the former on Article 27:

> This is an important Article which prohibits the exercise of the State's taxation power if the yields thereof are intended to be appropriated in payment of expenses for the promotion and maintenance of any particular religion or religious denomination. That means that State's revenue cannot be utilized for the promotion or maintenance of any particular religion or religious group.[15]

Incidentally, Article 25(2)(b) has been the victim of some misunderstanding, if not deliberate misinterpretation. It has been held to be discriminatory against the Hindus who are alleged to have been singled out for reform giving Hinduism a bad name. The truth is that the reference to 'the throwing open of Hindu religious institutions of public character to all classes and sections of the Hindus' has a definite context: the temple entry movement of the 1920-30s. It has also to be read along with Article 17 that abolishes untouchability. For the same purpose the Sikhs, the

Buddhists and the Jainas are included within the span of the Hindus because they have, positively or negatively, been connected with the *varna* system and may become victims of untouchability. Both Buddhism and Jainism revolted against the *varna* system. Several conversions of the dalits to Buddhism in the recent decades definitely highlight the untouchability aspect. The Sikh religion has untouchable castes within its fold.

Article 25(2)(a), it should be noted, has two parts. It enables the state to throw open the Hindu religious institutions of public character. Before that, it generally authorizes the state to provide for social welfare and reform. Much of the state assistance toward the religious places, pilgrimages and festivals go in the name of 'social welfare'. It is the word 'reform' that proves to be the bone of contention. On the one hand, allegations have been made that only Hindus have been targeted for social reform (like women's succession and marital rights and prevention of *sati)* while a common civil code has not been established encompassing the Muslims. On the other hand, a section of the Muslims feel that their personal law is ordained by the scriptures and cannot be changed. The issue is contentious. What needs to be noted, however, is that there is no prohibition on the state with regard to social reform of any religious community. There is no prefix to the word 'reform' in Article 25(2)(a) other than 'sonit'.

The Constitution of India issues the directive to the state to endeavour to secure for the citizens a 'uniform', *not* a common, civil code (Art. 44). Like most other directive principles of state policy this directive is yet to be implemented. The most cogent explanation of this failure is obtained from a statement of P.V. Narasimha Rao on the floor of the Lok Sabha:

> The law of evidence is common, the civil procedure code is common, the Criminal Procedure Code is common, every law in the civic field is common. What is not common is the personal law part of it. Unless the affected people concur, the personal law will not be changed. Personal laws in India vary widely. The Hindu *dattak* system, for instance, is legally untenable (paraphrased).[16]

Contemporary debates in the social sciences point out that group rights may be oppressive on individual citizens. Muslim personal law in India is certainly oppressive on Indian Muslim women, in fact, more oppressive than in Islamic states, as pointed out by several women's organizations. It needs a strength and determination on the part of a Government to modify them. However, this is not sufficient reason for the majority community to demand the preservation of archaic systems of oppression like the *sati* and the dowry. At the same time it does not justify the cultivation of minority sensitivities for the sheer purpose of electoral politics as happened in 1987, following the *Shah Bano case* judgement of the Supreme Court of India. The Muslim Women (Protection of Rights on Divorce Act) was a deliberate defiance of the judgement. It literally adopted the provisions of the *shariat* into secular law.[17]

Several political observers have commented that the 1987 legislation was intended to offset the anger of the orthodox Muslims who had been infuriated by the opening of the gate of the Babari Masjid to Hindu religious worship in 1986. It gave a boost to the Ram Janambhoomi movement of the Bharatiya Janata Party (BJP) and its *Sangh Parivar* associates and led to the *Ratha Yatra* of L.K. Advani with the election symbol of the party - the lotus - at its head in October 1990, fall of the V.P. Singh Government and ultimately, on 6 December 1992, the demolition of the Babari Masjid in the presence of Advani and other BJP leaders resulting in horrible communal riots throughout the country. The status of minorities permanently changed to that of second-class citizens.

Constitutionally, the fact of being a member of a minority community does not disqualify or downgrade anyone as a citizen. Article 14 forbids the state to deny to any person equality before the law or the equal protection of law within the territory of India. Article 15 forbids it to discriminate against any citizen on grounds only of religion, race, caste, sex, place of birth or any of them. The fact that the special provisions about the minorities and the backward classes are listed after the general provisions of Articles 14 and 15 means that they are in addition to the general rights. The second point about Article 15 is that it does not mention language. This indicates two things: The Constituent Assembly hoped that the language rights would be taken care of by the eventual linguistic reorganization of states. But it also put a premium of concern on religious difference over linguistic difference.

If minority rights are, therefore, a sub-set of fundamental rights of the citizens, minority politics is a subset of general politics. The basic truth about rights is that they are to be protected by the state. The attitude of the state anywhere depends upon the ideology of the Government, the prevailing social attitude and pressures from the citizens. This requires the state to be secular in India. Minority politics, on its part, is a part of the pressure tactics of the minority group that sees the state to be failing in its assigned role. The most violent manifestation. of conflict on language is the language riots for which Assam is famous but to which many other states and regions are no strangers. The rise of the Shiv Sena in Maharashtra is partly associated with the language riots in the city of Bombay and the Maharashtra-Karnataka border in the recent decades. While most of the language riots are intra-state and inter-state affairs, it required the language riot of 1965 in Madras (Tamil Nadu) to checkmate what was called 'Hindi imperialism'. But the pride of place (!) is held by religious-communal riots if we exclude the recent caste wars as out of the scope of the present article.

Communal Conflicts and Conversion

The question of the prevailing social attitude about the minorities leads one into the question of what in the West is generally known as the 'race relations' and in India 'the communal problem'. In a simplistic logic 'communalism' is counterposed to secularism in India. The object of communalism is secular gain. It differs from secularism only in respect of strategy - the symbol(s) that it uses. It is not necessary for a communalist to believe in religion at all. In fact, the really devout people are rarely communal. No one can accuse Moulana Abul Kalam Azad as a communal person though no one will doubt his attachment to religion. On the other hand, Mohammad Ali Jinnah, a communal leader par excellence since the late 1920s, was hardly known as a devout person.[18] The difference between communalism and secularism lies in the fact that communalism is a social phenomenon, secularism is an institutional phenomenon. They operate at different levels. A contradiction takes place between two forces when they operate on the same plane.

Communalism has different manifestations: cultural, social and political. Culturally it seeks hegemony of the community or fights the hegemony of the other communities. Socially it seeks to exclude the others from a community's sphere of operation. Politically it seeks to control and dominate the other groups. In the days of the growing role of the state every community seeks to control the state and use the levers of its power. Elections, mobilization, agitations and virtual wars - communal riots - are the means that the communalists adopt.

Between the Great Calcutta Killings of August 1946 and the post-Godhra communal carnage of February-March 2002, the two party-sponsored virtual wars, hundreds of communal riots have occurred in this country. Paul Brass has calculated the number of communal riots between 1954 and 1982 as 6933.[19] His comments indicate the close connection between communal riots and politics.

> The numbers of communal incidents and of persons killed in them increased significantly between the mid-1960s and 1982 - the last year for which official figures are available.... It is evident from the figures that, with rare exceptions, the numbers of Muslims killed were usually much higher than the numbers of Hindus. Moreover, in most major riots police firings are directed disproportionately at Muslim mobs and many of the Muslims killed in these riots are killed in the police firings themselves, rather than by Hindu rioters.[20]

Not all communal riots originate out of politics. There may be strong social and economic causes of a communal riot. But the truth is, whenever a major communal riot takes place, political parties enter the field. A recent phenomenon in the communal situation in the country is the number of violent incidents in connection with conversions of dalits and tribal people to Christianity and Islam. In the immediate post-Independence period Hindu organizations, with the backing of the state, tried to politically discourage conversion of the tribals to Christianity. Christian Missions were not allowed in the North-East Frontier Tracts though the Rama Krishna Mission was allowed to set up Schools there. In 1967 Orissa and, in 1968, Madhya Pradesh passed their Freedom of Religions Acts to check conversion. There is no evidence of their being implemented rigorously as there is no evidence of any large-scale conversion of the tribal people in these states thereafter. In October 2002, three weeks before the convening of the Legislative Assembly session the Government of Tamil Nadu issued the Tamil Nadu Prohibition of Forcible Conversion Ordinance requiring the reporting of every conversion to the District Magistrate. An unusually high penalty was fixed for such conversion, particularly in the case of dalits. Doubtless, the Ordinance was turned into an Act immediately after the convening of the Assembly session after a debate of three hours.[21] (Ibid.).

The conversion issue was brought to the centre-stage of Indian politics in 1982 when a batch of dalits converted themselves to Islam at the village of Meenakshipuram in Tamil Nadu. In 1954, when B.R. Ambedkar had converted himself to Buddhism the incident was only noted with a benign remorse probably because Ambedkar was too important a personality to be browbeaten and of a self-indulgent theory that Buddhism was, after all, a branch of Hinduism. There was no Ambedkar at Meenakshipuram and the beneficiaries of the conversion were the Muslims. The Vishwa Hindu Parishad, an innocuous organization set up in 1964 with moderate Hindu leaders like Dr Karan Singh, at once dropped its moderate garb and became active against the depletion of the Hindu rank. Very soon it became the vanguard of the Ram Janambhoomi movement. It was alleged to be involved in the murder by burning of Grahan Staines, a health missionary working in the tribal belt of Orissa, along with his minor children, and massacre of Christian tribals in the Dangs district of Orissa in 1998. Its influence grew so fast that some of its *sadhus* got elected to the Lok Sabha in 1991 on the ticket of the Bharatiya Janata party.

Ironically, when five dalits were lynched by upper-caste Hindus in the district of Jhajjar in Haryana, in the evening of the *Dasserah* day (15 October) of 2002, the Viswa Hindu Parishad leaders publicly defended the lynching with the false plea that the dalits had actually skinned a live cow. About a hundred dalits' immediately responded by converting themselves into Buddhism, Christianity and Islam. The conversion, as already noted, was not the first incident of its kind. Its history can be traced to at least the Meenakshipurm conversion in 1982. Its significance lies in the fact that the dalits were ready to pay its price. Under the Indian Constitution, while a Scheduled Tribe person retains his/her reservation benefits, a member of a Schedule Caste, on being converted, loses them.

Incidentally, the *Hindutwa* zealots vehemently protest against the enjoyment of the benefits of reservation by the Christian members of the Scheduled Tribes as they are held by the former to be converts. The fact is that there is no earthly reason to consider the members of the Scheduled Tribes to be 'originally' Hindus. They were never part of the *varna* system that is the mark of Hindu status.

2003

NOTES AND REFERENCES

1. See B. Shiva Rao, *The Framing of India's Constitution: Select Documents, Vol 2,* New Delhi, Indian Institute of Public Administration, 1967, p. 336-37.
2. *Ibid.*, Vol. 1, 1966, p. 558.
3. Acharya Dr. Durgadas Basu, *Introduction to the Constitution of India,* Seventeenth Edition, New Delhi, Prentice-Hall of India, 1995, p. 405 (Emphasis in original).
4. Shibani Kinkar Chaube, *Constituent Assembly of India: Springboard of Revolution,* (1973) , Second Revised Edition, New Delhi, Manohar, 2000. Ayesha Jalal, *The Sole Spokesman: Jinnah, the Muslim League and the Demand for Partition,* Cambridge, Cambridge University Press, 1985.
5. James Wilford Garner, *Political Science and Government,* 1935), Indian Reproduction, Calcutta, The World Press, 1951, p. 150 fn.
6. *Ibid.*, pp. 151-54.
7. For a further discussion of this question see S.K. Chaube, 'The Domain of Secularism,' *Social Science Probings* SSP, Vols. 7-8 March 1990-December 1991; 'Communalism and Secularism in India,' in K. Raghavendra Rao, Ashok K. Maiti, Debabrata Panda and N.P. Chaubey (Eds), *Fifty Years of India's Freedom,* Allahabad, Indian Academy of Social Sciences, 1997, pp. 177-85; 'Indian Secularism: The Place of Religion in Human Life,' *The Statesman,* 21 January 1997.
8. S.K. Chaube, 'Democracy and Co-existence of Civilizations' in D.D. Khanna and Gert W. Kueck (Eds), *Conflict Resolution, Human Rights and Democracy,* Delhi, Shipra Publications, 2003, pp. 58-73.
9. B. Shiva Rao, op. cit., Vol. 5, p. 743.
10. Ayesha Jalal, op. cit., pp. 1 0-11.
11. See Shibani Kinkar Chaube, *Constituent Assembly,* pp. 40-41.
12. Paul R. Brass, *Language, Religion and Politicas in India,* New Delhi, Vikash Publishing House, 1975, pp. 404-05.

13. Durga Das Basu is angry with the creation of Muslim-majority districts in Kerala in 1967-69 and 1983. He considers this trend to be paving the way for the creation of a second Pakistan. See Durga Das Basu, op. cit., p. 421.
14. See S.K. Chaube, 'The Scheduled Tribes and Christianity in India', *Economic and Political Weekly.* Vol. XXXIV No. 9, February 27-March 5, 1999.
15. *Judgements Today,* Vol. 2, No. 8, 21 March 1994. See also S.K. Chaube, 'The Supreme Court, Federalism and Secularism in India, ' *Trends in Social Science Research,* Vol. 1, No. 1, June 1994.
16. *Lok Sabha Debates,* 12 June 1996, Column 76.
17. Paul R. Brass, *The Politics of India Since Independence,* Cambridge University Press, Second Edition, 1994, p. 233.
18. Bipan Chandra, 'Communalism—The Way Out' and 'Communalism as Ideology' in Bipan Chandra, *Essays on Contemporary India,* New Delhi, Har-Anand Publications, 1993, pp. 127-36 and 148-59, respectively.
19. *Ibid.,* p. 240.
20. *Ibid.,* p. 239.
21. *The Hindu,* 30 October 2002.

16

Tribal Movements : Social and Political

Tribal Solidarity

It is perhaps a reflection of the problems of defining a tribe that 'tribes' never emerged as a legal category in British India. They were used as descriptive terms like 'agricultural tribes' and 'criminal tribes'? but they never found place in the various 'reforms' like the Indian Councils Acts, and the Government of India Acts. In the British period they were merely residents of 'backward tracts'. Under the partial exclusion scheme they were given a restricted representation in the legislatures first through nomination (1919) and subsequently (1935) through election. The Indian Constitution too did not define a tribe but left it to the government to identify them. Under the Indian Constitution tribal rights are partly all-India and partly location-specific; but tribal administration, including tribal development administration, is only location specific.

From Jarwa to Mina the variety of tribal socio-economic conditions virtually tell the entire story of India's historical development from the primitive to the modern life. The challenges to their life range from scarcity of the basic needs of life like food and shelter, through the degeneration of their environment, to the reservation in jobs and higher education. Interestingly, however, the two ends of the scale are singularly free from what S.C. Sinha called 'the tribal solidarity movement'. The tribes of Andaman and Nicobar are too weak to assert their solidarity and rights. The Minas are too advanced to need a solidarity movement. They are a conscious pressure group.

Number and location are important factors of a solidarity movement. The tribes of Andaman and Nicobar are not only small in number but also fragmented by the Bay of Bengal. The tea garden tribes of Assam were uprooted from their homeland a century ago and are heterogeneous. They are on the way to forming an industrial working class. Solidarity movements grow where the tribes are substantial in number, localized and homogeneous.

The major concentration of tribal people in India forms an interesting pattern - along all the hill ranges from the Eastern Himalayas, including the Patkai and the Barail, to the Meghalaya, then, across the Ganga, to the Vindhya, including Chhotanagpur, to the Aravali with small protrusions to the south (the Eastern Ghats and the Deccan).

Roy-Burman points out that the Scheduled Tribes are mostly found 'in the meeting points of dominant lingua-political formations like Assam and West Bengal, West Bengal and Bihar, Bihar and Orissa, Orissa and Andhra Pradesh, Andhra Pradesh and Madhya Pradesh, Madhya Pradesh and Maharashtra, Maharashtra and Gujarat. These are the regions where the bulk of the known natural resources of the country, of great economic value, are concentrated. The implications of this pattern of distribution for the cultural, economic and political processes of the country have of late come up to sharp focus thanks to Bodoland movement, Jharkhand movement, Gondowanaland movement, Adivasijhan movement and similar other movements'.[1]

The 1991 census shows the Scheduled Tribes as constituting 8% of the Indian population with a decennial growth rate slightly higher than the all-India average. Yet the number of the Scheduled Tribes is estimated differently. In 1970 Roy Burman, as the Deputy Registrar-General, calculated it to be 427. In 1990 the Ministry of Welfare, Government of India, put the number at 258. This discrepancy is due to the overlapping enlistment of several tribes.[2] A group may be identified as a tribe, a sub-tribe or a caste in different states. In the absence of a rigorous definition of the tribe, ethnic identities are politically created and recreated all the time.

Social Movements

The theoretical premise of this paper is that there can be no social movement totally devoid of politics. In the first place all social movements ultimately involve power. They are aimed at either supporting a social structure or reforming it or destroying it. Therefore the existing system of authority is either positively or negatively involved.

This proposition enables us to prepare a classificatory scheme for the movements. Social movements may be in the nature of protest. All protests are against 'undesirable' changes and are, therefore, aimed at restoration of an older order perceived to be comparatively better.

There can equally be movements in support of changes proposed or already introduced. Such movements are reformative. A movement for reform may originate outside the structure of authority as well as within it. Usually, however, persons in authority oppose such reform. Depending on the intensity of the reformists' desire, successive frustrations or a persistent stand-off may lead to a revolutionary situation. Whether the revolution succeeds or produces the desired result is another matter.

The other reason why social movements tend to be mixed up with politics is the all-encompassing nature of the modern states' power. Within the civil society interested people may try to build their 'community' outside the domain of the state. But this effort itself involves politics. The task is somewhat easier in the colonial context where the rulers and the ruled form distinct classes/ segments in the polity. A democratic system, on the other hand, works against such insulation in two ways.

First, it extends individual rights to members of all 'communities' and drafts or, at least, seeks to draft them into the system. On the other hand, using this logic of individual rights, democracy fosters a majoritarian ideology under which group rights become difficult to assert.

A people under an alien rule tends to carve out its own community. Hence one finds frequent use of the term 'samaj' in the nineteenth century discourse. This 'samaj' is different from the civil society and very often identified with castes. Because of the absence of the caste system in Islam the community was straightaway identified with religion with the name of Anjuman. Both these concepts served as the foci of social reform and even of resistance to colonial pressure. The Associations, Leagues and even the Congresses that began to emerge since about the end of the nineteenth century were the generalized, secularized and political forms of the samaj and the Anjuman. They did not keep themselves insulated from the Empire. Rather, they took part in it and bargained with its rulers.

Pure social movements, therefore, all but disappeared in the twentieth century India except in the tribal belts where certain degrees of autonomy prevailed. Even these movements came to the verge of politics, when they articulated their dream of pristine independence, and came to be suppressed by imperial might.

When I undertook a study of the political situation in northeast India[3] there were two kinds of 'approaches' available: (1) anthropological, thorough but fragmented, and (2) political, entirely journalistic. Verrier Elwin had tried to integrate the macro and the micro views but was handicapped by his office.

I was personally so impressed by the sophisticated level of politics that characterized northeast India at the time that I refused to regard it as tribal politics and called it 'hill politics'. Besides, I am still convinced that, I was able to identify some broad economic factors of the volatility of north-east India. I was, in any case, struck by the political consequences of the social developments in northeast India.

In 1996 K.S. Singh classified the tribal movements in India (outside NE India) into the following groups:

(i) Movements for political autonomy,

(ii) Agrarian and forest-based movements.

(iii) Sanskritization processes, and

(iv) Cultural movements based on script and languages.[4]

Theoretically a process is a much broader concept than a movement. Therefore, the Bhagat movement, based on the purity-pollution model and anti-drink thrusts may be regarded as a movement but the general process of Sanskritization should not be treated as a movement. In any case, there is no cut-off point of its antiquity.

The initial resistance that almost all tribes of India put up to the colonial rulers or the Jarwas and the Sentinelese are still putting to penetration of administration, often violently, also cannot be regarded as a movement. They were gut reactions, total and unpremeditated wars against the encroaching system.

A movement is intra-systemic, mostly pre-meditated though possibly warlike, being based on rejection of a system. Tribal economic movements are older than tribal autonomy movements. Such economic movements have had three major issues : Money-lenders' exploitation, land-grabbing and forest rights. The British could act against money-lenders with less hesitation than against land-grabbers for, though their own revenue system had forced the tribals to borrow money, they were not money-lenders themselves. Action against land-grabbing was softer because the government itself had grabbed land. On reserved forests, however, there was a virtual denial of tribal rights as forests had been turned into state property. The position remains more or less the same today with restriction on land alienation of different degrees being enforced in several states but little restoration of tribal land.

Boundary and reference point

The first pre-requisite of a social movement is that the community must have an identity or must aim at defining it. In other words, the community must have a boundary. This leads to the second requirement, namely, a comparative reference point. The Renaissance had a reference point in the Graeco-Roman past of Europe. Hindu social movements in the nineteenth century were based on the dream of a golden age as well as a response to the Western rule. The same can be said of the Wahabi and the Faraizi movements except for the fact that their dream related to the Turko-Arab golden age. The Aligarh movement was more influenced by the West than by an Arab golden age as is evident from Saayed Ahmed's criticism of the Khilafat. The tribal groups of Central India had their non-tribal neighbours for reference. Their solidarity movements borrowed heavily from the non-tribal neighbourhood in order to establish their tribal identity.

Social bases of autonomy movement

This happened when the process of Hinduization stopped. In the 15-16th century a wave of state formation based on the 'Rajput model' eswcept central India. The process is noticed even in the eastern frontiers like in Manipur, Tripura, Cooch Behar and Jaintia.

State formation in tribal societies is a universal phenomenon springing from surplus generation. Hinduization in actual terms meant caste-formation with the ruling class assuming the Kshatriya status. A number of ruling classes, however, wavered between the caste and the tribal statuses like the Bhumij in Jharkhand and Tripuri or Koch Rajbanshi in northeast India. It seems that autonomy movements have a fertile ground in regions which have not been adequately casteized.

This proposition is independent of the linguistic state movement. In the first place, no tribe has been able to develop a language commanding a substantial following. Secondly, formation of linguistic state was roughly completed by 1966, but the autonomy movement was not over. In 1972, the large-scale reorganization of northeast India was actually a challenge to the linguistic principle. Thirdly, casteization of a tribal polity leads to its feudalization and is unfavourable to the middle class demand of linguistic state. (The formation of Rajasthan, it may be noted, was more an administrative than a political act).

Here a distinction between regionalism and autonomy movements is necessary. Caste is of course a regional phenomenon and Charan Singh's advocacy of partition of UP was partly dictated by considerations of caste but he did not stand for autonomy of any region. By that token the movement for greater power of the states is different from tribal autonomy movements.

Politicization

It is not necessary to give a record of the numerous tribal unrests in India since the British took over control of this country. Upto the middle of the 19th century what happened in the tribal belts was total rejection of and war against the British. Revolts did take place even after 1858. All of them were unsuccessful in most cases resulting in the loss of nerve and in some cases resulting in violent messiahnic movements e.g. of the Birsa movement of the Munda in 1899-1900 and the Jadonang-Guidinlieu movement of the Kabui in the early 1930s.

In more cases, however, there was introspection among the enlightened sections of the tribes. Many of them chose to be converted to Christianity in pursuit mainly of worldly progress. Some educated Christians formed associations for the promotion of education among their brethren like the Lutheran graduates of the Jharkhand area who founded a Christian Association in

1898. Some took upon themselves the task of revival of their communities through sustained cultural movements. They adopted Hindu as well as Christian rituals but rediscovered and, in some cases, invented religious symbols akin to their culture. The All-India Kurmi Kshatriya Mahasabha (1894) in Bihar and the Seng Khasi in the Khasi hills (1899) were the first such bodies.

It was in this context that politics appeared in the tribal world, particularly in eastern India. The correspondence of this appearance with the politics of the country is remarkable. Closely on the heel of the partition of Bengal Presidency, in 1906, a Catholic Cooperative Society was formed for 'civilizing' the aboriginals. At the next crucial juncture of 1911-12 a students' conference was held at Dacca, the seat of Muslim League politics deeply concerned with the annulment of Bengal partition. J. Bartholomew, another Jharkhandi of Anglican Mission, attended the conference and in his native area formed a branch of the Dacca Students' Union to raise funds for education of poor Christian students.[5]

During World War I, and on the eve of the Non-cooperation movement, a Chhotanagpur Improvement Society is formed to demand that 'Whatever may be done in the way of reform elsewhere, the aborigines of Chhotanagpur may be left to the administration of European officers'. Shortly, thereafter, the Naga Club demands of the 'Montagu-Chelmsford Commission exclusion of the Naga hills from the scope of the reforms. The Mont-ford Reform provides for total or partial exclusion of the backward tracts from the scope of the Reforms. In 1923 the Khasi National Durbar is formed. During the visit of the Simon Commission British officers go out of their way to suggest exclusion of the tribal-inhabited areas of British India from the scope of Reforms.

It was during the Civil Disobedience Movement of 1930 that satyagrahas were reported from some of the tribal belts. After the collapse of the Civil Disobedience Movement Gandhi paid attention toward constructive programme in the Central Indian tribal belt. Neither the Civil Disobedience Movement nor the constructive programme could enter the hills of northeast India because of travel restrictions on outsiders. Yet, in 1930, Guidinlieu used Gandhi's name in the Manipur hills. It was at this stage that some forest and land movements were started among the tribal population of middle India.

It was around the introduction of the 1935 Reforms that political autonomy movements started cropping up. In 1934 the Khasi States' Federation, in 1938 the Adivasi Mahasabha of Jharkhand and the demand for a Gond land in 1941 were the precursors of the tribal autonomy movements of today.

Autonomy movements today

There are two active, though somewhat disoriented, autonomy movements among the tribal people : the Bodoland movement and the Jharkhand movement. Both of them gained certain results from the respective state governments of Assam and Bihar of course through the good offices of the Union government. The partial success fractured both the movements which had never been monoliths anyway. Fulfilment of autonomy movements in northeast India earlier had left their dissidents too. The most powerful dissidence was in Nagaland where the unspecified 'remaining issues' (of agreement) have been made use of by the opposition. A related question has been the settlement of the Manipur Naga areas on which there is sharp intertribal disagreement.

After the consolidation of the British Raj the tribal protests were gradually contained. The tribals reorganized, or at least tried to reorganize, themselves through, first, socio-cultural movements and then economic movements. The autonomy movements come late as a result of several factors. There was frustration of their socio-economic demands. There was a realization of their numerical weakness compounded by their inability to meet the electoral requirement. There was some hope in their territorial concentration and insulation. Missionary education gave them a further hope of fulfilment of their dreams by collaboration with the Empire and carving their niches away from the humdrum of nationalist politics.

The Empire was partly successful, by blocking the tribals' communication with the non-tribal world, to create a mutual distrust. To a certain extent the legacies persist.

The protections of the Constitution of free India have of course removed some of the causes of their grievances. But their land is under constant assault of outsiders who make use of the loopholes of law. And they are deprived of access to forest.

But the Constitution has given them a new set of rights and opportunities which they are utilizing. Why, then, still the ethnocentrism or regionalism? The answer is simple. Electoral democracy in the prevailing economic scarcity is generating them not only among the tribals, but also among virtually all sections of the society. The fact that the tribals are ready to make use of them is, on the other hand, a sure sign of growth.

1999

NOTES AND REFERENCES

1. B.K. Roy Burman, *Tribes in Perspective,* New Delhi, Mittal Publications, 1994, pp. 6-7.
2. *Ibid,* p. 1.
3. Shibani Kinkar Chaube, *Hill Politics in North-East India,* Calcutta, Orient Longman,1973.
4. K.S. Singh (ed.), *Tribal Movements in India,* Vol. 2, New Delhi, Manohar, 1983, pp. xx.
5. K.S. Singh, 'Tribal Autonomy Movements in Chhotanagpur' in K.S. Singh, op. cit.

17
Interethnic Politics in Northeast India*

In this paper interethnic politics implies the politics of conflict and collaboration among ethnic groups within a political system. Political power in modern times is organized within a territorial limit and inevitably cuts across as well as limits several ethnic groups. The enquiry is devoted to an analysis of the extent to which primordial ethnic affinities survive or, constrained by the overwhelming power of the state, merge into new alignments and develop alternative aspirations. The story of interethnic politics in northeast India is the story of disintegration of a once composite state of Assam. It has not made Assam, long in quest of linguistic homogeneity, a unilingual state but has given birth to a number of relatively homogeneous states dominated by different Scheduled Tribes or their alliances but hardly tribal in content. Abandoning the dream of "tribal" freedom the dominant elite in the hill areas aspire for territorial autonomy within India. The territorial system of government has drastically altered the orientation of ethnic aspirations of the northeast Indians and has given birth to new political identities. The chief instruments of this reorientation are an educated and modernized elite who, notwithstanding their desire to preserve regional autonomy, became the agents of integration.

This situation may be compared with the North West Frontier Province of Pakistan where ethnic aspirations are being fused into secular democratic movement.

*This is a revised version of a discussant paper submitted to the VIIIth World Congress of Sociology, Toronto, August, 1974. Undertaking sole responsibility for the views expressed here, the author wishes to thank Barun De, Amalendu Guha, Partha Chatterjee, and Sunil Munsi of the Centre for Studies in Social Sciences, Calcutta, and S. K. Ghosh of Burdwan University for their comments and suggestions.

Interethnic politics in northeast India, now comprising five states (Assam, Manipur, Meghalaya, Nagaland and Tripura) and two Union territories (Arunachal Pradesh and Mizoram), have assumed a critical dimension due to three reasons: (1) the ethnocultural background of the region, (2) loss of direct contact of much of the territory with the Indian mainland after creation of East Pakistan (now Bangladesh) and (3) nationalist sensitivity about territorial integrity of the country. Foreign influences have been noticed in particular sectors of the politics of the region. Economic backwardness and a communication gap have been considered to be the objective factors, while tribalism, Christianity, elite conflict and subnationalism have been identified to be the native subjective limitations. It is our hypothesis that no foreign influence can be effective on a soil which is not prepared to receive it. At the same time, no native category is permanent since every historical situation is subject to the process of change.

Thus Fürer -Haimendorf (1945), while characterizing the many rebellions of aboriginal tribes of peninsular India as "defensive movements", distinguished the occasional risings of the frontier tribes as "more in the nature of resistance to the establishment of Government's authority than a challenge to the administration." While the tribes in central and peninsular India had long lost their political freedom and were struggling merely for economic survival, the frontier tribes were waging a *political* struggle against British rule. Even such rebellions became infrequent since the beginning of this century.

The Political Heritage of Northeast India

Once "the North-East Frontier of Bengal" (Mackenzie, 1884), this region, in 1947, consisted of one composite province (Assam), two mostly hilly native states (Manipur and Tripura), 25 lesser chiefships in the Khasi hills and an unadministered Naga "tribal area". With the partition of British India a Bengali-speaking and Muslim-majority district of Assam (Sylhet) went to East Pakistan. The Khasi chiefships were annexed to Assam while Manipur and Tripura were left as separate states within India. Plains Assam retained the Bengali-dominated districts of Cachar and a substantial Bengali-speaking population in the entire Brahmaputra Valley. Partition brought in thousands of Bengali refugees, mostly

Hindu, but the Muslim population of Assam did not emigrate. The lesser ethnic groups in the Valley were the "plains tribes" and "other backward groups", and the non-Bengali immigrants, trading and working (mostly in tea-gardens). There was bulk emigration of Muslims from Tripura.

Part of the ethnic complexity of the region must be traced in the ethno-cultural factors. Migrations from different directions from the pre-historic period have completely confused the racial picture. Hinduism penetrated the organized states of the area long before the British advent but hardly cast its spell below their feudal hierarchy and its paraphernalia. This explains the presence there in large number of half-Hindus. But since the British period, needs of administration, tea plantations and oil industry caused the bulk of immigration in the 19th century and even the 1961 census showed the urban areas of Assam as mainly non-Assamese. Reclamation of waste land brought in Muslim peasants from East Bengal since the early twentieth century. The fact that there was no major tension over the Muslim question, in spite of an administrative "line system" meant for checking settlement of Muslim peasants, introduced in the wake of the national Khilafat agitation of 1919-21, shows that the ethnic tension is but a function of modern politics. Discrimination between "local" and "domiciled" people was introduced early in this century in the wake of agitations in Bengal.

Ethnic Politics and Elite Articulations

The grievances were clearly confined to the emerging middle class. Their demand for Assamese as an additional court language of the Brahmaputra Valley was accepted only in 1872. From the 1920's the Muslim question became significant partly because of the electoral potential of Muslims vis-à-vis the reformed provincial legislature and partly because an independent Assamese Muslim, Saadulla, emerged into the ministerial leadership and inducted some Brahmaputra Valley Muslims into the Government services. About the time of transfer of power, the Pakistan question increased suspicion against the Muslims. The same fears have been directed against Bengali Hindus after partition, Bengali Muslims in the Brahmaputra Valley having mostly declared themselves Assamese. In spite of several "language disturbances", however, due to the sparse distribution of the Bengalis as well as the cross-cutting cleavage of religion, there has been no major demand of Bengali separatism, except occasionally in Cachar, dominated by the Bengalis.

The "plains tribal movement" in the Brahmaputra Valley is stigmatized by the lack of regional compactness as well as of an articulate middle-class elite. The hill districts of Assam, administered separately from the plains since the British days, have, on the other hand, emerged into *separate* hill states precisely because of their compactness of elite articulation. The "frontier tracts" have become Arunachal Pradesh purely through administrative initiative and without any agitation. Arunachal Pradesh is much less self-governing and much less politicized than the other Union territory, Mizoram.

The Manipur kings used to control parts of the neighbouring Naga and Kuki-Mizo hills until their take-over by the British at about the end of the 19th century. To some extent, administration of these hills resembled that of the Assam hills, both inhabited by numerous tribal groups. In both these areas Christian churches got official encouragement. Slightly falling behind the Assam hills, the Manipur hills have recently obtained District Councils. Hill Tripura, on the other hand, was always under the rule of a Hindu tribal Raja who settled Bengali Hindus and Muslims. After partition Bengalis have far out-numbered the tribals, who are in a miserable stage of battle for survival, expressed through occasional violence and leftist politics. Absence of protection has disinherited the Tripura tribal of their only wealth, i.e., land.

Administrative protection and Christianity appear to be the common denominators of the new identities that are growing in northeast India while Tripura and Assam without these benefits, seem to be the losers in the game. Assam has shed a large part of its alien ethno-cultural element in a desperate search for linguistic homogeneity which is yet nowhere in the horizon. But it would be misleading to view the denominators solely in terms of exclusiveness vis-a-vis the dominant culture of India and treat them as instruments for the reinforcement of tribalism, ignoring the conflicts between the two. Such a view would be based on an inadequate understanding of the fact that the "tribal" states that have emerged are hardly indicative of a return of a tribal "golden age" but are the synthesis of complex and dynamic social forces.

There is something in "tribalism" which is out of tune with the modern political order. The first is based on kinship relations, the second on territorial loyalty. Political boundaries inevitably cut across the ethnic, religious or linguistic boundaries, and create minority problems. Border adjustments of Assam with Bengal, Manipur and Tripura in the 19th century not only created problems for the Assamese but also split numerous tribal groups (Garo, Khasi, Mizo and Naga). Separation of Burma (1937) and partition of British India gave international significance to their borders and restricted the mobility of the tribal people living on shifting cultivation and doing trade with neighbouring countries. Finally, the establishment of district boundaries affected most of the tribal groups and created multi-ethnic districts. With the transformation of administrative districts into political entities, inter-district borders created political problems (Chaube, 1973).

Elite Conflict in a Tribal Society

No less significant was the institutionalization of tribal authority traditionally based on customs. Rules for administration of justice and police vested the village chiefs, usually the chiefs of the dominant clans, with administrative, judicial and police powers under the overall control of the District Officers, thus combining lineage with territorial authority. Where there was no chief a "head-man" was created. As a result, paradoxically, the authoritarian structure was strengthened at the village level and, at the same time, a district orientation was given to the political outlook of the hillmen. The District Officer being virtually the supreme authority, all appeals from the verdicts of the village chief were sent to these officers. Naturally the recourse to such appeal was taken more frequently by the educated sections than the uneducated and the District Officers' decisions were not always appreciated by the chiefs. An agitation to replace the system of executive appeal by the jurisdiction of the High Court was started by the chiefs with the beginning of reform moves in the name of preservation of tribal autonomy (Chaube, 1973).

A second paradox resulted from the virtual delegation of welfare works to the Christian Church, chiefly to the Protestant sects. Activities of the Church were not always conducive to the objectives of administration. It was the Church which gave the people of north-east India their linguistic consciousness. It was the Church which raised the first voice of protest against the system of tribal slavery in the Mizo hills (Chaube, 1973). Most important, however, was the creation of an educated, modernized elite whom a former British officer called "the black coat revolutionaries" (McCall, 1949), and who challenged the allies of administration in the hills: the chiefs. The chiefs abhorred the Church and the education that it gave. Education came to a few commoners who joined the junior services of government or the Church. As in the chiefs/Church controversy, the policy of administration was to support tradition, the handful of tribal officials took the side of the chiefs. The bulk of the educated hillmen joined the Church services and the professions and became the agency of modernization going to the extent of demanding constitutional reform about 1930 (Chaube, 1973).

Archetypal leadership of this modernized elite was provided by J. J. M. Nichols-Roy, an educated Khasi, Christian, pastor, businessman and politician,who became the first tribal minister, agitated for the curbing of chiefly rights and became the guiding spirit of the concept of district autonomy for the hill areas *within* Assam at the time of transfer of power. The Khasi National Conference that he formed was in contact with similar elite organizations in the other hills, like the Garo National Conference, the Mizo Union, and the Naga National Council. The "grouping" controversy of 1946 forged alliance between the Christianized elite and the Indian National Congress. On the other hand, the chiefs, inspired by an official scheme for a"crown colony" (Coupland, 1944) demanded complete autonomy of their tribal existence. After failure, some of them toyed with the idea of joining Pakistan, some others sought to go to Burma where the chiefs had secured special rights (Chaube, 1973).

The result was the constitutional plan for District Councils—territorial and secular local bodies—as the guardian of tribal affairs and the overlords of the chiefs, in the hill districts other than the "frontier tracts" and the Naga Tribal Area. The chiefs opposed the District Councils which initially came under the control of the new elite and in some places demanded secession. The irredentist grievances came in handy for such movements. The successes of the challenge were not uniform. The moderates lost control of the Naga National Council itself to the secessionists, while the Mizo Union, ruling the Mizo District Council abolished chiefship with payment of compensation. There were compromises in the Garo and the Khasi hills. In the Garo hills a village resettlement scheme could not be implemented due to the opposition of the chiefs and in the Khasi villages no elected village councils could be constituted while the big Khasi chiefs *(siems]* obtained the status of Additional District Council Judges. It was from the Garo and the Khasi hills that a movement for a hill state within India emerged. The Mizo Union kept aloof from it until the Mizo National Front, backed by the former chiefs, compelled them to demand a state for the Mizos. The moderates went under a temporary eclipse in the Naga hills where no council could be elected due to separatist activism.

What we find as the salient feature of politics in the northeast Indian hills is a confrontation between tradition and modernity. At the material level, tradition has vested interest in the old order of chiefship and its related oligarchy. Modernity stands for an elective "open" elite system and demands an individualistic property system to replace the so-called system of communal property through which the chiefs and their retenues appropriated most of the communal lands. This is not to suggest that the tribal elite is clearly demarcated by the line dividing tradition and modernity. It must be noted that in the hill areas of northeast India the traditional elite has a strong populist base, and the class of professional politicians that has cropped up as the functionaries of the modern state has to reckon with them.

In many ways therefore the District Councils failed and popular expectations about the Councils were frustrated. A scapegoat was conveniently found in the mistakes of the Assam government and the Assamese language movement was used as the pretext for demanding the hill state. Since 1947, however, the effort to run an all-hills agitation could not fructify in spite of appeals to racialism and even religion. The hill state agitation only united two hill districts—the Khasi-Jaintia and the Garo—which made Meghalaya. The other hill states are only hill districts: Naga hills are Nagaland, Mizo hills are Mizoram. Khasi Garo competition has already vitiated the alliance in Meghalaya. To the extent that the hill states are no more than political versions of the hill districts, the territorial orientation of modernity has won the round. The hill state however synthesized much of the traditional aspirations of political freedom in the statehood but feels uncomfortable with the irredentist slogans of recovery of the neighbouring areas now or once inhabited by cognate groups.

The politics of secession is fundamentally circumscribed by the powers of the modern state. The old chiefly class is no longer powerful enough to retain the secessionist stand and has inevitably been remoulding its aspirations. The emaciated secessionist movements are surviving through recruitment from the disgruntled section of the educated elite. According to the Naga underground's own admission, the educated Naga youth was generally apathetic to the movement in its early phase. But recently more and more educated young men are joining it as the employment opportunity is decreasing in the state. The revolt of the frustrated youth becomes secessionist only because of the geographical situation of the Naga and, for that matter, the Mizo hills.

The North-West Frontier Province: A Comparison

Grant of regional autonomy in the form of states has on the whole reinforced the new elite of northeast India who have stood for integration with India. The story of Pakistanese North West Frontier Province, however, is of regional integration confronting the broader political entity of Pakistan.

The five settled districts of the N.W.F.P. were within the Punjab until 1901. The transfrontier tribes were brought under British control with the drawing of the Durand Line about which Afghanistan was aggrieved as were many frontier tribes who cherish ethno-cultural connections with that country (Spate et al, 1967: 492-495). Ethnically, most of the people belong to the ascriptive category of Pathan, which means, in Pashtu, one who has a share in the village land as distinct from a Fakir who has none. Pathan identity is associated with the belief in a common descent, Islam and the observance of the conventional Pathan code (Barth, 1959, 1969; Caroe, 1962).

Spate and his colleagues suggested connection of the authoritarian tradition of Pathan leadership north of the Kabul river with the high and rough terrains compared to the lower and evener landscape to the south where tribal *jirgas* (assemblies) and *maliks* (masters/patriarchs) run a more or less democratic village system. Although the *malik* is no more than the first among equals, in most clans the leading *malik* ship is vested in a particular family (Spain, 1963: 41), suggesting the synthesis of the kinship lineage and the territorial systems in indigenous leadership. In the settled districts the title is usually *khan* (Spain, 1962: 49), a feudal honorific. There is evidence that British rule in the north-west frontier, as in the northeast frontier, encouraged the growth of authoritarianism. Even in the unadministered tribal agencies, there was at the beginning of this century only one organized state under a ruler, Chitral, ethnically not Pathan (Spate et al, 1967). Three other native states were recognized by Government before the transfer of power: Dir, Swat and Buner. The process of the birth of Swat is analyzed by Barth (1957). The title of *nawab* and *khan* were also bestowed on lesser chiefs.

There is another group of leadership, the *Pir* and the *Mulla*, described as the counterpart of the "warrior-bishop" of the middle age (Spain, 1962: 49) as well as "holy men-cum-arbitrators" (Sayeed, 1964), and extremely influential. The social life of the frontier, however, has been little affected by the Quranic *shariat* and an attempt of Dr. Khan Saheb to bring the customary laws of the Pathans under the codes of Islam was unsuccessful (Sayeed, 1964).

As in northeast India, in the N.W.F.P., the British rule created an articulate middle class which protested against the loss of a legislative council since the separation of the N.W.F.P. from the Punjab. The most moderate among them, a commoner conferred the title of *nawab*, Abdul Qayyum, placed the demand at the Round Table Conference. He was later nominated to the Central Legislative Assembly. Olaf Caroe, a former Governor of the N.W.F.P., regarded him as the leader of Pathan enlightenment (Caroe, 1958: 426) while a nephew of Abdul Ghaffar Khan called him a "collaborator" (Yunus, 1947). Abdul Qayyum's successor in the Central legislature, Akbar Khan, *nawab* of Hoti, was more collaborator than reformer and belonged to the vanguard of Muslim League politics in the N.W.F.P. Yunus (1947: 74) called such landlord chiefs the representatives of the vested interests.

The emergence of the *Khudai Khidmatgar* movement under the leadership of the "saintly" Abdul Ghaffar Khan and his western educated brother, Dr. Khan Saheb was considered to be a reaction to British "immobility" (Caroe, 1958: 431). Abdul Ghaffar, son of a rich *khan* of Peshawar, connected with an anti-British big *mulla* by marriage, entered politics by starting the *mulla*-backed "national education movement" and joined hands with the Indian National Congress through the Khilafat agitation moving the Sunnis that constituted almost 98 percent of the N.W.F.P.'s population. The party defeated the Muslim League in the elections of early 1946. But its appeal to religion backfired when the Pathans were given the option to join Pakistan after the partition decision. Anticipating defeat, the *Khudai Khidmatgar* boycotted the plebiscite of 1947 (Azad, 1959). The Khan brothers had failed to secularize their movement and now demanded a separate state of Pakhtoonistan with an appeal to racialism. On the other hand, the government servants, the soldiers, the traders and the professionals had a greater stake in Pakistan than in India.

The failure of the Pakhtoonistan movement cannot be explained by religion or even the fact that the people of the N.W.F.P. were not given the option. In spite of its ethnic affinity with Afghanistan, the political connections of the N.W.F.P. with the once-British India for over a century had firmly established a set of economic nexuses in which the new elite was deeply involved. This applies also to the tribal agencies ethnically as much affiliated to Afghanistan as to the settled districts of the N.W.F.P. It has to be noted that the Pathan political movement became significant only when Abdul Ghaffar's son, Wali Khan, fused the Pakhtoonistan movement into the subsequent, and broader, democratic agitation in Pakistan.

Conclusion

An Indian anthropologist who used to apply the geo-political concepts of bridge and buffer to the little communities surviving between the frontiers of great communities (organized states), now considers such roles with regard to the tribal areas of Northeast India "dysfunctional" in view of recent changes in the political organization of the concerned states (India, Burma and China) as well as in the modes of transport and communication (Roy-Burman, 1972: 72). It is submitted that this point is eminently applicable also to the Northwest Frontier Province, but not the northern frontier of India where the smaller states of Nepal, Bhutan and Sikkim largely eliminate the "tribal problem".

In a territorial society, ethnic categories are under the constant pressure of political power. Ethnic distinctions through *ascriptive* alliances do persist, according to Barth (1963: 10), despite changing participation and membership in the course of individual life histories since "Ethnic distinctions do not depend on the absence of social interaction and acceptance, but are quite to the contrary often the very foundations on which embracing social systems are based." The socio-cultural aspirations of each ethnic group, are, on the other hand, perennially moulded and reviewed according to the circumstances proximal to the conditions of its existence. This is how inter-ethnic conflicts within a political system seek to be resolved and new fields of collaboration and conflict are discovered. The process is however likely to be determined more by the *internal* relation of forces than by external agencies.

In northeast India as well as in the N.W.F.P., the greatest integrative role was played by the market economy of the regions they joined. Government continued to play a dominant role as almost the sole source of patronage and non-agricultural employment. In north-east India, creation of the new states has increased that opportunity. One hill state would do so to a lesser extent. The hill states of northeast India may, consequently, clamour for more Central attention or readjustment of political boundaries, but will have little capacity to obtain secession.

1975

REFERENCES

1. Azad, Maulana Abul Kalam, 1959, *India Wins Freedom*, Calcutta.
2. Barth, Fredrik, 1959, *Political Leadership among the Swat Pathans*, London.
3. Barth, Fredrik (ed.), 1969, *Ethnic Groups and Boundaries*, Oslo.
4. Caroe, Olaf, 1958, *The Pathans 550 B.C.-A.D. 1957*, London.
5. Chaube, Shibani Kinkar, 1973, *Hill Politics in North-East India*, Calcutta.
6. Coupland, Reginald, 1944, *The Constitutional Problem in India*, 3, London.
7. Fürer -Haimendrof, Christoph Von, 1945, "Aboriginal Rebellions in Deccan", *Man in India*, XXV, 4.

8. Mackenzie, Alexander, 1884, *History of the Relations of the Government with the Hill Tribes of the North-East Frontier of Bengal*, Calcutta.
9. McCall, Anthony Gilchrist, 1949, *Lushai Chrysalis*, London.
10. Pyarelal, 1966, *Thrown to the Wolves: Abdul Ghaffar Khan*, Calcutta.
11. Roy-Burman, B.K., 1972, "Integrated Area Approach to the Problem of the Hill Tribes of North-East India", *Tribal Situation in India*, edited by K. Suresh Singh, Simla.
12. Sayeed, Khalid B., 1972, "Pathan Regionalism", *South Atlantic Quarterly*, LXIII, 4.
13. Spain, James W., 1962, *The Way of the Pathans*, London.
14. Spain, James, W., 1963, *The Pathan Borderland*, The Hague.
15. Spate, O.H.K., A.T.A. Learmouth and B.H. Farmer, 1967, *India, Pakistan and Ceylon: The Regions*, London, Third Edition.
16. Yunus, Mohammad, 1947, *Frontier Speaks*, Bombay.

18

India and Her Neighbours : Linkages and Fissures

One of the significant contributions of the non-Congress governments to Indian state craft has been in the domain of Indian foreign policy evinced in the attention paid to India's immediate neighbours that was theoretically formulated by I.K. Gujral as India's Foreign Affairs minister on 20 January 1997 in a speech at Colombo as 'the Gujral doctrine.' In the post-independence period India's relationship with her neighbours has had a mixed record, in some cases pleasant, in some cases hostile and in some cases indifferent, with considerations of security and co-operation playing alternately against a grand vision of leadership in the non-aligned movement at the background.

Security and Sovereignty

The general proposition guiding this paper is that security is a concept of defence of a political system emanating from what generally is termed national interest and specifically economics today. In the earlier systems it was tied up with the survival/aggrandizement of a regime. Monarchs traded territories in order to buy peace, make gains or even (as in the case of Mumbai/Bombay) as marriage gifts. As power shifted from the rulers to the people, or at least the articulate/influential sections of them, more tangible considerations entered political gains. For the ruling class now the question of security arises over a stake of a state — life and/or property. Life is almost an axiomatic concern of a state because it is made up of people. Property of the people is a secondary concern. It becomes primary to a state when the scale of its operation is significant enough to generate revenue. The state claims the ultimate right over land and other natural resources like water and minerals primarily with a view to earning revenue from them. By extension of such interests the state claims the right to (protect/guard) routes of travel (by land and sea), means of communication and even the modes of popular thought. This is how political systems get linked up with territory, class and ideology too.

The security problem arises when there is a perception of threat to such stakes. Perception of the 'stakes,' however, may be defensive or aggressive, depending upon the nature of a regime. An ordinary peace-loving state may consider its population, its established territory, its normal trade activities and socio-economic stability as a sufficient area of concern. An imperialist/neo-imperialist country, on the other hand, may not be satisfied before having the world conform to its requirements.

Yet, attachment to territory cannot be older than where human groups would grow into food producers. It is true that archaeological evidences suggest that some Andamanese food-gathering groups used to travel in secular circles within the same territorial limits in the pursuit of sustenance. But this can be explained by the natural limits set by the geography of their island habitat. Even such groups are believed to have migrated there from their original habitat in the Indonesian islands by canoes. Some of the pastoral nomads in West Asia rotated within territorial limits in order to feed their animals. The shifting cultivators rotate their sowing and reaping activities within definite geographical territories. Conflict on possession of the areas of such nomads or shifting cultivators probably caused the first tribal wars. People's attachment to land developed only after the evolution of permanent/sedentary agriculture.

This attachment, which is the core of territorial nationalism, needs to be distinguished from the feudal mode of tribute collection from loyal chieftains and revenue collection from land which encompassed not only settled agricultural land but even remote forests and hills at the same time dividing people into fiefdoms. In the era of capitalism economic value mainly attaches to the productivity of a territory in terms of the available technological means and its usefulness in trade and transit. Exploration of gas and other mineral resources today, for instance, has created claims on sea beds and the polar regions of the earth and, before long, this may be extended to other planets. The development of sea routes in the late fifteenth century reduced the traditional importance attached to the land routes. Air transport reduced the importance of both of them. Yet certain natural limitations continue to hold the traditional attachment to land. In 2004 an earthquake created an artificial lake on the Tibet side of Sutlej river (Paree Chu) causing devastating flood in the Himachal Pradesh in the same year and the following. The Sindhu and, more so, the Tsangpho/Brahmaputra rivers originating from Tibet pose similar problems to India making water management in the Himalayas a formidable task.[1] There is still a huge amount and variety of trade which require travel by land. Hence the continued need for territories.

The concept of the 'nation state' that sought to reconcile political dominion with national aspirations in the wake of the emergence of industrial capitalism in the eighteenth century always left out as well as contained 'minorities' while forest dwelling *(antevasaayin/seheranaseen)* populations remained at the best isolated, if not hostile to central powers, leaving for the social scientist the task of their 'acculturation,' 'integration,' 'sanskritization' and 'mainstreamization.' When capitalism reached its highest stage in the nineteenth century imperialist powers took upon themselves the further task of 'civilization' as ' the white man's burden.' At this late stage of capitalism territorial nationalism got diluted by what in the recent political discourse is called globalization. It is by no means eliminated.

Through this entire course of history of the world political economy the one theoretical point that is established beyond doubt is the ultimate primacy of economics over politics. Nothing proves it better than the amazing facts that Vietnam and China, two sworn enemies of the USA till the early seventies of the last century, are having her as the major trade partners and the two rapidly successive visits of the Prime Minister of China and the President of Pakistan in March-April 2005 to India leading to the virtual burial of five to six decades of hostility over territorial claims by the sheer logic of economics. At the climax of the process came, on 11 June 2005, during Prime Minister Manmohan Singh's visit to Kargil, the proposal to link Kargil with Skardu in the Pakistan-occupied Kashmir (*The Indian Express*, June 13, 2005, the second editorial: 'Peace, broadbased'). Already, India's ideological opposition to the military junta of Myanmar (Burma) has been considerably diluted by the economic policy of looking east.

To comprehend this new direction of political economy India has to be situated in a specific historical context of the broadly south Asian civilization. India today is the sum of about two-thirds of the former British India, five hundred and fifty four former princely states, a 'tribal area' in the far eastern part of the country (now comprising the Tuensang district of Nagaland), the former French and Portuguese colonial possessions in the sub-continent and Sikkim. Her extended northern border from Gujarat to Mizoram, skirting the Himalayan heights, separates her from the sovereign states of Pakistan, China (Tibet), Nepal, Bhutan and Myanmar besides Bangladesh (which dents its territorial integrity without destroying it). The west-north segment of this frontier separates India from Pakistan. Except for Nepal and Bhutan the entire northern frontier separates her from the Tibet region of China while the hills of northeast India, viewed notionally as the south eastern projection of the Himalayas, separates her from Burma (Myanmar). The point that needs to be stressed is that this entire territorial configuration is a product of a hundred years of colonial rule that largely destroyed India's traditional cultural and economic linkages and imparted the concept of territorial power to the Asians.

India's Traditional Linkages

From the ancient city of Taxila (now in Pakistan) to the modern industrial town of Tinsukia (in Assam) the entire hilly border was cut across by numerous trade routes connecting India with Afghanistan, Central Asia, Tibet, China and Myanmar by land. South to north these routes have connected the sub-continental highway known as the Grand Trunk Road from Taxila to Bhagalpur and Kolkata and the Lhasa-Leh road running almost parallel to the Grand Trunk Road. Until the partition of India in 1947 the sub-continental highway crossed the Ganga and, through Gaur/Malda, moved northeast, through Dinajpur, Rangpur, Goalpara, Kamrup and Tinsukia, to Ledo in today's Arunachal Pradesh and further, through the Hukong Valley, into Myanmar and south-east Asia. Another east-ward route from Dhaka moved through Sylhet and Cachar into Manipur, touching Silchar, Lakshmipur, Jiribam, Bishenpur (Vishnupur) and Imphal, and finally joined the aforementioned Indo-Myanmar road. Of course there were sea routes of almost equal vintage connecting India with the West, Southeast Asia and the eastern sea-coast of China to which the Arabs and the Western powers paid greater attention in the later days because of their natural proficiency in maritime transportation. But the growth of the volume of trade in the late eighteenth century forced the West to look for greater access to inland Asia through the land routes.

The Trans-Asian highway from Chang an, the Han-period capital of China, to Antioch in Syria known, originally, as the Royal Persian Road and, since the 19th century, as the Silk Road extended to the east up to Korea and to the west up to Egypt and Rome. It had a minor company that may be called 'the minor silk road' that ran parallel along the northern fringe of the Himalayas from Lhasa through Shigatse and Gartok in Tibet, along the north of Nepal, to Leh in Ladakh and Srinagar in Kashmir (India) and moved through Peshawar to join the arterial road at Kabul in Afghanistan. From Kabul through Bamyan and Balkh a road moved to Samarkand and Tashkand while, from the Gartok-Leh-Srinagar segment, another route moved through Gilgit, Khotan, Yarkand, Kashgar and Aksu to Almaty on the main silk road. While Shigatse was the nodal point for passage to central and north western India, Gyantse on its southeast, forming a triangle with Lhasa and Shigatse, provided an opening to Sikkim, Bhutan and northeast India. Gartok was another nodal point on the Lhasa-Leh route for travel to central Asia on the north and to Rampur and Shimla of India to the south. Midway between Shigatse and Gartok two major routes branched off southward: (1) through Nyi-lam in Tibet and Kuti pass in the Kodari district of Nepal to Kathmandu, Gorakhpur and Benares, and (2) through the Lipu Lekh pass of the Kali valley to Almora, Rishikesh, Garh Mukteswar, Delhi and Agra.[2]

Another road came up from Chang an to the south, moved through Chungking to Kunmin and, while a branch of it went as far as Mandalay and Prome in Burma, the main road moved into Vietnam and Thailand. The fact that Sadiya was an important traffic node before its demolition by the 1950 earthquake on Assam suggests that the Sadiya-Rima-Walong route was in use long for minor trade between the Sikang province of China (formerly 'Inner Tibet') and northeast India. Another route of equal significance was the Chittagong-Rangamati-Demagiri-

Lungleh-Haka route to the Chindwin valley, Shwebo and Mandalay of Myanmar. There is no doubt, however, of the great importance of the two roads from eastern India: the Tinsukia-Ledo-Hukong Valley route to Myitkina, Lashio and Mandalay and the Dhaka-Sylhet-Silchar-Lakhmipur-Jiribam-Bishenpur (Vishnupur)-Imphal-Moreh route joining the India-Myanmar road at Swebo. The Dimapur-Kohima-Imphal road was developed in the late nineteenth century.[3]

There is no reason to assume that the entire road system cropped up at one go or that it was built by China alone. The so-called Silk Road was actually known as the Royal Persian Road in the West linking, at the first stage, Greece, Rome and Egypt with central Asia where Indian, Chinese and other Asian traders met their European and African co-laterals. Asoka's emissaries went to China, central Asia and probably to Europe and Egypt through this central Asian land route though some others travelled by sea to Sri Lanka and southeast Asia. The Chinese side of this continental road appears to have grown by the first century A.D. when Chinese hegemony extended up to the north of the Kuen Lun mountains. Linkage of central China with Lhasa appears to have developed by about the seventh century A.D. when Songtsen Gampo (Sron-btsan-sgam-po) brought a wife (Wen Cheng) from China along with an image of the Buddha. The other wife (Bhrukuti), with another image of the Buddha, had earlier come from the Kathmandu valley. The association of Buddhism with empire/state building activities in Asia is an interesting subject of enquiry not quite within the scope of the present study. The only point that may be suggested was that Buddhism offered the first philosophy of life that went beyond the level of ethnic culture and preached a universalistic view of life. It also fitted well with the culture of commerce that defied ethnic and territorial boundaries. There is reason to believe that increased political and commercial activities of Tibet since the seventh century A.D. led to the linking up of Lhasa with Gartok (in today's Tibet) and Leh (Ladakh).

Although Gampo extended great patronage to Buddhism and the Sanskrit language, institutionalization of Buddhism in Tibet began in the eighth century with king Trisong Detsen bringing Santirakshita and the Tantrik Guru Padma Sambhava from India[4].

Right from the beginning the new religion came into conflict with the prevailing Bon religious beliefs and got mixed up with internecine conflict in the Tibetan royal family leading to the assassination of king Ral-pa-chen, an otherwise successful ruler who extended his kingdom and got the first history of Tibet written, by his brother Glan-dar-ma. Glan-dar-ma repressed Buddhism, patronized Bon and was himself assassinated by a Buddhist monk. The country split into lay and ecclesiastical fiefdoms. Finally, in the tenth century, Dpal-bkhor-btsan, Glan-dar-ma's last successor to the Lhasa throne left for Western Tibet and set up an independent rule on Guge and Ladakh.

'When the PLA (People's Liberation Army) took charge of Lhasa in 1951, there was hardly any roads in Tibet. Lhasa and its environs were better connected to India than China,' says a recent report. 'In May 1954, the roads from Qinghai to the north of Tibet and Sichuan to the east were formally linked up in Lhasa. Two other roads - linking Tibet with Xinjian to the north-west and Yunnan to the south-east - were also completed soon after.'[5] This is an exaggeration for indeed Tibet, as we have seen, was connected with the central part of China from early days though not with Yunnan. Of course Tibet was better connected with India.

India came to be politically defined in a sub-continental term (from the Himalayas to the Indian Ocean) only during the British period. No Indian ruler/dynasty could unite such a huge territory before the British. No Indian ruler other than Chandragupta Maurya held territory outside India though many rulers of central Asian origin from Kanishka to Shah Jehan held territory in the Hindukush valley with capital in India. 'That this was an unnatural geographical agglomeration was again and again demonstrated when after a generation or two the extra-Indian territory had to be given up in favour of India.'[6] Instead, India sent her traders to central Asia and beyond, followed by missionaries. The Chinese, since the first century A.D., expanded their control westward to reach this central Asian heartland through Mongolia.

Contribution of Colonialism

During the peak of British supremacy in the sub-continent at the end of the nineteenth century 'the Indian empire' consisted of British India, including Burma (Myanmar) and 566 princely states. The British allowed Nepal, Sikkim and Bhutan to survive as satellite states and created a 'trans-border' area between this empire and Afghanistan (which they could not annex). They did not annex Tibet but tried to retain substantial political and economic control over it. The main reason for the survival on sufferance of these small states was the presence of two big states - Tsarist Russia and China - with which their relationship was ever uncertain. In 1937 Myanmar was turned into a separate crown colony. A small tract of territory corresponding to the Tuensang division of today's Nagaland as well as the former trans-frontier area between British India and Afghanistan was re-designated as a 'tribal area' outside British India but within India and under the executive authority of the Governor-General of British India.[7] In 1947 Myanmar became independent and the two wings of Pakistan came into this picture creating several political and economic problems.

The first of these problems that immediately started a war between India and Pakistan, inaugurating unending hostility, was Jammu and Kashmir. The second but simultaneous problem was the huge refugee influx, subsequently accompanied by illegal migration. The third was the drying up of legitimate trade and rise of smuggling. The fourth was the conflicts in river water sharing. The fifth was a political stand-off responsible for three major wars between the two countries and numerous skirmishes culminating in the split of Pakistan in 1971. Although the emergence of Bangla-desh in 1971 gave a respite to India, it was short-lived - only up to 1975 when the assassination of Sheikh Mujeeb unleashed a new chain of unrest. The only accumulation of India during this period - but totally unrelated to these incidents - was the merger of Sikkim with India.

Right from the time of Warren Hastings the East India Company was looking for land routes to Tibet. In 1774 Charles Bogle was sent to Tibet through Bhutan (He went as far as Shigatse). After the Anglo-Gorkha war of 1815 the British annexed the Kumaon-Garhwal areas of today's Uttaranchal state and the hill territories further west up to Shimla now comprising the Himachal Pradesh and brought Sikkim under their control. In 1850 Dalhousie ordered the construction of the Great Hindustan-Tibet Road from Shimla. Soon another road linking Srinagar and

Leh with Kashgar was undertaken.[8] After the Anglo-Bhutanese war of 1865 that resulted in the annexation of today's Kalimpong sub-division to British India the Kalimpong-Yatung-Shigatse route was developed and two trade marts were established at Gangtok and Gyantse. The urge for developing the Kalimpong route had been growing since the closure by China of the Shigatse-Kathmandu route following the Anglo-Chinese conflict involving Nepal and Tibet in 1792.[9]

It is a known fact of history that the British did not conquer India; they annexed it through stages by questionable means and then declared their sovereign status over British India only in 1858. The territorial claim involved in this process was uncertain and they adopted the expedient of 'the frontier.' The annexation started immediately after the battle of Plassey (1757) when the East India Company acquired the zemindari of Calcutta and its neighbourhood from Mir Zafar to secure its trading base and eliminate/control Portuguese and French competition upstream of the Hoogly river. In 1760 they acquired from Mir Qasim the zemindari of the districts of Burdwan (the rice bowl of Bengal) and Chittagong which housed the second biggest sea port on the Bay of Bengal (after Madras) of the same name on the sea route to southeast Asia and China.

Seven years after the Company acquiring the dewani of Bengal (1765) Warren Hastings was appointed the first Governor of Bengal in 1772 and the first Governor-General of British India in 1773.'Hastings undertook an exploration of the Bhutan route to Tibet. Not much was achieved immediately.[10]

'A Flexible Frontier'

Britain's annexation of territories west, north-west and south-west of the Bengal *suba* is a well-documented story. As far as the eastern frontier of British India was concerned, the Moamaria revolt of 1792 brought the British to Assam for the first time and the 1794 report of Captain Welsh on trading possibilities with Assam merely strengthened the East India Company's interest in Assam. On the spurious ground of the 1826 Treaty of Yandabo the Company annexed Assam along with the hills. By 1885 (the third Anglo-Burmese war) it annexed the whole of Myanmar (Burma).[11] As far as the northern frontier was concerned the focus was confined to Bhutan from which territories were annexed up to 1865 and Nepal which was placed under a subordinate relationship after 1815. Tibet remained an open question till the end of the nineteenth century except for a British intervention on Nepal's side during the Nepal-Tibet war of 1792.

Up to about the end of the nineteenth century British India's relations with her immediate neighbours were governed by a flexible 'frontier policy' that prevented the neighbours from exercising any undue influence/authority on her soil but kept the reverse door open (a policy reminiscent of the colonial expansion in north America). It was in the far north western part of British India that a new phase of frontier policy was opened up by the drawing of a 'frontier' with Afghanistan, through an agreement with the Afghan government in 1893, the actual Durand Line being drawn in 1902. Since 1883 an Inner Line was being drawn on the foothills of northeast India to prevent the travel of un- authorized plainsmen into the hills but allowing the travel of hillmen into the plains territories. The Inner Line was an administrative arrangement without any political significance for, though in the northern area administration did not extend much beyond the Inner Line till after Independence, in the southern areas it did penetrate almost the entire hills. With the annexation of Myanmar (Burma) the eastern frontier of British India moved from the Patkai-Barail range to the Salween river that separated the Thai territories. The southern part of this Myanmar-Thai border was further secured by Anglo-French agreements in 1896 and 1904 on neutralization of Thailand while the northern parts were secured by the relatively autonomous status of the Shan and the Kachin states as well as the weakness of China.

India-Myanmar relations

Existence of Saivism and Vaishnavism[12] along with Buddhism as well as substantial settlement of people of south Indian origin from ancient times attest to more pervasive Indian contact with southeast Asia in general and Myanmar in particular than with Tibet. The reason is the accessibility through the sea. Accessibility through land has brought more people from the east than sent them the same way. Myanmar was not always a united country. Her smaller shape (compared to Tibet's) and proximity to the sea placed her under a great deal of foreign influence. It is identified with the *suvarnabhumi* of the early Buddhist literature where Asoka is said to have sent an emissary. In the first century B.C. (the animist/Vaishnavite Pyu period) the country was fragmented into city states/kingdoms of which Sri Kshetra was the most prominent. The 'Burmese' population appeared on the scene from the north in the eleventh century and founded the kingdom of Pagan (Bagan). By the middle of the twelfth century almost the whole of southeast Asia came under the control of two empires: the Pagan (Myanmar) and the Khmer (Kampuchia). In the thirteenth century Myanmar was occupied by the Mongol ruler Kublai Khan and the Mongol incursion probably induced large population movement out of the region toward India (including that of the Ahoms). In the fourteenth century the country was divided into two major regions: Ava in the north and Pegu in the south. Pegu/Bago was originally known as Assa, a word believed to have been derived from 'Orissa.' While upper Myanmar was long known as Ava. In the sixteenth century Myanmar was again united and its expanse went upto Manipur. In the seventeenth century Myanmar defeated a Portuguese attempt at domination.

In 1752 Pegu revolted against Ava but was recovered in 1758. By the middle of the eighteenth century Yangon (Rangoon) had grown into a port due mainly to European contact[13] and it became the capital of the reunited kingdom. The Burmese government soon grew powerful enough to launch upon an imperialist venture up to Arrakan and Tenassarim to the south. By 1824 they annexed Assam bringing the British East India Company face to face with them. By the Treaty of Yandabo, 1826, they had to abandon their claim on Assam, Manipur and their neighbouring areas and cede Arrakan and the Tenassarim coast to the British. In 1852 lower Burma (Pegu) was annexed (Second Anglo-Burmese War). The capital of Ava was shifted to Mandalay. In 1885 upper Burma was annexed and the whole country was constituted as a Lieutenant-Governor's province within British India with Yangon as the headquarters. It was freed at the end of 1947.

The British undertook an ambitious railway building programme in Myanmar. By 1886 Yangon was connected with Prome and Pegu in lower Burma. By 1893 Pegu was connected with Mandalay and Myitkina on the traditional Assam-Burma Yunnan road.

Simultaneously a railroute between Assam and Burma was conceived with three probable alignments: (1) Chittagong to the Chindwin river, (2) Lamding through the Kubaw valley across the Chindwin and (3) Dibrugarh through the Hukong valley across the Patkai range. The report came out in 1922 favouring the Hukong valley route. But then the post-war nationalistic upsurge in India and Burma poured cold water on the plan. In 1923 the Montagu-Chelmsford scheme was implemented in Burma which had been constituted as a Lieutenant-Governor's province in 1899. In 1937 Burma was separated from British India and constituted as a Crown Colony.[14]

When, in 1937, Burma was separated from British India as a crown colony, only a small patch of territory lying between the two crown colonies was left un-administered. Under the Government of India Act, 1935, this area was designated as a 'tribal area' beyond British India and Burma but within India and under the executive authority of the Governor-General of British India.[15] Such a tribal area was created beyond the North-West Frontier Province bordering on Afghanistan too. On the other hand, although the North-East Frontier Tracts of Assam were legally 'excluded areas' to be administered by the Governor of Assam through his secretaries, they were actually treated as 'tribal areas.' In 1942 an Advisor was appointed by the Governor of Assam to look after the statutory and the actual tribal areas.[16]

Tibet

The British were never sure of the strength of China's relationship with Tibet or over its ability to annex Tibet which bordered the Himalayan frontier tracts. It was only with the Younghusband mission of 1904 under Curzon's viceroyalty that a positive initiative over Tibet is noted. And it was only after the Chinese civil war of 1912 that the initiative produced some results. The Younghusband mission obtained three trading posts (Yatung, Gyantse and Gartok) besides a temporary occupation of the Chumbi valley in Tibet but what the Simla conference of 1914 obtained was more on paper than on territory. Neither the Chinese nor the Tibetans were fully reconciled to the conclusions of the Simla convention. In the late 1930s the British government in India tried to build a supply route to China through Tibet for the war purpose but was thwarted by the Tibetan government. Hence the revival of the Hukong valley route under the command of the US general Stilwell. It was only in the 1950s that the fate of Tibet was sealed China arrived at the border of independent India.

There is a certain amount of romantic anguish in India about 'the loss of Tibet.' Tibet was within the cultural zone of India predominantly due to the spread of Buddhism. It was never a part of political India even during the British days. On the other hand, because of the Chinese 'imperial' practice of regarding any gift from a foreign land as a tribute, China always claimed a 'sovereign' right over Tibet. Even Songtsen Gampo's taking of a Chinese wife is claimed to have been a sign of subordination/ submission. China's historical claim on Tibet is vicarious. It flows from the fact that Kublai Khan, the Mongol conqueror of China, who established the Yuan dynasty with his capital at Beijing (Peking), took a Tibetan Buddhist monk, Lodo Gyaltsen, as his Guru (preceptor) and set him up as the ruler of central Tibet in 1253. This record can at best make China a secondary patron of Tibet, but it hides a chequered history of politics in China and central Asia at least until 1720 when China sent an army into Tibet to establish the seventh Dalai Lama and station an Amban (provincial governor) in Lhasa. The Mongol rule was overthrown by the Ming dynasty of China in 1368 and the Mongols were subordinated by the Qing (Manchu) dynasty long after they came to power in China in 1644 - in 1691. The Mongols were neither ruling China nor under China's authority in 1578 when Altan Khan conferred on Sonam Gyatso of the Drepung monastery of the Gelukpa sect the title of the Dalai Lama to be posthumously rewarded by the appointment of a member of his family, Yomten Gyatso (1589 - 1616), as the fourth Dalai Lama. Ghusri Khan of the same clan (1584 - 1656) set up Dalai Lama V as the religious head of Tibet with sovereign rights over the resources of the country. If Tibet had any socio-political linkage it was not with China but with Mongolia. For China, to set the 1720 military conquest and the 1727 border treaty with Tsarist Russia as the basis of her sovereignty over Tibet is tantamount to claiming the right of imperial succession. This does not establish any legitimacy of the Dalai Lama either as it does not prove his claim to historical independence. (Political power cannot be held long by mere religious authority anywhere in the world). The losers in the present Chinese programme of modernization of Tibet are its people who are being swamped by settlement of the Chinese on their territory.

Though Gampo adopted Buddhism or, at least, patronized it, Tibet was not a theocracy all the time. It did not become a theocracy when Gedun Khan, a grand son of Chengis Khan, appointed the grand Lama of the Sakya monastery, Kunga Gyaltsen (Sakya Pandita), his viceregent in central Tibet before Kublai Khan's appointment of Lodo Gyaltsen. The power of the Sakya sect came to an end in the middle of the fourteenth century and the Mongol chieftains continued to play the kingmakers until the lay hegemony of Phagmo Drupa of the Tsangpo valley came to rule. By 1350 its control spread over virtually the whole of Tibet from Lhasa. In 1481 the Rimpung family of Tsang (South Tibet), supported by the Karmapa sub-sect of the Kargyu sect of Buddhism of Tibet seized power from Phagmo Drupa and ruled till 1565 when its minister, Karma Tseten Dorji, overthrew it and assumed sovereignty over the whole of Tibet.

It was Altan Khan, chief of the Khoshot/Tumet Mongols of Amdo in the Kokonor region, close associate of the Chahar Mongols in the region of the upper bend of the Manchu (Huang Ho/Yellow River) in the east and scourge of the Mings (1368 - 1644), who invited in 1577 Sonam Gyatso, hierarch of the Drepung monastery of the Gelukpa sect, and conferred on him the title of Dalai Lama in 1578. Yonten Gyatso (1589-1616) of the Altan family was installed as the IVth Dalai Lama. His successor, Dalai Lama V of Drepung, Ngowang Lobsong Gyaltso (1617-82), was declared the religious head of Tibet with sovereign rights over the resources of Tibet by Ghusri Khan (Khoshot Mongol) who declared himself *Po Gyalpo* of Tibet retaining in his own hand the defence of Tibet and the security of the Dalai Lama.[17]

There are two broad objectives of war: (i) punishment or destruction and (ii) occupation though in most cases the two objectives are combined in different measures and different methods. Several memoirs and reports have delved into the reasons of the 1962 disaster of India. It is true that the Chinese withdrew their 1962 incursion 'voluntarily.' They did not want to destroy India; they merely wanted to punish India's territorial pretensions. It is, however, undeniable that 1962 saw the proclamation of China's territorial claims on India's borderlands and the building of bridges with Pakistan enabling her to construct the Tibet-Xinjian road. As far as the technology of war is concerned K.M. Panikkar, the great geo-political historian, considered 1498 as the dividing line between land and sea as India's major threat to security. World War II, however, had brought up the sky in the picture. The dropping of atom bombs on Hiroshima and Nagasaki crushed the Japanese resistance in 1945 as did the bombing of Iraq in 2003. But occupation is a job of the infantry and the US failed to conquer Vietnam. Therefore, the Himalayan wall is still a major defence for India.

Less so is the Himalayan terrain. 'The mountainous area to the north of India has to be considered strategically as one, a great quadrilateral, the middle of which is an elevated plateau 15,000 feet above sea level and the southern ramparts an invulnerable range of an average height of 20,000 feet.'[18] That is a natural advantage per se. But, compared to the power in occupation of Tibet, the advantage dims. For the entire Indian Himalaya is a gradient from north to south. That may be one reason why the British failed to annex Tibet. Comparatively, the eastern border of British India was much more accessible from the Indian mainland. The average height of the Patkai range is 2,000 metres (about 6,700 feet)[19] allowing better road links between India and her eastern neighbour. Naturally, British territorial aspirations developed faster toward the east than toward the north.[20]

Exclusion and administration in northeast India

Until the partition of India with the end of British power 'India' was constituted by three broad kinds of regimes. British India, 566 princely states of different sizes and power and two 'tribal areas.' About a third of British India went to Pakistan in two parts (east and west); 554 princely states joined India while 12 went to Pakistan and one tribal area each went to India and Pakistan[21] (The Naga Tribal Area in the east, today's Tuensang area of Nagaland, went to India and the North-West Frontier Tribal Area, today's 'federally administered tribal area' went to Pakistan) Within British India the tribal-inhabited areas were divided into excluded areas and partially excluded areas.

In the north-east travel of non-tribal outsiders was restricted in most of the excluded areas by means of the Inner Line under the Bengal Eastern Frontier Regulation, 1873, and the Government assumed the right to regulate habitation of non-tribal population in not only the areas covered by the Inner Line but also some other areas by means of the Chin Hills Regulation, 1896. The excluded and partially excluded areas were insulated from the power of the provincial legislature to different extents as well as nationalist politics. Administration, under the control of the Governor's secretaries, was similarly thinned out in excluded and partially excluded areas. In the tribal areas the Governor-General exercised only political control through his agents.[22]

The two north-east frontier tracts - Balipara and Sadiya - were excluded areas; but the Government, as has been noted, treated them as tribal areas. In 1942, in the wake of Japanese threat, an advisor was appointed for the frontier tracts as well as the Naga tribal area. But ever since the introduction of the 1919 reforms in Burma in 1923 and, particularly, after the rise of nationalist movement in Burma British officials began to 'worry' about the vast hill tract lying between the Irawaddy valley and the Assam-Bengal plains and the Simon Commission was presented with several official and non-official memoranda proposing the exclusion of the hills from the scope of the forthcoming reforms and by 1944 the idea of a Crown Colony crystallized with the backing of Reginald Coupland.[23]

No other part of independent India was as much affected by the partitions of 1937 (with Myanmar) and 1947 (with Pakistan) as Northeast India. The first partition created a wall, though not severed all communications, to the east particularly affecting the Nagas and the Mizos who lived on both sides of the border integrated community lives. The second partition turned the whole of northeast India virtually into an island with only a 20 kilometre wide land connection with the rest of India (the Siliguri bottle-neck). The tribal communities of today's Meghalaya, (Garo and Khasi), Tripura (Tripuri and Reang) and Mizoram (Mizo, Hmar, Kuki, Chakma) like the Bengalees, besides smaller tribal groups, were divided into two sovereign states of India and Pakistan. After the 1965 India-Pakistan war border trade was disrupted ruining cash-crops like orange. Particularly tragic was the fate of the Chittagong Hill Tracts which, by virtue of its administrative association with the Chittagong district alone, went to Pakistan and was subjected to demographic assault.[24]

While partition of India in 1947, like the partition of Bengal in 1905, was a political decision resulting from communal conflict in India, the transfer of the Chittagong Hill Tracts, a non-Muslim majority area, to Pakistan, defies all logic particularly against the fact that the Sylhet district of Assam was partitioned on the ground of its communal demography. Like most of the hill districts of Assam Chittagong Hill Tracts, under the Government of India Act, 1935, was an excluded area and had no voting right. It did not choose to be in Pakistan as Sylhet did in the 1947 referendum, Neither the Pakistan government nor its successor, Bangla Desh government, respected the communal rights of the local people in land or granted them much of administrative autonomy in the pattern of the northeast Indian hills. On the other hand, both the governments encouraged non-tribal (Muslim) settlement in the area causing migration of Buddhist Chakma and other groups toward the Mizo hills of Assam and Tripura and the birth of the *Parbattya Chattogram Jana Sanghati Samity* with a militant wing by the somewhat paradoxical name of Shanti Bahini. This Shanti Bahini took a major part in the 1971 struggle for Bangladesh but was alienated by that government after the assassination of Sheikh Mujibur Rehman in 1975. With alleged support of the Research and Analysis Wing (RAW) of the Government of India they became very active and, in turn, persecuted.[25] In 1976 the Bangladesh army was deployed in the Tract but a full-scale operation took place in 1986 and was repeated intermittently after that. To a large extent the Chittagong Hill Tracts situation is responsible for Bangladesh playing host to insurgent groups of northeast India.

The Government of India settled a large number of Chakmas from Chittagong Hills Tracts and Hajos from Mymensing of East Pakistan and Bangladesh in the thinly populated Arunachal Pradesh hills. The economic success of these sedentary cultivators, before long, produced jealousy as growing ethno-politics in Arunachal Pradesh after its achievement of statehood in 1975 is creating tension in that region.

Security and Economy

For a long time the security perception of India was dominated by Pakistan and China. Whereas there is a thaw in India-China tension for the time being and some improvement of Indo-Pakistan relation, Pakistan continues to be the major source of threat to India's security through the promotion of sabotage and killings by militants and ISI agents directly across her borders. What is growing as another major headache for India is the ISI's surreptitious promotion of anti-India militancy through Bangladesh and even Nepal. Both Bangladesh and Nepal have suffered from a certain fear complex about India. Internal politics of the two countries have merely aggravated the distrust.

Nepal, a land-locked country, can have access to the sea only through India, Kolkata being the closest port. It feels that India takes undue advantage of this geographical shortcoming of the country. Ever since the 1951 'coup' of King Mahendra against the country's Ranacracy suspicion persists about India dabbling in the country's internal politics—a suspicion periodically stoked by (well-intentioned but ineffective) leftist (socialist as well as communist) interventions in Nepalese politics. Gyanendra's accession to the throne through a mysterious disaster in early June 2001 has taken things to a crescendo.

There is a great divide in Nepal's agrarian political economy. The Nepalese ruling Ranas, living in the Kathmandu valley, largely depended on their estates spread over the poor villages around it. Such villages are also home to the ethnic minorities of the country. The strength of the monarchy descending from Tribhuvan Shah was drawn mainly from the rural areas whose people saw the king as the embodiment of Lord Vishnu of the Hindu pantheon. The principle of heredity was central to this assumption. The controversial accession of Gyanendra took away this divine sanction to monarchy giving a boost to the Maoist communist movement which has, in addition to its traditional demand for land reform, taken up the cause of republicanism, a demand erstwhile confined to a small section of the Kathmandu valley-based middle class.

This has not, however, lessened the suspicion of India which is seen to be 'arm-twisting' Nepal with regard to her trading rights. Generally speaking, India's close neighbours view India as seeking to monopolize the trade relations envisaged by the South Asian Association for Regional Cooperation (SAARC) by means of its geographical centrality. Nepal will certainly like free and direct access to the market and sea port (Chittagong) of Bangladesh if not to Pakistan. (This does not mean that relations among the non-Indian members of the SAARC are completely satisfactory. The Nepalese refugees from Bhutan have soured the Nepal-Bhutan relations and the free transit of fugitives from north-east India to Bangladesh and Bhutan is creating uneasiness between the two countries).

India is by no means in an enviable situation. Sharing of river water with Bangladesh and Nepal is a constant headache for her. The refugees and infiltrators from Bangladesh and migrants from Nepal are major worries for India severely affecting peace in the north-east. Escape of north-east Indian militants to Bangladesh, Bhutan and Nepal unsettles India's security drastically while recent infiltration of Nepalese Maoists has caused grave concern in India. Interestingly, while Nepal is not unduly worried about their fugitives crossing over to India, Bangladesh accuses India of sheltering her fugitives from the Chittagong hill.

Though there is nothing like an LoC (with Pakistan) or an LoAC (with China) between India and Bangladesh, border demarcation, occasionally involving the shifting river bases,[26] have caused quite a few skirmishes. The open and freely accessible border between India and Bangladesh has not only facilitated illegal immigration but also encouraged smuggling of good and arms and theft of cattle resulting in exchange of fire between the border forces. Finally, the internal politics of Bangladesh has aggravated the tension between the two countries. While the modernised Bangladesh elite have always been uncomfortable with India's regional 'big brotherhood,' the orthodox religious groups held India responsible for the dissolution of the Islamic unity of Pakistan in 1971. Since the killing of Sheikh Mujeeb ur Rehman in 1975 this group is gathering strength with the support of the ISI.[27] While Sheikh Hasina is seen to be too weak to confront them, Begum Zia ur Rehman is suspected to be indulgent to, if not in league with, them. The latter, however, cannot permit them total freedom on pain of losing international donations on which the economy of the country heavily depends.

Only Bhutan, a country slowly moving toward constitutionalism, has a satisfactory relation with India. But her economic backwardness, coupled with an extremely narrow elite structure, evokes local aspirations for a larger participation of the country in the world affair beyond the 'see' of India. She wants greater access to Bangladesh through North Bengal and China through the Chumbi valley.

The Pakistan factor

Partition of British India in 1947 was rapidly followed by Pakistan's aggression on Jammu and Kashmir. Pakistan not only occupied a part of Jammu and Kashmir but gifted the northern part of this occupied territory to China to facilitate the construction of a highway between Tibet and Xinjiang. The Pak-occupied territory in Jammu and Kashmir is now governed in two parts - Azad Kashmir and the Northern Area (comprising Gilgit and Baltistan). The almost perpetual hostility between the two countries not only strained the trading relation between them but also closed India's land link with (1) West Asia through Lahore, Peshawar and Kabul and (2) central Asia through Gilgit, Yarkand and Kasgar. The difficulty was aggravated by the 1962 India-China war and Pakistan's gift of the northern part of Kashmir followed by the India-Pakistan conflicts since 1965. Nothing less than a paradigmatic shift in India-China-Pakistan relation can revive India's land trade with western and central Asia.[28] Immediately, the Pakistan position is impeding effective supplies to Afghanistan for her reconstruction. An alternative route to Afghanistan is through Iran by sea.

To understand the Pakistani reluctance to allow transit facility to India for Afghanistan one has to refer to the historical as well as contemporary politics of India, Pakistan and Afghanistan. The Durand Line that was formally established by the British as the border of India with Afghanistan by a treaty in 1893 was reluctantly accepted by the Afghan government but resisted by the Pushto-speaking population on the two sides of the border and fed the nationalist movement led by Khan Abdul Ghaffar Khan. It had created the abnormal situation that, while the Pushto speakers constituted the largest linguistic group in Afghanistan, the Durand Line put more Pushto-speakers on the eastern side of the line. The British were never able to govern the entire territory lying between the North-West Frontier Province and the Durand Line effectively, the tract being in fact controlled under the Foreign Jurisdiction Act of 1890 till 1937 when the Government of India Act, 1935, declared it as a 'tribal area' outside British India but within India and under the executive authority of the Governor-General of British India. In 1949 the Loya Zirga of Afghanistan declared the Durand Line invalid and laid claim to the territory of the north-west frontier tribal area of British India. The people of this Federally Administered Tribal Area of Pakistan never took part in a Pakistan election until 1996 when the area came under the Taliban occupation. However, when the USA began bombing of Afghanistan, the Taliban took refuges in the Tribal Area and repudiated Pakistan's claim to the territory. The Pakistani operation against the Taliban has merely aggravated the tension. The problem is grave in Baluchistan where the once powerful Khanate of Kalat, which had to be forced to merge with Pakistan in March 1948, is spearheading a strong 'anti-Punjabi' movement in Pakistan in the past several years and has sympathisers in Sindh and the North-West Frontier Province.

The British and Pakistan always suspected Iranian design on Afghanistan. Iran under the Shah, however, was the centrepiece of the CENTO and Pakistan joined it. The Khomeini revolution in Iran changed the situation and Pakistan wanted to cope with it by promoting the clerical authority in Pakistan during General Zia's rule. The US affection for Iran ended. Pakistan, where the clerical authority is still strong - inviting for itself the acronym of 'fundamentalist' - tried to maintain the 'Islamic' link with this oil-rich country which has not denounced Pakistan's militarism.

The long-term impacts of partitions in India were severe in respect of the economy in the country. In 1937 the separation of Burma (Myanmar) from British India was not immediately felt as both the crown colonies remained under one sovereignty. But when, in 1947, Burma became independent like India the border peoples (Naga and Mizo) were divided under two sovereignties, upsetting their kinship linkages as well as trade relations. The partition of 1947 did the same mischief with the Chakma, the Khasi, the Garo, the Hajo, the Rabha of Assam and the Tripuri, the Reang and several other small tribes of Tripura. But for a narrow stretch of 20 km-wide plain territory in North Bengal the whole of northeast India was cut off from the rest of the country. Its traditional trade links with the port city of Calcutta through the plains of eastern Bengal (East Pakistan/Bangladesh) were severed. The fate of the Mizos was the worst as they were sandwitched between two sovereignties (Myanmar and Bangladesh). Even today the fastest overland transport from Lungleh in Mizoram to Calcutta will take not less than 48 hours.

At the Foreign Secretary level talk in September 2005 Pakistan agreed to open the Srinagar-Muzaffarabad route to trucks for facilitating commerce between the two parts of Kashmir. The devastating earthquake in Jammu and Kashmir and the Pak-occupied Kashmir forced Pakistan to modify the stand in order to receive Indian assistance. On the other hand, Pakistan has declined to grant India the right of passage through her territory to central and western Asia. India is looking forward to Iran for allowing the passage to Afghanistan (and, eventually, to central and western Asia) by developing the Chahbahar port in Iran and thence a road to Zaranj on the Afghan border. The Border Roads Organization of India is already working on a 218 km road between Zaranj and Delaram in Afghanistan as a part of the Afghan reconstruction programme of India. The Zaranj -Delaram road, in turn, will join the Afghanistan Garland Highway that connects the major towns of Afghanistan and moves on to Central Asia.[29] If the Iran-Pakistan-India pipeline materializes that will make the first crack in Pakistan's resistance to the Indian right of passage. Politics and economics are directly in conflict here.

Looking East

In the east, however, India has a dual problem. It needs the right of passage through Bangladesh to her northeast, particularly for Tripura and Mizoram and partly for Manipur which can develop a faster contact with West Bengal through National Highway No. 53 through Jiribam and Silchar. The reluctance of Bangladesh to allow this right has compelled India to seek a sea route to Mizoram through the Akyab/Sittwe port of Myanmar and the Kaladan river a survey for which was conducted in the beginning of this century. The other - and greater - focus of the survey was the exploration of a huge amount of natural gas reserve at the east coast of the Bay of Bengal. There the problem is political too for, although India and Myanmar have no political rivalry, the military-dictatorial political order in Burma induces strong reaction in the Indian democratic attitude.

At the thirteenth SAARC summit in November 2005 at Dacca India proposed, among other things, free air and overland passage of SAARC countries through each other. The impact of the proposal will be heightened by the decision of the SAARC summit to invite Afghanistan to be a member. Interestingly, Nepal, with the tacit support of Pakistan, demanded the association of China with the SAARC along with Afghanistan's membership. Immediately after the SAARC summit Pakistan openly advocated the same thing. There is no doubt that Afghanistan's membership of the SAARC will make it more India-centric, reduce Pakistan's influence on Afghanistan and even, to some extent, choke its opening to central Asia.

As and when Myanmar is brought into the SAARC India is bound to gain more and the linkages of the old British India will be restored. As of now Myanmar's political system stands in the way of such integration even though the mutual benefit of the two countries stemming from such association is undeniable. India is trying to develop a working relationship with the Myanmarese junta but China, ignoring the democratic predilection, has established a much better relationship with that country. Even the other SAARC countries have so far desisted from advocating Myanmar's membership.

This is, however, not the ultimate dilemma of India's quest for a friendly neighbourhood. All of India's northern, western and eastern neighbours are despotic to varying extents and, therefore, essentially unstable. It is difficult to establish a permanent bridge with any of them. The only hope is that economics will ultimately prevail over politics. However, as Afghanistan slowly moves toward democracy with unqualified Indian support, the prospect of Indo-Afghan co-operation has been challenged by great power politics. The USA which has provisionally accorded India a nuclear status, is strongly opposed to Indo-Iran cooperation including India's land access to Afghanistan via that country. India's stake in a democratized Afghanistan is much more important than even the uncertain prospect of nuclear collaboration with the USA or a gas pipeline from Iran to India through Pakistan.

2006

NOTES AND REFERENCES

1. 'HP floods show Beijing-Delhi link is dry,' by C. Raja Mohan, *The Indian Express*, June 28, 2005.
2. There is a third, ancient, route connecting Beijing (Peking) with St Petersburg and the rest of Europe through Mongolia, known as 'the tea road,' roughly along the Trans-Siberian railway, which also brought the Mongols into China in the thirteenth century. The Mongol ruler Kublai Khan moved China's capital to Beijing from Chang an.
3. On 22 November 2004, at Guwahati, Prime Minister Manmohan Singh flagged off the India-ASEAN Motor Car Rally, which moved through Kohima (Nagaland), Imphal and More (Manipur)-Tamu (Myanmar) border to Mandalay (Myanmar) and then, through the Shan state of Myanmar and the Taichilek (Myanmar) - Mai Sei (Thailand) border, then through Phitsanulok, to the Thai-Lao border of Nong Khai-Friendship Bridge, to Vientiane, Paksan and Densavanh (Laos), to Lao Bao, Hue, Nha Trang, Ho Chi Minh City (Viet Nam), and, through the Moc Bai (Viet Nam)-Bavet (Cambodia/Kampuchia) border, to Pnom Penh (Cambodia/Kampuchia) and, through the Siem Reap (Cambodia)-Aranya Prahet (Thailand) border, to Bangkok, Surat Thani, Nakhon Si Thammarat and Dan Nok (Thailand), to Kayum Hitam, Putrajaya and Johor Bahru (Malayasia), to Singapore and, finally, reaching Batam in Indonesia on December 10 (See *The Indian Express* 21 November 2004 and *The Assam Tribune* 23 November 2004). Earlier, in June 2004, a 12-member survey team travelled in car from Imphal along the same route, to Nong Khai (Thai-Lao border) and, then, splitting into two routes - one through Vietnam and the other through Cambodia/Kampuchia - met in Bangkok. ('Asean ... by Road' by Tutu Dhawan. *The Hindu*, June 20, 2004). There is already a plan to connect by air Bangkok with Dibrugarh and Guwahati in Assam.
4. While Santirakshita belonged to the Nalanda Mahavihara and came through Nepal, Padma Sambhava, who was invited on his suggestion, probably belonged to the Swat valley in northwest India. See *2500 Years of Buddhism*. General editor: Professor P.V. Bapat. Publications Division, Ministry of Information and Broadcasting, Government of India, 1956, pp. 66-67. Also see Shibani Kinkar Chaube, 'Religion and Politics in the Himalayan Kingdoms' *North Bengal University Review*, Special Issue on the Himalayas, Vol. 2, No. 1 & 2.
5. C. Raja Mohan, 'Many roads to China's Tibet policy.' *The Indian Express*, June 20, 2005.
6. K.M. Panikkar, *Geographical Factors in Indian History*. Bombay, Bharatiya Vidya Bhavan, 1955, pp. 33-34.
7. Section 311 of the Government of India Act, 1935.

8. Partial occupation of Jammu and Kashmir by Pakistan in 1957 turned the Srinagar-Leh route vulnerable as it fell close to the Line of Control. The Kargil war of 1999 exposed this vulnerability inducing India to develop the alternative trade route from Shimla via Manali and, across the Rhotang Pass by means of a tunnel, Darchu,Padam and Nimu to Leh ('Centre paves way for new Leh route via Manali,' *The Indian Express*, 1 September 2005).
9. Parshotam Mehra, *The North-Eastern Frontier: A Documentary Study of the Internecine Rivalry between India, Tibet and China:* Delhi, Oxford University Press, 1980, p. 112. In the 1880s plans were floated for building a railway line to Lhasa through Kalimpong.
10. See S.K. Chaube, *Hill Politics in Northeast India*, New Delhi, Orient Longman, Revised Second Edition, 1999, p. 3.
11. *Ibid.*, pp. 4-7.
12. There is a dilapidated Vishnu temple of thin bricks of the Bengali *chouchala* type at the Bishenpur village near Moirang, the old capital of Manipur. The once-presiding deity, having had several movements, is now lodged in the palace temple of Manipur raja. According to some local historians the idol had been donated by the king of Pong, a Shan state, in the fifteenth century.
13. The other, and older, port city was Akyab, at the mouth of the river Kaladan that flows from the Mizo hills to the eastern coast of the Bay of Bengal northwest of Yangon and closer to Chittagong, now known as Sittwe.
14. See Chaube, op. cit, pp. 220-21.
15. *Ibid.*, pp. 26- 27.
16. See 'India and the Mongolian Fringe: Note by Foreign Secretary.' Parshottam Mehra, *The North-Eastern, Frontier: A Documentary Study of the Internecine Rivalry between India, Tibet and China.* Vol. 2, 1914-54, Delhi, Oxford University Press, 1980, pp. 111-24, at 117-19. Also Chaube, op. cit., pp. 90-91.
17. Ram Rahul, *The Government and Politics of Tibet.* Delhi: Vikas, 1969, pp. 2-3.
18. Panikkar, op. cit., pp. 54 - 55.
19. S.C.Bose, *Geography of the Himalaya*, New Delhi, National Book Trust, India, 1976, p. 42.
20. One of the considerations behind Britain's annexation of Burma is believed be the rising French influence in Thailand, on the east of Burma. But Burma herself offered many lures besides being a possible entry route to South China (Yunnan).
21. According to Section 311 of the Government of India Act, 1935, 'tribal area' was an area lying between British India and Afghanistan or British India and Burma but belonging to neither British India, nor Afghanistan

nor Burma nor any princely state but belonged to India. As distinguished from the princely states the tribal areas were under the executive authority of the Governor-General of British India.

The following princely states joined Pakistan: Bahawalpur. Khairpur (Punjab and Sindh states); Kalat, Las Belas, Makran, Kharan (Baluchistan states); Amb, Chitral, Dir (Dhir), Hunza, Nagar and Swat (Frontier states).

22. See Chaube, op. cit, pp. 17 - 27.
23. *Ibid.*, pp. 74-78.
24. At the time of Independence the non-tribal population of the Chittagong Hill Tracts constituted 9% of its total population, by 1991 it became the majority thanks to the policy of settlement of non-tribal population in the hills since Kaptai hydro-electric project beginning in 1951 and several amendments to the 1900 Regulation on the administration of the Chittagong Hill Tracts. Quantitatively, the Chittagong Hill Tracts are still a better place for the tribals than Tripura where the tribals have been reduced to virtually a quarter of the total population. Qualitatively, however, the situation is worse because (1) non-tribal settlement in Tripura started long before Independence, under the patronage of the tribal king, but was (2) accentuated after Independence and partition, without state encouragement, by the influx of refugees.
25. Subir Bhaumik, 'The external linkages in insurgency in India's northeast.' B. Pakem (ed.), *Insurgency in Northeast India,* New Delhi: (Omsons Publications, 1997), pp. 89 -100, at 97-99.
26. There was an exchange of fire between the Border Security Force of India and the Bangladesh Rifles on 20 August 2005 arising out of embankment of the Mahananda river at the Malda district (West Bengal).
27. This group backed several extremist organisations at least one of which - the Jamayet Mujaheedin - were believed to be behind the series of bomb blasts in Bangladesh on 17 August 2005.
28. A slight hope about West Asian links is raised by the UPA government's initiative in opening a gas pipeline from Iran through Afghanistan but the main hurdles are the huge expense and the violent political situation in Afghanistan and the north western part of Pakistan besides the traditional India-Pakistan distrust.
29. 'IMEA sluggish in funding Afghan road project?' *The Times of India,* 1 September 2005.

19

Social Tensions in Calcutta—A Comparative Study within the Frame of Urban Crimes in India*

ABSTRACT

Social tensions in Calcutta are sought to be quantified, comparatively with those in four other cities of India, on the basis of crime data. Three criteria for gauging the social aspect are adopted: participation, openness and sporadic occurrence.

Calcutta has a high rate of harm-oriented, but low rate of gain-oriented crimes. Their incidences vary according to political fluctuations. Apparently, organized labour movement has no positive relationship with urban crimes.

There is perhaps no other city in the world today which has inspired so much awe and concern of the national and international community as Calcutta. Calcutta's cultural sophistication has frequently been counterweighed in polite minds by waves of violence the last of which appeared shortly before the West Bengal Legislative Assembly election of 1982.

It is not easy to sociologically define violence particularly because of its implicit roots in the concept of crime. Mackenzie defines violence as 'the exercise of physical force so as to inflict injury to cause damage to persons or property; action or conduct characterized by this; treatment or usage tending to cause bodily

*An earlier version of the paper was presented in a seminar on Calcutta organised by the French Cultural Centre, Calcutta, in November 1979. The author is indebted to his former colleagues at the Centre for Studies in Social Sciences, Calcutta, for their help and comments in preparing the paper.

injury or forcibly interfering with personal freedom' (Mackenzie, 1975: 39). Yet Domenach applies the term to the use of force, whether overt or covert, in order to wrest from individuals or groups something that they are not disposed to give of their own free will' (Domenach, 1978: 719).

Apparently both these definitions mix the question of instrumentality with that of motive: Mackenzie mixes force with harm and Domenach mixes it with gain. In both these definitions, however, stress is laid on the use of force, direct or indirect, physical or otherwise. This abstraction, instead of simplifying the definition of violence, complicates it. For 'violence'—as distinguished from 'force'—is a value-loaded concept, designating the use of force to change a state of affairs that is accepted as legitimate. The problem ultimately involves the very basis of criminology as a social science, for almost every 'legitimate' state of affairs in society is based on certain forces and the sociological test of crime rests in the perception of the forces that confront each other. Thus, Pierre Spitz calls famine and inequality 'silent violence' (Spitz, 1975: 768) and Ted Robert Gurr considers political violence as 'normal self-adjustive mechanism of society' (Gurr, 1970; 160). Khan emphasizes that violence in general is not only a personal affair, it has a cultural and a situational dimension (Khan, 1978: 834-37).

The Meaning of Crime

Though in law crime is characterized by 'mens rea' (criminal motive), in a general sense crime as such can be regarded as an 'adjustive' or 'remedial' action on the part of the 'criminal'. A crime is a crime because it goes against a prevailing norm. A crime is, further, viewed by different parts of the world, even by different sections of the same people, differently. Every criminal has a grievance against a particular state of affairs. The most significant point about such grievances is that they are hardly uniform in their specificity. The grievance may be aimed at one individual or more, one group of individuals or more, a government, a law, a situation or even an attitude held individually or collectively. The grievance may be borne by one individual or more (usually in varying degrees). It may — in fact, it does — vary in intensity from time to time and from place to place.

This will be evident from a classification of the 'crimes' that are considered here for an understanding of the social tensions in Calcutta. Murder, robbery, ordinary theft and riot, as defined in Indian law, are rather unsophisticated urban crimes. We are not considering 'culpable homicide not amounting to murder' as the motives for such crime are by no means clear. Crimes like 'cheating' and 'forgery' are complex, while 'dacoity' (involving five or more persons organized for the purpose of forcible capture of property) is a predominantly rural crime. So, they are ignored.

Crime can be studied from two angles: motives and instrumentality. Motivationally crime arises out of different degrees of desire either to gain some profit or property or to cause harm or injury, or out of a combination of both. Theft represents the simplest form of gain-oriented crime though, in many cases, it may arise out of the desire to harm people too. In robbery both these motives are present, but probably the second to a greater degree than the first. Murder is the most serious of the harmful offences, but, in many cases, it may be associated with the desire to gain. Riot is usually aimed at harming others. But even riot may emerge from a desire to gain indirectly by destroying the strength of the rivals. In other words, there is no 'purely' gain-oriented or harm-oriented crime.

Instrumentally, theft is scarcely violent, and it needs to be treated separately from the more violent crimes. In the Indian criminal law riot involves five persons or more, while robbery involves four persons or less. Murder is defined by the motivation and the effect of the crime, and not by the number of persons involved in it. In the cases of murder and robbery, further, the criminal intentions are much more prominent than in the case of riot. The *nature* of the crime in murder and robbery, therefore, is regarded to be more serious than that in riot. The main criteria of 'riot' are two: (1) there is a gang-up, and (2) there is violence. In other words, from the social scientific angle, theft falls primarily within the domain of psychology, riot falls primarily within the domain of social psychology, while murder and robbery hold somewhat intermediate positions.

The Social Psychology of Riot

Viewed thus 'riot' under the Indian criminal law falls within the category of what the social psychologists would call an 'out-burst of excited crowd action' and encompass a *mob* ('a hostile crowd acting concertedly toward a goal, which is usually that of inflicting "violence" on somebody'), a riot as such ('a free-for-all of crowds and individuals in violent conflict') and a crowd *panic* ('a precipitous flight in which coordination breaks down and individuals act for themselves without concern for others') (Klapp, 1972: 45). The important elements in the production of a riot, that is a crowd turning violent, are identified to be the following: (1) common attitudes, (2) tension, (3) mood, (4) imagery, (5) trigger, and (6) circular interaction (Klapp, 1972: 49).

Common attitudes involve some homogeneity, or sharing of values. Tension stands for 'the tendencies in the organism that are pressing for release by a suitable trigger' (Klapp, 1972: 137). The mood is something beyond common attitude, it sets, a range of what is possible and probable in crowd behaviour at a time, and the imagery helps to set the crowd mood (Klapp, 1972: 53-54). Trigger means the various stimuli, including 'acts of leaders, that precipitate crowd action or new stages of feeling at various points in the development process (Klapp, 1972 : 55). Circular interaction establishes rapport and loss of self-awareness through repeated 'cheering, jeering and haranguing. All these components are present in the crowds of football fans that, for the past few years, have kept the guardians of Calcutta's law and order anxious on every day when a leading team is in the field.

Social psychologists thus regard riot as a sub-set of 'social unrest'. Social unrest signifies a state of affairs in which

(1) people are restless, tense and disturbed,
(2) feelings are expressed in overt behaviour (signs) that can stimulate other people, and
(3) action in fact becomes contagious (Klapp, 1972: 191).

Indices of Social Tension

In common use 'tension' is frequently confused with 'conflict'. According to our definition tension is a subjective phenomenon while conflict has an objective as well as a subjective dimension. Springing from specific social conditions tensions manifest themselves in conflicts. As all tensions are rooted in society, how do we distinguish 'social tension'? The author adopts three criteria for such distinction: (1) strength of participation in a conflict, (2) the openness of its occurrence and (3) the sporadic nature of such occurrence.

Social tension is likely to instigate people to violate the law as well as the rights of others with a certain amount of boldness and often in collusion with sympathisers. Such conflicts inflate the volume of 'crime' in a society. Circumstantially, however, a situation of intense social tension cannot be permanent. Either there is separation, or the conflicts are controlled by the authorities within limits. Yet, such subdued tension occasionally gets released in the form of large-scale conflict. The 'trigger' for such large-scale release is expected to be much bigger and effective than that in an *occasional* riot or vandalism. In other words, the larger and the more sustained a conflict is, the trigger increasingly turns into mobilization. If war is a bigger form of conflict, mobilization is the bigger form of trigger. The important point is that social tensions are reflected by *occasional* rise of crimes rather than in their steady trends.

Finally, increased participation may substantially affect the specificity of a 'crime'. It reduces the prospects of direct gain of the individual participants from any particular act. In such a situation the desire to harm takes precedence over the desire to gain at least for the participating 'rank', if not for the ring-leaders. In other words, the mass of the participants become motivated mainly by the element of protest than by a desire to obtain immediate remedy. Sociologically, the dilution of the gain-orientation in crime may be called *anomie*.

The above analysis enables us to attempt the following relativistic classification of the four kinds of 'crime' under consideration. As an index of social tension, on our criteria, theft is the least qualified. Murder, when committed by individuals or very small groups, and in secret, will be of more or less, similar status. Mass involvement in murder, often in the open, are more qualified. In urban societies, however, more murders are committed in secret and by individuals; or small groups than in public and by big groups. Robbery frequently involves small gangs and some public knowledge. Riot involves a group and is open.

One is here confronted with a conflict between quantity and quality. Not only is murder likely to be more harm-oriented than robbery. In the prevailing urban ethics of India, murder is less likely to be ignored than robbery. There is, however, a greater probability for one's getting away with a murder than robbery. Individual and secret murders represent lesser 'social' tension than robberies. But a *significant* rise of the volume of murder in a particular period represents a greater amount of social tension than a similar rise of robbery.

Murder of course represents the highest amount of tension. But as we have chosen to define 'social tension' in terms of participation in overt conflicts, riot, which always has large participation, gets precedence over murder. Robbery has a maximum participation of four persons, and it is more clearly gain-oriented than murder or riot. Hence it gets the third place. Theft comes fourth.

Crime and Social Tension

1. RIOT
   High participation
   High-low harm-orientation
   High-low violence
2. MURDER
   High-low participation
   High harm-orientation,
   High violence
3. ROBBERY
   Medium-low participation
   High gain-orientation
   High-low violence
4. THEFT
   Low participation
   High gain-orientation
   Low violence

A Comparative Estimate

It should be clear by now that we attach no 'value' to the crimes, but seek to understand the sociological significance of these legal categories. In the following pages we make a comparative estimate of the social tension underlying the four urban 'crimes' from the crime figures, as reported by the police, during the fifteen years from 1961 to 1975 (See *Crime in India)* in the four metropolitan cities of Bombay, Calcutta, Delhi and Madras. As none of these cities can be considered predominantly industrial the reports on Kanpur, the most industrial major city of India, are also compared. It should be stipulated that the reports of the cases are merely numerical. They do not reflect the spread and intensity of each incident. Further, one incident may lead to the recording of a number of cases. A riot may be accompanied by murder and/or robbery. Finally, it is the singular practice of Calcutta Police to record cases of 'snatching' as 'theft' rather than robbery. This slightly raises the 'theft' figures of Calcutta at the cost of 'robbery'.

The years covered correspond to the 1961 census at one end and the beginning of the emergency at the other. By 1961 the cities of Greater Bombay and Delhi got the present shape. The territorial limits of the three other cities (Calcutta, Kanpur and Madras) correspond to the respective corporation jurisdictions. With a view to the comparative purpose the figures are presented as 'per lakh' of the estimated mid-year population. This conversion is worked out in the records themselves from 1972 to 1975. The conversion for the earlier period had to be worked out

Table 19.1 : Average of Crimes in Cities 1961-75

Cities	*Riot (per lakh of pop.)*	*Murder (per lakh of pop.)*	*Robbery (per lakh of pop.)*	*Theft (per lakh of pop.)*
Bombay (Maharashtra)	5.15	2.72	4.89	254
Calcutta (West Bengal)	18.11	2.38	1.88	172
(excluding (1970-71)	15.03	1.65	1.11	175
Delhi (Delhi Union territory)	4.15	2.42	3.98	362
Kanpur (Uttar Pradesh)	13.86	3.74	9.81	337
Madras (Tamil Nadu)	8.07	0.89	0.45	201
(excluding 1962)	4.72			

Source: *Crime in India.*

of the estimated mid-year population from the figures of population census. On the graph, the figures showed some interesting correspondences.

Theft, for obvious reasons, has a much higher intensity than robbery, murder or riot. Further, the theft figures, except for a jump in Delhi (254 to 428) between 1969 and 1970 are relatively steady. There are however two great slumps in 1965 at Kanpur (3.10 in 1963 to 0.09 in 1965) and Madras (1.81 in 1964, 0.07 in 1965 and 2.33 in 1966). The fact that the theft figure for Kanpur in 1964 is not available at all gives rise to the suspicion that there was no reporting for a period in 1965 about theft in Kanpur. The 1965 slump in Madras cannot be explained, but may probably be ascribed to faulty recording too.

Robbery

Not only is 'theft' figure not available for Kanpur in 1964, 'robbery', 'murder' and 'riot' figures for that year are not available either. On the other hand, if this non-availability has adversely affected the 'theft' figure of Kanpur in 1965, there is an unusual rise of the robbery figure of Kanpur in 1965 (3.00 in 1963, 7.50 in 1965) which takes Kanpur to the top, position in 1965. In 1966 Kanpur (5.10) again yields the first position in robbery to Bombay (5.82), the first in 1961-64 (average 4.37), itself holding the second position. From 1967 to 1974, however, Kanpur is decisively at the top (average 7.21). In the first year of the emergency (1975), it is at the bottom (0.9).

Throughout, Madras has a low profile in robbery (average 0.45), though in 1975 (1.7) it leads Kanpur. It also has a slight lead over Calcutta during 1961-63 (Madras average 0.31, Calcutta average 0.08). Calcutta shows up in 1964 (0.43) and again falls to the lowest position in 1965 (0.09). From 1966 Calcutta's robbery rises slowly (0.27 in 1966, 0.56 in 1967, 0.75 in 1968 and 1.13 in 1969). The rise is substantial in 1970 (3.60), but extraordinary in 1971 (10.18). In 1972 the figure falls and remains steady (between 1.90 and 2.12) Calcutta holds the fourth position in 1972-74 and third in 1975. Delhi is second in robbery during 1972-74 (average 7.61) but at the top in 1975 (5.3). Bombay is third during 1972-74 (average 5.37), but second in 1975 (4.5).

Calcutta's robbery figures may have been affected by the non-inclusion of snatching in robbery. But the extent of such deviation must have been marginal, for it did not substantially raise the theft figure of Calcutta.

Murder

There is much variation in the murder rates in the cities. Bombay holds the first position in 1961-62 (average 2.93) and the second position from 1963 to 1969 (average 2.54). Kanpur leads in 1963-75 (average 3.78) and is superseded only by Calcutta in 1970 (5.06) and 1971 (9.19). Calcutta is the fourth in 1961-63 (average 1.19), 1965-66 (average 1.12) and 1972-75 (average 1.87). It holds the second position in 1964 (2.27) and (third position in 1969 (2.19). Delhi holds the third position in 1961-66 (average 2.17), 1968 (2.00) and 1971-72 (average 2.57). Calcutta pushes Delhi to the fourth position in 1967 (1.50) and 1969 (2.03). From 1973 to 1975 it holds the second rank (average 5.90), Madras is uniformly at the bottom.

Riot

Generally speaking, the riot figures are the most fluctuating. Barring theft, they also generally hold the highest place in the cities being superseded by only the robbery figures in Delhi in 1970-71 (riot average 5.04, robbery average 7.79) and 1974-75 (riot average 4.40, robbery average 6.50), in Kanpur in 1968 (riot 8.64, robbery 9.27) and 1972 (riot 17.80, robbery 18.30) and in Bombay in 1962-65 (riot average 4.38, robbery average 5.48), 1967-68 (riot average 4.91, robbery average 5.71) 1972 (riot 3.39, robbery 3.94). and 1975 (riot 3.2, robbery 4.5). Madras keeps the lowest position in 1961, (1.76), 1963-66 (average 1.81) and 1969-70 average 5.48), 1967-68 (riot average 4.91, but a very high score in 1962 (61.94). In 1967-68 it (average 3.50) supersedes Delhi (average 2.36). After 1970 Madras, Bombay and Delhi frequently change position. Calcutta holds the top rank in 1961 (7.79), 1967-72 (average 26.22) and ranks second to Kanpur in the other years. (This statement does not apply to 1964 when the Kanpur figure is not available).

The Peak Periods

We are seeking to measure social tension in terms of sporadic rises in murder, robbery and riot. The focus falls on the 'crisis' years when particular crimes are at the peak. The method is simple averaging over the 15 years (see Table 2). The method has its drawbacks, since about the mid-sixties 'crimes' in cities seem to take off. It is, however, simple and still points out some significant phenomena. There are two exceptions. No particular period in the recent history of the Indian cities is as distinguished as 1970-71 in Calcutta. We have therefore singled out those two years in working out Calcutta's crime average. There is another exception similarly singled out — riot in 1962 Madras.

There is also a close correspondence of the volumes of riot and robbery in Kanpur and, to a lesser extent, in Bombay and Delhi. The largest gap between riot and the other crimes is in Calcutta, followed by Madras. This suggests an impersonal character of the protests expressed by riot in Calcutta and Madras. The fact that the robbery figures are about the lowest in these cities further suggests a middle-class *(bhadralok)* element in the prevailing value systems.

In the history of the cities there are a few years when robbery, murder and riot simultaneously exceed their averages. Bombay has it in 1964-65 and 1967 (3 yrs.), Delhi and Kanpur in 1971-74 (4 yrs.), Madras in 1973-74 (2 yrs.), and Calcutta in 1970-71 and 1973-75 (5 yrs.). *This analysis will give Calcutta the first place in respect of social tensions, Delhi and Kanpur the second, Bombay the third and Madras the last.* Excess of riot and murder together is reached by Calcutta in 1967-68, by Bombay in 1969 and by Kanpur in 1975. In terms of the lesser combination of riot and robbery, Bombay exceeds its average in 1973-74 and Calcutta in 1969 and 1972, Kanpur, making it in 1970. The respective averages in robbery and murder together are exceeded by Bombay in 1962, Delhi, in 1975, Kanpur in 1967 and Madras in 1975. The riot average alone is exceeded by Bombay in 1966 and 1970 and Madras in 1962 and 1971. The robbery average alone is exceeded by Bombay in 1968. The murder averages alone are exceeded in Bombay in 1961 and 1963, by Calcutta in 1964 and by Kanpur in 1969. This is of course not a measure of the volume of the 'crimes'. On the other hand, the clustering of the crimes is likely to indicate the social climate in which they are committed. Thus, it is only in Calcutta that rise in robbery is always associated with rise in riot. On the other hand, in Calcutta, murder, while mostly accompanying riots, rises alone only in 1964.

Crime and Urban Unrest

Table 1 has shown that Kanpur, the most industrial city has the highest average of murder and robbery but is second in theft followed by Bombay. Delhi leads in theft but is third in murder and robbery. Madras has the lowest murder and robbery average; she is fourth in theft and, excluding the 1962 figure, riot. Calcutta has the lowest theft average and is above only Madras in respect of murder and robbery. On the other hand, Calcutta is at the top in respect of riot, followed by Kanpur.

At this stage we eliminate theft as an insufficient indicator of social tension in Calcutta. The most probable causes of urban unrest in the Indian context, are believed to be inter-communal conflict, labour trouble and/or high politicization of the people. Although the figures of Kanpur and Bombay are apt to suggest association with urban crime, the role of 'labour unrest' behind such crime is not established.

A perfect quantification of these factors is impossible. But we have some data about 'labour unrest' in terms of the man-days annually lost, due to strikes and lockouts arising out of specific demands of workers from 1961 to 1975, in the states in which the respective cities are located (source: *Indian Labour Yearbook).* The figures used are in absolute number and relate to the organized sector. They can at best give an impression of the environs of the cities under consideration and may not faithfully reflect the labour situation in the respective cities.

The most remarkable feature of the statistics is a sudden jump of the figures in 1973 in the cases of Delhi (243.36%) and Uttar Pradesh (121.19%) and in 1974 in the cases of Maharashtra (139.97%) and West Bengal (123.40%) which is perhaps explained by the imposition of emergency in June 1975. The jump had occurred in Tamil Nadu in 1967-68 (246.31%) and, after a slump in 1969 (218.72%), and in 1970-72 (510.01%). On the other hand there was, to quote an official report, nationally, a 'marked decline' in the number of mandays lost in 1975 by 46.6 per cent over 1974 and in 1976 by 41.8 per cent over 1975 *(Indian Labour Yearbook* 1975-76: p. 84). The decline can obviously be ascribed to the emergency which was in force during the second half of 1975 and the whole of 1976. However, West Bengal and U.P. record higher numbers of mandays lost in 1975 (14.25% and 14.3% respectively). In 1976 there were substantial declines even in those states (West Bengal: 33.73%; U.P. 21.17%). As the monthly statewise figures were not available, the reasons may be conjectured. The rise in the first half of 1975 may have substantially reduced the overall annual figures for those states. Local political situations may have softened the impact of emergency in 1975 in them. The critical point about labour unrest in Calcutta is that, before 1974, the peak period was reached in 1970 by a steady ascent from 1967.

Table 2. Years showing more than Average Incidence of Crimes and Labour Unrest since 1961

	Riot (1961-75)	*Murder (1961-75)*	*Robbery (1961-75)*	*Labour Unrest in state (1961-75)*
Bombay (Maharashtra)	1964-67, 1969-70, 1973-74	1961-65, 1967, 1969	1962, 1964-68, 1973-74	1966, 1972-74
Calcutta (West Bengal)	1967-75	1964, 1970-71, 1973-75	1969-73 1975	1967-70, 1973-75
Delhi (Delhi U.T.)	1970-74	1970-75	1970-75	1966, 1968-69, 1971-74
Kanpur (Uttar Pradesh)	1970-75	1967, 1969, 1971-75	1967, 1970-74	1966-67, 1971, 1973-75
Madras* (Tamil Nadu)	1962, 1971-74	1967-68, 1970, 1972-75	1971-75	1968, 1970-75

*The riot average for Madras worked out excluding 1962.
Source: *Crime in India and Indian Labour Yearbook.*

It will be seen that excess in labour unrest in the state in which a city is situated is not reflected in the crime situation in Kanpur in 1966, in Delhi in 1966 and 1968-69 and in Bombay in 1972. In most other cases, labour unrest is accompanied by riot. There are two exceptions: Kanpur in 1967 and Madras in 1968 and 1970. In 1967 in Kanpur, robbery and murder and in 1970 in Madras, murder alone, accompany labour unrest. Riot, robbery and murder together accompany labour unrest in Calcutta in 1970, 1973 and 1975, in Delhi in 1971-74, in Kanpur in 1971 and 1973-74, and in Madras in 1972-75, but never in Bombay. Riot and robbery accompany labour unrest in Bombay in 1966 and 1973-74, in Calcutta in 1969 and in Madras in 1971. Riot and murder accompany labour unrest in Calcutta in 1974 and in Kanpur in 1975. On the other hand, without the company of labour unrest, riot and robbery exceed their averages together only in 1970 in Kanpur and in 1972 in Calcutta. Without the company of labour unrest, riot and murder exceed their averages only in 1969 in Bombay, and murder and robbery do so in 1962 in Bombay and in 1975 in Delhi. Such excesses take place singularly in riot in 1962 in Madras and in 1970 in Bombay, in robbery in 1968 in Bombay and in murder in 1961 and 1963 in Bombay, in 1964 in Calcutta, in 1967 in Madras and in 1969 in Kanpur. On the other hand, without the company of labour unrest, riot, murder and robbery together exceed their averages only in 1964-65 in Bombay, in 1970 in Delhi and in 1971 in Calcutta, the most politically active cities of the country.

Among the singular excesses, however, all are not equally significant. It is not possible to judge the 1961 murder figure for Bombay for want of 1960 figure, but 1963 actually holds the lowest point in a curve running from 1961 to 1965. The Madras 1967 figure is also 20 per cent lower than the 1968 figure. The 1969 excess in Kanpur in murder is marginal (2.2%). And it is less than that in 1967 (by 7.33%). However, labour unrest in the state of U.P. in 1969 is lowest among all the years from 1964 to 1974. The year 1970 actually shows the descent of the riot curve in Bombay since 1969. Robbery in Bombay in 1968 was also lower than that in 1967. This leaves us with the task of explaining the 1962 excess in riot in Madras and the 1964 excess in murder in Calcutta.

Communalism

In 1964 Calcutta not only exceeds its murder average, but reaches the peak of murder for the entire period excluding the two exceptional years of 1970-71. Though robbery in Calcutta was much below the average, in 1964, it was at its peak for the period 1961-66. Neither riot nor labour unrest did rise to any significant proportion. It was the year of the last communal riot in Calcutta when the lives and properties of the Muslims of the city were affected.

The singular rise of riot in the city of Madras in 1962 to a rather alarming degree is explained by the anti-price-rise agitation of the Dravida Munnetra Kazagham *(Crime in India,* 1962: 12) which alarmed the national leadership so much that in 1963 the Sixteenth Amendment to the Constitution of India was passed to ban all secessionist demands. This perhaps testifies to the specialized character of a middle class movement— for 1962 has the lowest record of labour trouble in Tamil Nadu between 1961 and 1975. The movement was, however, parochial and it is interesting that at the pre-1967 period murder in Madras rose slightly in 1962 (9.21% over 1961). On the other hand, in 1965, the year of the language agitation when 66 persons reportedly died of police firing, the rate of murder was the lowest, those of robbery and riot were low. The state's labour disputes too were moderate in volume.

In 1969 riot reaches its peak in Bombay, murder does not reach its peak, but exceeds the average, robbery is lowest in the period since 1962 and labour trouble considerably low. This was the year of the height of the Shiv Sena agitation, a parochial middle-class phenomenon.

Labour Unrest and Crime

In the year 1968 murder reaches its peak in Madras. That year labour unrest also reaches its peak for the period 1961-71. This may give rise to the impression of an exclusive association of murder and labour unrest in Madras unless we take into account the fact that, inspite of the exclusion of 1962 from the riot average of Madras, the average remains affected by a great rise in the period 1971-74. In fact 1968 sees the peak of the riot curve for the years between 1963 and 1970. Similarly, the riot curve of Madras reaches its second highest point for the period. Thus murder *and* riot accompany labour unrest in 1968 and 1970 in Madras. One major difference between Calcutta and Madras may however be noted in this connection. In Calcutta, large-scale communal tension never appeared after 1964. On the other hand, the tensions appearing in Calcutta are, except in 1971, stated clearly in terms of class conflict. In Madras, however, linguistic tension and labour troubles have frequently appeared at short intervals. Thus the labour disputes in Madras in 1968 related chiefly to the textile worker's strike in February 1968, while there was a spurt of linguistic tension in May-June 1968.

The following associations of urban crimes with labour unrest are suggested by the above analysis:

(1) Labour unrest has the greatest association with riot.

(2) Robbery alone never accompanies labour unrest.

(3) Murder and robbery together rarely accompany labour unrest.

(4) Robbery and riot do have a greater association with labour unrest.

The fact that riot, murder and robbery exceed their averages without the company of labour unrest in Bombay, in 1964-65, Delhi in 1970, Calcutta in 1971 and Kanpur in 1972 tend to disprove a positive correspondence of labour unrest with urban crime in general. No negative correlation between labour unrest and urban crime in general can, however, be established at the same time for they are frequently associated since 1970 in all the cities except Bombay. Such a uniform rise in crime in general along with labour unrest can probably be described as 'crisis' in which organizational failure in the labour movement may have a part to play.

Crime in Calcutta

It appears, that while uncontrolled labour agitation has some association with the simultaneous rise in riot, robbery and murder, controlled labour movement seeks to avoid robbery and murder while middle class agitations tend to avoid property-oriented crimes more than murders. The first part of the last statement may go a long way in explaining the simultaneous rise of riot, robbery, murder and labour unrest in Calcutta since 1967. There are however some important points to be noted about Calcutta, while considering crimes within the frame of the general hypothesis stated above:

(1) There was no communal conflict on a large scale after 1964.

(2) 1967 ushered in the most radical phase of West Bengal politics. In 1967 and 1969 two United Front governments were installed in the state. The state was, however under Governor's rule in 1970-71.

(3) The Naxalite urban agitation and the counter-active police action was a major concern of 1970-71 Calcutta.

(4) In Calcutta alone the gap between the riot curve and all other curves has always been wide. Except in 1962 there has never been such a gap even in Madras. In the three other cities riot and robbery go almost hand in hand.

(5) Calcutta's social tensions also seem to have positive correspondence with communal conflict as well as political mobilization.

Calcutta presents a generally low profile in urban crimes comparable to that of Madras. But with regard to riots Calcutta can compare only with Kanpur. Yet, generally speaking, 1967-71 has been the most tumultuous period in the socio-political history of West Bengal in general and Calcutta in particular. The specific features are, however, most interesting. The labour scene became tense in 1966 with a rise of mandays lost by 119.29 per cent over 1965, due to strikes and lockouts in the organized sector of industry in the state. Between 1966 and 1967 there was a jump of 55.26 per cent of the mandays lost. In 1968 there was a jump of 23.73 per cent over 1967. In 1969 the jump was 34.24 per cent over the previous year. The corresponding jump in 1970 was 12.22 per cent. In 1971, however, the figure slumped by 60.71 per cent. In 1972 it fell further by 6.82 per cent. But 1973 saw a rise by 40.48 per cent over 1972, and 1974 by 124.14 per cent over 1973.

Calcutta's crime profile during this period, however, does not perfectly correspond with the trends in labour unrest in the state. It is only in 1969 that Calcutta reaches the figure of more than 1 robbery per lakh of population. The robbery figures are, of course, subject to the qualification that snatching in Calcutta is recorded as theft and are, therefore, inadequate for comparison with other cities. But Calcutta's *trend* can be revealed by the figures. In 1970 they jump by 218.58 per cent and in 1971 further by 182.77 per cent reaching the all-time high figure of 10.18.

In respect of murder, Calcutta crosses its 1964 record of 2.27 per lakh only in 1970 (5.06), when it registers a rise of 131 per cent over 1969. In 1971 it reaches the peak by a jump of 81.62 per cent over 1970. Thus in respect of labour unrest while there is a distinct fall in 1971 from the 1970 level, murder and robbery reach their peak in 1971.

A part of the rise in murders is explained by a sharp rise in political murders in Calcutta and four industrial districts of West Bengal from 9 in 1968 to 66 in 1969, to 291 in 1970 and 840 in 1971. The figure slumps to 73 in 1973 (Bandyopadhyaya, 1974). But the significant point about these figures is that while in 1971 labour unrest falls distinctly from the 1970 level, murder and robbery reach their peak, suggesting that labour unrest may rise along with murder and robbery through political activism. On the other hand, labour unrest as such is not positively correlated with murder and robbery.

There is however a much greater correspondence of riots to labour unrest. Riots increase in Calcutta upto 1970 along with murder and robbery as well as labour unrest. But in 1971 riots decrease along with labour unrest, though murder and robbery do increase.

Conclusion

Calcutta thus presents a low profile in gain-oriented crimes. There are more protests embodied in Calcutta's crimes than the desire to gain or even do harm to others.

One reason of this aversion to gain-oriented crime may be a middle-class scruple about property. This indicates, further, the greater influence of tension than what the lawyers call *'mens rea'* (criminal motive). Except in the year of last major communal conflict in Calcutta (1964) and the year of an unusual number of political murders (1971) even the incidence of murder is not alarming. Crimewise, 1971 must be treated as exceptional for Calcutta and may be, partly at least, explained by influences that are not systemic to Calcutta. Only twice in Calcutta's history, in 1971 and 1975 (the first year of the emergency), has robbery surpassed murder.

But Calcutta seems to have lost its middle class innocence in 1970 since when, till 1975, murder and/or robbery is a regular feature of its crime statistics.

1991

REFERENCES

1. A. *Official Reports. Crime in India,* Bureau of Police Research and Development, Government of India, Delhi (Annual). *Indian Labour Yearbook.* Labour Bureau. Government of India (Annual).

   B. *Secondary sources*

2. Bandyopadhyaya Debabrata, Labour Secretary, Government of West Bengal : "A Decadal Survey of the Labour Scene in West Bengal", paper in *Symposium on Problems of West Bengal Economy and Planning,*

26th February 1974. Forenoon, Session No. 5: Labour. Centre for Studies in Social Sciences, Calcutta.

3. Domenach, J.M. 1978 : "The Ubiquity of Violence", *International Social Science Journal*, Vol. XXX, No. 4.
4. Gurr, Ted Robert 1970 : *Why Men Rebel*, Princeton: Princeton University Press.
5. Khan, Rasheeduddin 1978 : "Violence and Socio-economic Change", *International Social Science Journal*, XXX, 4.
6. Klapp, Orrin E. 1972 : *Currents of Unrest : An Introduction to Collective Behaviour*, New York: Hall, Reinhart and Winston Inc.
7. Mackenzie, W.J.M. 1975 : *Power, Violence, Decision*, London : Penguin.
8. Spitz, Pierre 1978 : "Silent Violence: Famine and Inequality", *International Social Science Journal*, XXX, 4.

20
Social Unrest in India

While narrating the situation on the eve of the French Revolution Ketelbey wrote:

> Privilege, concession, exemption - not law - was the basis of French society; expedient, not principle, the policy of its rulers. It is not to be wondered at that the earliest demand of the Revolutionaries was for a "constitution," by which they meant a system, an organization.
>
> The effect upon the people was to create distrust, suspicion and discontent. Class was divided against class, group against group; not one was satisfied; each maintained itself in as great an isolation as possible, distrusting the class above, despising the one below (Ketelbey: 30-31).

Unrest of Different Kinds

The world's first political scientist, Aristotle, while discussing the causes of political revolution, bracketed it with dissension. At the same time, he identified them with political disturbances and quarrels. According to him the universal and chief cause of this revolutionary feeling is the desire for equality or, more accurately, the varying desires of sections of the people for equality and perceptions of inequality. 'Inferiors revolt in order that they may be equal, and equals that they may be superior' (Aristotle: 212).

Though Aristotle's analysis was essentially political, the scope of his enquiry covered the entire span of social unrest. Aristotle's analysis, however, suffered from neglecting the slave revolts that played critical role in the Greek society. He ignored the phenomenon of exploitation (that, two millennia later, became the crucial analytical category) and conceived revolution/dissension/unrest in terms of competition.

All unrests that matter to the society are social as far as their spread is concerned. All unrests are rooted in tension and all tensions are rooted in suffering, perceived as well as actual. Individual unrests may lead to crime, suicide or similar actions generally regarded as 'aberrations.' Even such unrests may occasionally take a social character as in the case of the spate of suicides that rocked Andhra Pradesh and Karnataka in 2003-04. A natural calamity produces unrest; it takes the form of social unrest only if such calamity is seen to have been the result of apathy/corruption of powers that be and when the society/state is seen to be apathetic towards remedial actions or sections of the society/government are seen to be taking advantage of it. Thus social unrest/tension is produced by inadequate/unfair treatment, deprivation or exploitation. More often than not its focus is diffuse making its classification difficult except from the point of view of the *main* focus. Thus an economic or a social problem may grow into a political unrest when the state is seen to be apathetic or a perpetrator. The great depression of the 1930s produced great political unrest throughout the West leading, through different twists of history, to the rise of fascism and nazism. The Age of Consent Bill, 1891, gave birth to a political turmoil that merged with the rising nationalist sentiment in India (Sarkar: 71). Whether such unrest will lead to violence will depend upon its intensity, its leadership and the availability of peaceful remedies.

Aristotle was dealing with the city states. Another social scientist, Karl Marx, in the nineteenth century, was dealing with the mass states. Aristotle's emphasis was on the demagogues; he did not have to bother about organization (Aristotle: 221, 223). Marx set great store by organization and considered sporadic acts of protest by the workers, the petty bourgeois and the unemployed, without organization and leadership, as counterproductive. *The Communist Manifesto* (1848) was essentially a call to the workers to organize. Subsequently, he blamed the failure of a workers' revolution upon the betrayal of the bourgeois leadership.

The Marxist concept of class struggle was a philosophy of history; it was also a strategy for the capture of state power by the working class. Formulated in the middle of the nineteenth century, when voting right was highly restricted or altogether absent in Europe the Marxist strategy essentially had to focus on revolution with the question of violence being left open. With the broadening of voting right attention of the Second International was shifted to parliamentary politics. In France and Italy, after World War II, the Marxists took part in the governments through elections. Through elections they came to power in the states of Kerala, West Bengal and Tripura. Latin America and Africa have occasionally seen elected Marxist governments too.

It is organization along with long-term goals that turns unrest into a movement/struggle. A social unrest, unless organized, often manifests itself into senseless violence or/and peters out. Such violence, when aimed more at harming others than at making gains, can be said to reflect social tension (Chaube 1990: p. 240). When such violence is even partly motivated by the desire to make gains, it can be, from a sociological point of view, designated as criminal.

Violence and Conflict: Vertical and Horizontal

Violence may be directed horizontally as well as vertically. A vertical violence involves class conflict in which the state takes the side of the richer few and its armed forces descend on the poorer many. When violence is directed horizontally it takes the form of group clashes. The concept of riot should be understood from this perspective.[1] A class conflict results in revolution or repression. It is only the horizontal group conflicts which result in riots.

By this token several peasant revolts like the Pabna (1872) and the Moplah (numerous in the nineteenth century) (Sarkar: 49; Lahiri: 89, 94) cannot be considered as communal riot even though the objects of their ire belonged to people of different communities. Nor can the different tribal revolts adversely affecting the Indian traders, money lenders and land-grabbers from the plains be considered as ethnic conflicts (Sarkar: 44-48; Chandra: 45-49; Lahiri: 49-57, 89, 93). The tribals were simply unaware of the role of the imperial government imposing land revenue and driving them to money lenders or even directly appropriating their land for plantation, mining and timber collection.

The attitudes that govern class conflict are generally categorized as class consciousness, the attitudes governing horizontal conflicts as identity consciousness. They generally do cross cut. The ethno-culturally heterogeneous tram workers of Calcutta gave exemplary demonstration of communal amity during the 1946 disturbances. Village life in India is by far free from communal tension because the agrarian people's struggle for existence favours communal amity. At the same time, it is undeniable that class consciousness grows well in an ethno-culturally homogeneous population. Indian villages are by far free from communal tensions partly because the residential segments within the villages are generally uni-caste/uni-communal and partly because agricultural land, the main means of agrarian production is relatively inalienable. There is less residential segregation in towns (Biswas, Chatterjee & Chaube) and greater competition in business and jobs that can be easier snatched.

In two inter-related cases, however, class conflict and identity conflict may coincide: racialism and imperialism. For quite some time British historian, saw Indian opposition to the empire as racialist. When the Indian National Congress was set up to provide a platform to Indian voices of unrest, it deliberately used the word 'national' to combine class contradiction with identity consciousness. The USA's black population is the living evidence of the fusion of class contradiction and identity consciousness.

All horizontal group conflicts, however, do not necessarily reflect social tension/unrest. Wars between two countries may cause unrest among the minority populations of the respective countries but are rarely caused by it (as in the case of Sudetan Germans before World War II suspected to have been partly instigated by Hitler). Germany and France fought several wars over the occupation of Alsace-Lorraine that caused unrest among the German and the French-speaking populations of the region at different times. Such wars, however, were parts of the grand state craft of the respective states and not caused by social sentiment of the respective communities. The Muslims of India have often been victims of suspicion during the several India-Pakistan wars. Hindu-Muslim relations in India or, for that matter, in Pakistan and Bangladesh, have never caused a war. Village clashes over the occupation of *char* lands in the riverine Bengal before partition were calculated war-like operations directed mostly by feudal lords who appointed their mercenaries *(lathiaals)* in several cases. Conflicts between the striking workers of a factory and new recruits of the employers (including musclemen) directed to break the strike may cause unrest but are not caused by it.

Communal Riots and Politics

A communal riot in India has come to mean a riot between religious communities, particularly, the Hindus and the Muslims. Christians have not taken part in these riots, one of the reasons being their small number. However, in the hill areas of northeast India, where there is a Christian concentration, there have been occasional cases of killing of non-Christian plainsmen settlers or even Christian hill-men from other tribes by the way of what looked like ethnic cleansing. There has to be a certain amount of resistance from the attacked side if an act has to be described as a communal riot. Otherwise, it becomes a pogrom/ mayhem. The violence that occurred at the Godhra railway station on 27 February 2002 was a riot, the violence that occurred throughout Gujarat following the incident was a pogrom/mayhem undertaken by local toughs backed by community/political leaders in the name of majority sentiment. Every riot needs a trigger, probably an agent provocateur. A pogrom/mayhem needs a planner and a manipulator.

The total Sikh population in India is less than the total Christian population. In today's Punjab they constitute a big majority. In the British period the Sikhs often joined the Hindus against the Muslims. After the virtual transfer of population in Punjab around the time of partition Hindu-Sikh riots have taken place with some intensity in the late 1970s and the early 1980s. The violence that one notices in Tripura between the tribes and the non-tribal population, or even between different tribes combines the attributes of mayhem and pure riot as they are aimed at ethnic cleansing but not very well planned and destined to succeed.

One of the reasons such violence has not succeeded in the hill states of northeast India is the lack of government support. The state governments in northeast India are severely dependent on the central government which has generally been sensitive to communal violence. In 1993, following the demolition of the Babari Masjid, the Union government superseded three state governments in plains India, on ground of their inability to control communal conflict. However the Union Government failed to act during and after the Gujarat pogrom in 2002.

Indirectly, however, the governments have been responsible for several communal flares-up. The Great Calcutta killing of August 1946 was sparked by the Muslim League's call for direct action on the sixteenth and the assurance of the Muslim League Prime Minister of Bengal, H.S. Suhrawardy in a public meeting at the Calcutta maidan on the same day of governmental indulgence (Sarkar: 432). On the eve of the Babari masjid demolition on 6 December 1992 the Chief Minister of UP made it known that he would not apply force against the *kar sevaks (India Today,* December 31, 1992: p. 53). In more cases, however, without instigating a communal riot, the governments turn their eyes to other directions when the mayhems occur. There have been several complaints in the past that the police remained inactive or, when they acted, they fired on the victims rather than the attackers. In 1946 Suhrawardy was physically present in the Lalbazar police control room at Calcutta and expressed his concern for the sufferings of the Muslims in the city (ibid.). Allegations were levelled against Gujarat ministers that during the post-Godhra mayhem of February-March 2002 they were directing police operations to the detriment of the minorities.[2]

Riots, including mayhems, have deep socio-economic causes not necessarily reflected by the occasions that ignite them, very often trivial. What distinguishes a mayhem from an ordinary riot is the calculation of long-term consequences which is different from planning. The Calcutta riot was started as a mayhem but, in the absence of calculation of the numerical strength of the Hindu-Sikh population of the city, boomeranged and turned into what Governor Burrows called a 'pogrom between two rival armies of the Calcutta underworld', about 5000 lives, more Muslim than Hindu, being lost (Sarkar: 432; Chandra: 494). The Bihar and the Punjab riots looked more like mayhems. The Bihar riots, taking at least 7000 lives, mostly Muslim, had been started in observance of the Noakhali day (25 October, 1946). The Noakhali riots, earlier in the month (October 10), that took Gandhi personally on a peace mission in the far south-eastern corner of Bengal itself had been the handiwork of mercenaries from outside and took 300 lives but the loss of property amounted to crores of rupees (Sarkar: 433). All these riots, however, were nothing in comparison with the Punjab 'holocaust' that took 180,000 lives (60,000 in the West, evidently mostly Hindu and Sikh and 120,000 in the east, evidently mostly Muslim) and causing a virtual exchange of population. The important point was that the desertion of land in the two parts of Punjab was in the inverse ratio: 6.7 million acres in the west and 4.7 million in the east (Sarkar: 434).

Attack on life of the opponent group indicates a certain amount of brutality, probably instigated by the desire for vengeance. Attack on property reflects more economic motives. Around the time of partition this could be explained by the requirement of politics and the economic condition of the contemporary Muslims and Hindu societies. After the partition, however, there seems to have been a trend toward appropriation of minority property as much as that of life, probably indicating increased participation of the lumpen elements, not necessarily the underworld.

A historical reconstruction of communal riots in India, is necessary for the purpose of theoretical analysis of the phenomenon but is extremely difficult because of the general tendency of British historiography to scandalize India.[3] It is necessary to distinguish the violence inflicted by a marauding body of invaders belonging to a religious/ethnic group other than that of the locals and the violent local resistance to such invaders from communal riots. Such things, as the Hun invasion of Europe or the European invasions of America, have happened in the life of most countries of the world. On the other hand, the 1857 uprising of Indians displayed remarkable Hindu-Muslim Unity.

There is a uniform tendency on the part of British chroniclers to attribute several tribal upsurges in the nineteenth century to exploitation and/or misbehaviour of plainsmen (money-lender and land grabber) suppressing the fact that money-lending was necessitated by the imposition of land revenue/house tax by the British government over the tribals possessing no money and the bulk of tribal land was acquired by the administration for mining or plantation or as forest reserve. The entire story of the Jadonang-Guidinliu revolt against the British administration was first suppressed and later depicted as a Kabui-Kuki clash even though Guidinliu used Gandhi's name in her struggle (Chaube 1978: 37).

Nor does class conflict between the zamindars and the peasants in which the two sides belong to the opposite communities qualify as communal riots.

The 'Pabna riots' of 1873 (Chandra: 54-56) and the Mappila (Moplah) outbreaks over the late nineteenth century (Sarkar: p. 49; Chandra: p. 58) were class conflicts but the Kuka rebellion (1872) had a distinctly communal character, having a main thrust for conversion and against cow-slaughter (Jones: 91-92; Sarkar: 78.) In the industrial cities of India communal riots that took place mostly concerned the unemployed or casually employed labourers, critical roles being played by *sardars* in charge of recruitment and the underworld agents of the employers.

Gains and Loses

The role of agent provocateurs and mercenaries *(lathiaals/ goondas]* has so far not been sufficiently studied by social sciences primarily because of insufficient documentation by intelligence agencies. For this paper it is enough to stress that the extent and depth of their participation in a communal riot would undermine the extent and depth of social tension/unrest In other words, the importance of agent provocateurs and that of social tension/unrest are inversely proportional. This is the reason for the Indian police to record an all-purpose riot and any other crime(s) separately when they take place together.

This may be said about the motivation for riots too. Whereas for the ordinary rioters the sense of competition, deprivation and/or exploitation may be the primary motive force, for the agent provocateurs and mercenaries the motivation is gain. Consideration of gain constitutes *mens rea* and turns the participant from an offender into a criminal.

To the extent that riots start with aggression on the others' life or/and property they resemble war. Like wars riots bring in resistance. The resemblance ends there. In a war, as in a pogrom/

mayhem, there is a calculation of gain on the side of the aggressor and a fear of loss on the side of the victims. There has to be a planning on the part of the aggressor while the victim may or may not have anticipated and planned for the aggression or, at least, planned well. A riot lacks a precise calculation of gains and losses and, therefore, is mostly unplanned. The most important difference between a war and a mayhem is that, in the latter case, the victims are too weak to resist.

From this point of view the inter-tribal conflicts that bedevilled the northeast Indian hills before the advent of British rule and occasionally erupted even after their departure are local wars while the 'caste conflicts' that take place in rural Bihar, Jharkhand, Chhattisgarh and Andhra Pradesh are class wars. Communal riots, on the other hand, are predominantly urban and sub-urban phenomena.

The 1857 war of the Indians with the English East India Company gives a lie to the sedulous campaign that communalism was ingrained in the Indian society. The first major communal unrest in British India was the violence in 1871 of the Kukas on the issue of cow slaughter in the city of Amritsar (Jones: 92-93). (The subsequent riots revolved around the issues of cow-slaughter, *suddhi,* music before mosques and the Muharram procession. Politics plays a major role in fomenting as well as preventing it.)

2006

NOTES AND REFERENCES

1. The Indian Penal Code describes any violence involving five persons or more as riot. But, in case such an act of violence is accompanied by murder or robbery, rape or any other offence they are registered separately by the police.
2. The Concerned Citizens' Tribunal, headed by Justice V.R. Krishna Iyer (Retired) was told by Haren Pandya, a former cabinet minister, that Chief Minister Narendra Modi, in a meeting in the evening of 27 February 2002 (the day of the Godhra train carnage), told senior government and police officers to go soft on rioters as the "Hindus [should] be allowed to vent their ire" ('Haren blew the whistle on Modi, says father,' *The Times of India,* 24 February 2005. The minister was subsequently murdered during morning walk.

3 An example of such distortion is Reginald Coupland's recording of a riot in Benares in 1809 caused by the rude behaviour of a Muslim *daroga* (police station-in-charge) as the "earliest" recorded communal riot in British India' followed by the gratuitous comment that in this incident 'the deliberate insult inflicted on that sacred Hindu city by the erection of a mosque on its most sacred site by the Mogul emperor, Aurangzeb, a century before, was at last avenged by the Hindus. Several hundred people were killed and some fifty mosques destroyed' (Coupland: p.34). Besides the historical fact that Benares had emerged as a multi-religious commercial city long before Aurangzeb, the temporal connectivity between the two incidents, to say the least, is far-fetched.

BIBLIOGRAPHY

1. Aristotle N.D. *Politics*. Translated by B. Jowett, The Modern Library.
2. Biswas, Arabinda, Partha Chatterjee & Shibani Kinkar Chaube 1976 'The Ethnic Composition of Calcutta and the Residential Pattern of Minorities:' *Geographical Review of India dedicated to late Professor Nirmal Kumar Bose*, Volume 38, No. 2. June.
3. Chandra, Bipan *el. al* 1989 *India 's Struggle for Independence*, Penguin, New Delhi.
4. Chaube, S.K. 1978 'Rani Gaidiliu: Profile of a Tribal Woman Leader,' in *Tribal Women in India*. Indian Anthropological Society, Calcutta.
5. Chaube, S.K. 1990 'Violence, Crime and Labour Unrest in Calcutta: a comparative analysis of social tensions,' in Jean Racine (Ed) *Calcutta 1981: the city, its crisis and the debate on urban planning and development*. Concept Publishing Company, New Delhi.
6. Coupland, Reginald 1944 *The Constitutional Problem of India:* Oxford University Press, Bombay.
7. Jones, Kenneth W. 1994 *Socio-Religious Reform Movements in British India*, Cambridge University Press, Cambridge *et.al.*
8. Ketelbey, D.M. 1945 *A History of Modern Times*. George W. Harrap & Co. Ltd., London, Toronto, Bombay, Sydney.
9. Lahiri, Abani 2001 *The Peasant and India's Freedom Movement:* V. V. Giri National Labour Institute, Noida and Manak Publication Pvt. Ltd.
10. Sarkar, Sumit 1983 *Modern India 1885-1947*, Macmillan India Limited, Madras *et al.*

Index